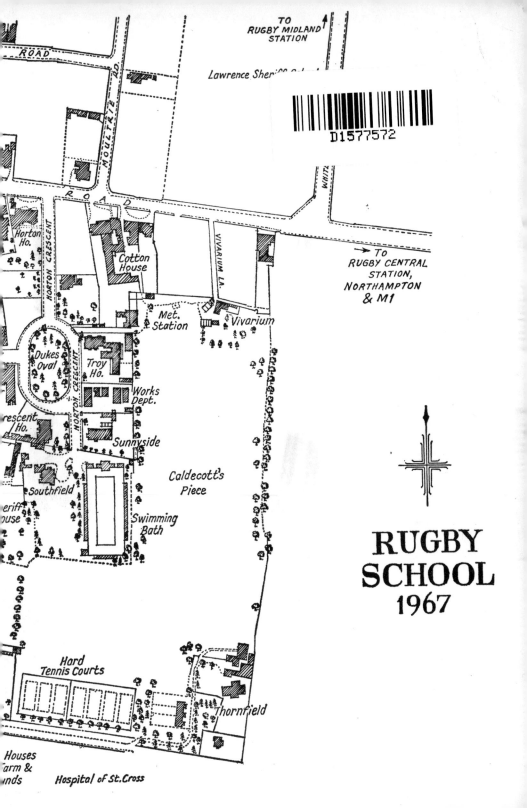

RUGBY
SCHOOL
1967

RUGBY SINCE ARNOLD

Rugby School

RUGBY
SINCE ARNOLD

A HISTORY OF RUGBY SCHOOL
FROM 1842

J. B. HOPE SIMPSON

MACMILLAN
London · Melbourne · Toronto

ST MARTIN'S PRESS
New York
1967

MACMILLAN AND COMPANY LIMITED
Little Essex Street London WC 2
also Bombay Calcutta Madras Melbourne

THE MACMILLAN COMPANY OF CANADA LIMITED
70 Bond Street Toronto 2

ST MARTIN'S PRESS INC
175 Fifth Avenue New York NY 10010

PRINTED AND BOUND IN ENGLAND BY
HAZELL WATSON AND VINEY LTD
AYLESBURY, BUCKS

Contents

Contents

Illustrations

MAPS

Foreword

It is nearly seventy years since the publication of W. H. D. Rouse's *History of Rugby School,* and Rouse, though he ended with a chapter entitled 'School life in Modern Times', gave no critical account of any headmastership later than Goulburn's. The way is open for a successor who will bring the history of the School as nearly up to date as tenderness for the feelings of living headmasters allows. No enterprise could more fitly mark the School's quatercentenary, and in Mr. Hope Simpson we are lucky enough to possess an historian whose talents and interests exactly match the occasion.

To Rugbeians this book will need no commendation. They will at last find in it something as close to the truth as can now be recovered about the unfortunate Hayman, and full accounts of such notable figures as Frederick Temple, Percival, David and Vaughan. Nor should it be without interest to a much wider circle of readers. At a time when the nature and function of the Public Schools are being subjected to intense and often hostile scrutiny, a book that concentrates on the history of a single school at the zenith of its prosperity and influence may hope to attract the attention of many besides the Public Schools Commissioners. When the single school in question is Rugby, which for better or worse has played so large a part in the development of what is called the Public School system, it is surely not conceited to think that its history is of considerably more than parochial importance.

Rugby's fifth century may well see changes as great as those which separate the present school from the humble foundation of Lawrence Sheriffe. Among the good things that we wish it on its four-hundredth birthday, let one be an historian of equal calibre for 2067.

WALTER HAMILTON

Preface

The history of a school, like the biography of a man still living, can never be complete. A great deal has been written about Rugby, but since the publication of W. H. D. Rouse's book in 1898 and H. C. Bradby's in 1900, only C. R. Evers, in 1939, has attempted a complete survey of the School's history. Each writer has had to tread very gently over the last thirty or forty years of his story. Up to and including Thomas Arnold, Rouse's admirable work must be regarded as the definitive history; Arnold himself, in biography, monograph and disputatious articles, has been examined in minute detail. But the period following his death has never received any very full treatment, for though Evers stood far enough away from the later nineteenth century to be objective, his book, not a very long one, covers the whole period from 1567, and the later stages of the story could not be allotted a greater share of the work than would allow for an outline treatment.

This is my excuse, if I need one, for attempting to write, in rather greater detail than has previously been done, a history of the last 120 years, to greet the School on its fourhundredth birthday. Inevitably I have covered ground that has been dealt with by previous writers, and to them I owe a very great debt. I have tried, not always very successfully, to be as little repetitive as possible, and much of my material comes from sources previously unexamined, or at any rate unpublished.

To thank all those who have helped me in this work would

require a chapter on its own, but to some I must record my gratitude: to Walter Hamilton for encouraging me to start and to persist; to the Governing Body for giving me access to their confidential documents and for allowing me a sabbatical term to break the back of the writing; to Peter Bennett, their Clerk, for the unfailing cheerful courtesy with which, for several years, he accepted the nuisance of my irregular but frequent visits to his office, and for allowing me space there to work; to J. C. Marshall, and those others whom he persuaded to the labour, for undertaking research into the history of the School games; to J. R. A. Smith for relieving me of the daunting duty of compiling an index, and for much information from his un-rivalled knowledge of the School over the last fifty years; to A. J. Hunt for valuable constructive criticism; to Mrs. Denis Buxton, Brigadier J. H. Penrose, Mrs. A. A. David, Mrs. W. W. Vaughan, Mr. H. J. Vaughan, the Rev. J. A. G. Haslam, Mrs. Doreen Atkinson, Mr. P. H. B. Lyon and the President and the Librarian of St. John's College, Oxford, for allowing me to examine manuscript material; to Mr. R. H. Huntingford for great help in producing illustrations; to Mr. J. Alldis for drawing the maps; and to Mrs. Mary Crowther for her admirable typing. My use of copyright material, for which permission has been kindly granted by authors or publishers, is acknowledged in the text or by footnote.

J. B. H. S.

February 1966

Introduction

> Rugby was made not by endowments but by its Masters alone. Except for a succession of distinguished and powerful administrators, it would have been nothing but an ordinary Grammar School.
>
> *The Times,* 31 January 1874

Nothing can be more certain than that the Rugby School of the nineteenth and twentieth centuries, whose progress is traced in the pages that follow, bore no resemblance to that which Lawrence Sheriffe had in mind when, in 1567, he drafted the 'Intent' by the terms of which it was founded. His vision can hardly have extended beyond the creation of a small local grammar school to serve the needs of a small market-town; and he would surely have laughed in impatient incredulity if he had been told that two of the 'honest, discreet and learned men' who were to be its Masters, and for whose salary he had provided £12 a year, and one of their assistants would successively occupy the throne of Canterbury[1] three centuries after his death. Nor could he have foreseen that the eight acres of a field called Conduit Close in the County of Middlesex, bringing in a rent of between £6 and £8 a year, which he left as part of the endowment for his projected School, would by that time be in London

---

[1] Archibald Campbell Tait: Headmaster 1842–50; Archbishop 1868–82. Edward White Benson: Assistant Master 1852–8; Archbishop 1883–96. Frederick Temple: Headmaster 1858–69; Archbishop 1896–1902.

and that Lamb's Conduit Street and Great Ormonde Street would cross one another in the middle of them.

The original foundation was, indeed, very humble and, for the first century of its existence, very insecure. The total endow‑ ment brought in less than £25 a year. The School House had been built opposite the parish church by Lawrence Sheriffe before his death and was to be the Master's residence; the School itself, alongside, cost £50 to erect and lasted for two centuries. Under the will of the Founder, the Trust was to be administered by two of his friends, George Harrison and Barnard Field, and their heirs 'for ever'. The two men saw to the building of the School and installed the first Master, Edward Rolston, in 1574, but after their deaths in 1582 and 1583 respectively things began to go badly wrong; the tenant of Conduit Close, Dakyn, ceased payment, and in 1600 actually conveyed away the property; the tenant of the parsonage of Brownsover, from which the remainder of the trust income was derived, withheld portions of the rent, and there followed, for over half a century, a stormy period of litigation. In 1602 the School's affairs were put into the hands of a body of twelve Trustees; but they neglected their duties, and the lowest point in the history of Rugby was reached in 1651 when the Master, Raphael Pearce, died, almost cer‑ tainly of privation. He had complained that both tenants had ceased payment, and that there was a year in which he had received only 2s. 7d. of his salary, 'whereby he was much dampnified'. His mastership had covered the troubled period of the Civil Wars, which must have been a difficult time in any case; and he appears to have been a weak man. The lawsuits dragged on for another sixteen years, and at last, on 26 November 1667, the Lord Keeper, Sir Orlando Bridgeman, confirmed a

'*Lawrence Sheriffe: Hys Dreame*'

Archibald Campbell Tait

E. M. Goulburn

settlement that vested the School property in the Trustees and compelled the defaulting tenants to repay what they had withheld or misappropriated. Thus it was not until a century after its foundation that the Trust was placed on a sound basis and the School was able to develop in conditions of greater security.

That it did develop beyond all expectation was due to a succession of remarkable Masters. The first really great one was Henry Holyoake, 1688–1731. He was Chaplain of Magdalen College, Oxford, and was expelled with the other Protestant Fellows by James II; he appears to have found the mastership of Rugby agreeable, for he refused to return to Magdalen when the Fellows were restored—though he did try unsuccessfully to cling to his chaplaincy; he was in fact something of a pluralist and at various times held the livings of BourtononDunsmore, Bilton and HarboroughMagna, putting in curates who spent part of their time helping at the School. These are the first assistant masters of whom we have any record. There had almost certainly been boarders before his time—even in the sixteenth century it cannot have been easy to live on £12 a year—but Holyoake was responsible for the increase in their number, and during his mastership fourfifths of the entries were not on the Foundation. Under him numbers in the School rose to little short of 100, and its reputation spread and attracted the sons of many of the local great families, as well as pupils from as far afield as Cheshire, Kent and Somerset. The process continued, and the brilliant Thomas Crossfield, who became Master in 1742 and died after two years in office, accepted 53 new boys in his first year, of whom only two were Foundationers.[1]

---

[1] Foundationers are local boys educated free under the endowment of the Founder.

By Holyoake's time the value of the Trust property had increased considerably; his salary, which started at £56, rose to £70. In 1742 the total annual income of the Trust was £116 17s. 6d., and the Trustees were considering how to raise a sufficient capital sum to move the School, for the old building was beyond repair. An Act of Parliament in 1748 empowered them to mortgage two-thirds of Conduit Close; by this means they raised £1800, which enabled them to purchase a manor-house that stood on the site of the present School House and to build a new School, much on the model of the old, alongside. Thither the School was moved in 1750.

For the next quarter of a century there was a gradual decline, and Stanley Burough (1755–78) handed over only 52 boys to his successor; but that successor was the second of the very great Masters—and the first to be called Headmaster—of Rugby School. He was Thomas James (1778–94), educated at Eton and a Fellow of King's College, Cambridge. It has been said that he brought to Rugby 'Cambridge scholarship and Eton methods'; certainly under him there was a very rapid develop-ment both in the reputation and in the numbers of the School, and he handed over to his successor some 245 boys and six assistant masters. It was he who introduced the tutorial system and who organised the curriculum with an efficiency that lasted at least until the time of Arnold. Under him we hear for the first time of Dames' Houses and of praepostors and fags (though these may well have existed earlier). His most distinguished pupils were Samuel Butler, later a great Headmaster of Shrews-bury, Charles Apperley ('Nimrod' of the *Gentleman's Magazine*) and Walter Savage Landor; the last two of these he expelled.

The great increase in numbers during his time made new

building a necessity. The rehousing of the School in 1750 had left a considerable debt, but in 1777 certain leases of the London property were due to fall in and a great increase in revenue was expected. The opportunity was taken to obtain a new Act of Parliament,[1] which not only clarified the constitution of the School, but enabled the Trustees to project a complete rebuilding when that should become necessary. In James's time new schools[2] were built west of the existing one, with rooms over them, presumably for boarders. It was left to John Wooll (1806–28) to see through the complete rebuilding, which took six years (1809–15) and cost in the end some £35,000. Henry Hakewill was employed as architect, and it is his design which produced, very largely, today's 'old buildings'. Wooll's headmastership saw numbers rise, at their highest to over 380, though there had been something of a drop before he was succeeded by Thomas Arnold.

Rugby, then, had already become before Arnold's day something much more than a local grammar school; it was one of those which Dr. Johnson called 'the Great Schools' and Rudolph Ackermann, in his illustrated *History of Rugby School* (1816), 'The Principal Schools of England', drawing its pupils from all over the country and distinguished for the quality of its scholarship.

What Arnold did was to make a radical change in the objectives of education. Previous Headmasters had aimed principally, some of them solely, at academic quality; Arnold's scale of values was different. He aimed to produce, in his own words, 'first religious and moral principle; secondly gentlemanly con-

---

[1] The Act is summarised in Rouse, *History of Rugby School*, pp. 121 ff.

[2] At Rugby a 'school' is a classroom.

duct; and thirdly intellectual ability'. In this order of priority lies the real revolution which he brought about. Though he had no opinion of mere brilliance, he believed that intellectual excellence and moral quality were closely allied, and that it was therefore his duty to get rid of unpromising material, intellectual as well as moral. 'Evil being unavoidable', he said, 'we are not a jail to keep it in, but a place of education where we must cast it out to prevent the taint from spreading'; and he cast it out by so vigorous a use of expulsion and the birch as to bring heavy criticism on him in his early days and even to endanger his position.

He found already in existence a tradition that gave the VIth form some authority, and he proceeded to develop it.[1] By purging the lower part of the School he hoped to make it unlikely that any would reach the VIth who were unworthy of trust, and he treated his senior boys as gentlemen and reasoning beings, discontinuing the use of the birch at this level, increasing both their power and their duties, and making them in some sense responsible for moral tone as well as for technical discipline. To say that all he did was to regularise and develop what he found is in no way to belittle him. His genius lay in his power of infusing into the School and into his assistant masters some of his own vigorous moral idealism. To bring this about, his main medium, apart from the infectious inspiration of his own personality, was the Chapel. In 1831, when C. A. Anstey resigned the chaplaincy, Arnold applied to the Trustees to be appointed to that office himself, and thereafter he preached weekly to the School. Reading his sermons today, one wonders why they were

---

[1] At this time all the members of the VIth form were praepostors, but from 1915 the term 'School Sixth' was used only for members of the School Levée.

so effective, but there is no question that his influence from the pulpit with those who heard him was really great. He was responsible, too, for the erection of the steps from the gravel to the Headmaster's study to enable boys, with the minimum of difficulty, to call on him whenever he was in, and he arranged that a flag should fly from the School House Tower staff as a sign that he was available. In this way he hoped—and to some extent his hope was realised—to have a more frequent and less formal contact with boys in the lower part of the School than had been encouraged by previous Headmasters. Thomas Hughes and Dean Stanley may have exaggerated Arnold's influence on the boys as a whole, but there is no doubt that it was great.

Of the practical changes that he brought about, possibly the most important were the elimination of Dames' Houses and the appointment of regular assistant masters to the Boarding Houses, and his insistence that all masters should give much more of their time to the School; from Arnold's period there dates the principle that has since been commonplace, that a master's work does not end with the lesson, but that he has a real concern with the general as well as the academic well-being of his pupils. Arnold's modification of the curriculum has sometimes been overstressed. It is true that he made mathematics, modern languages and modern history a part of the regular routine, but these had been taught before—James had been particularly interested in the first two—and in any case Arnold had them taught by his classical form-masters. This may have been to ensure that the subjects were not regarded with contempt by the boys, but few of the form-masters were capable of efficient teaching of so wide a range, and they remained very much 'by-subjects', except for modern history in the VIth where Arnold, who became in 1841 Regius Professor of Modern History at Oxford, did his own teaching.

Arnold was a national figure. His enthusiastic adoption of 'broad church' principles, his poor opinion of the clergy as a body and the Establishment as a whole and his voicing of these opinions in a pamphlet published in 1829, when the dispute over Roman Catholic emancipation was raging, entitled *The Christian Duty of Granting the Claims of the Roman Catholics,* had brought him fully into the limelight and had made him the target of attack by the Tory Press. His later published views on Tractarianism did nothing to appease his critics, and it was natural that the attack should shift its aim from Arnold's own opinions to his management of the School where, in his early years of purging, there were plenty of incidents that could be worked up into suitable ammunition. By the late 1830s the storm had subsided, but Rugby School and its remarkable Headmaster had become national news. One result was seen in very great pressure for entry from the liberal portion of the educated population, and Arnold found it impossible to keep the numbers in the School down to the limit of 260 non-Foundationers which, in 1830, he had persuaded the Trustees to fix. It was a school of over 360 that he left to his successor.

Henry Holyoake, Thomas James, Thomas Arnold—these three great Headmasters had been responsible for the rise of Rugby School. Under the weak Raphael Pearce it had all but collapsed; under the indifferent Stanley Burough it had suffered a grave decline. If the chapters that follow give pride of place to the Headmasters and may even seem to lay undue weight upon them, it is because, in the fortunes of the School, the personality of the Headmaster has always had an overriding importance.

The assistant masters, particularly the Housemasters, have had their great importance too, as also have the boys for whose benefit the place exists; without the co-operation of both, as was shown in the case of Henry Hayman, no Headmaster could do anything of value. But, in the last resort, it has always been the Headmaster—his personality, his ability, his influence—who has had the final say in creating the character of the School which it is his office to govern, and it is difficult to see how, in any great school, it can ever be otherwise.

I

A Parenthesis

ARCHIBALD CAMPBELL TAIT, 1842–50
EDWARD MEYRICK GOULBURN, 1850–8

Arnold was no easy man to succeed. In recent years attempts have been made, notably by T. W. Bamford,[1] to drag him from the pedestal that, for over a century, he has occupied almost unchallenged in the educational world; and it is certain that his vigorous broad-churchmanship had made enemies and that the results of his management of Rugby had led to criticism at the universities and elsewhere. Berdmore Compton,[2] writing half a century after Arnold, held that the School 'had gone down in the social scale [and] was no longer what it used to be—the public School for the county families of the Midlands', and spoke of 'conceited boys of the Arnoldite stamp, who set up for being "thinkers", poor lads, before knowing enough of the thoughts of older and wiser people'. It is also true that Arnold's reputation was enhanced by the publication in 1844 of the great biography by A. P. Stanley,[3] whose admiration for his old Headmaster fell little, if at all, short of adoration. But when all

---

[1] *Thomas Arnold.*   [2] *Edward Meyrick Goulburn.*
[3] *Life and Correspondence of Thomas Arnold.*

this is said, contemporary evidence leaves no doubt that when Arnold died suddenly on 12 June 1842, he was widely regarded as outstandingly the greatest Headmaster in the country, a figure of national as well as educational importance, and one whose place it would be very difficult to fill adequately.

There was no lack of candidates of distinction: Bonamy Price, already on the staff of the School, Herbert Kynaston, later High Master of St. Paul's, J. W. Blakesley, later Dean of Lincoln, were all men of outstanding scholarship; but the choice of the Trustees eventually was limited to two men, C. J. Vaughan, later Headmaster of Harrow, and A. C. Tait. Between these two the debate was long and anxious; Vaughan had been one of Arnold's most distinguished pupils; though five years junior to Tait he was quite certainly his superior in technical scholarship and no less vigorous a personality or capable an administrator, and to many it came as a surprise when the decision went against him and Tait was appointed.

Archibald Campbell Tait, the first Scottish Headmaster of Rugby (as he was to be the first Scottish Archbishop of Canterbury), was born in Edinburgh in 1811; he was a club-footed child, whose disability was cured by James Taylor, a remarkable farrier of Whitworth, in Lancashire. Taylor was one of a family whose success in treating horses had led them on to treat humans, and they had acquired more than a local reputation. In the case of Tait, then eight years old, and of his elder brother, the crude orthopaedic treatment was certainly entirely successful. In 1821 he was sent to Edinburgh High School, and three years later became a foundation member of the newly opened Edinburgh Academy. From there he went to Glasgow University in 1827, and three years later, as Snell Exhibitioner, to Balliol, where he gained an open scholarship and in 1834 became a Fellow. In 1835, at the young age of twenty-four, he became Tutor of what was coming to be recognised as the leading Oxford college. Among his early pupils were men who were later to make their mark, including the Rugbeians W. C. Lake, later Dean of Durham, A. P. Stanley, Dean of Westminster, and A. H. Clough, as well as E. M. Goulburn, later Dean of Norwich, who was to succeed him as Headmaster of Rugby; and Benjamin Jowett, later Master of Balliol. It was partly owing to the urging of Lake and Stanley that he was persuaded to become a candidate for the Rugby post. Oxford was at this time going through the turmoil and enthusiasm of the Oxford Movement, and Tait's name had in 1841 come to public notice as the drafter and one of the signatories of the famous 'Protest of the Four Tutors' against Newman's *Tract XC*, a protest that was instrumental in causing Newman to discontinue the *Tracts for the Times*. This action of Tait's may well have influenced the Trustees in his favour. Lake, writing of these events in 1888, said that Tait

> was almost the only tutor at once of a powerful intellect, and of a high moral tone, who was hardly in the least influenced by the spirit which moved almost every young man of thought in Oxford from about 1835 to 1845 . . . the only persons who were left outside the charmed circle being a somewhat apathetic race, the twenty or twenty-two heads of houses, and a few tutors, of whom Tait was the only one of real power.[1]

Tait, as Headmaster, has had rather a poor Press; there has been little positive attack on him, but he has been damned with

[1] R. T. Davidson and W. Benham, *Archibald Campbell Tait*, vol. 1, p. 105.

faint praise by more than one pen. Thus J. C. Shairp, Principal of St. Andrews, who had served under him, stated that he 'was by no means a born schoolmaster', and Arthur Butler[1] held that his 'teachings, sermons, government, were all good and sensible but somewhat cold and repressive; of a kind rather to create respect and confidence than affection and admiration'; though he added that 'behind his reserve and dignity there was, we all felt, a deep fund of power and feeling, which it only needed the occasion to bring forth'. With the faintness of the praise it is a little difficult, on the evidence, to agree. There were bound to be difficulties in the early days of any successor to Arnold's post. The assistant masters were individually brilliant; many of them, to quote Shairp again, 'had been devoted pupils and friends of Arnold, and they were apt to fancy themselves exalted beyond other men by their contact with him'. It would be natural for such men to be suspicious of the new-comer and to find difficulty in accepting any deviation from Arnold's principles and methods; and it is a measure of Tait's success that in certain respects he did so deviate—'We have other things to do at Rugby', he once said, 'besides exalting the Arnold tradition'—and yet that his relations with his assistant staff rapidly became cordial; and that, in spite of initial difficulties, the School grew and prospered under his management.

There was much to be done at Rugby in the 1840s. In 1830 Arnold had persuaded the Trustees to limit the number of non-Foundationers to 260, which had meant a School of not much more than 300 boys, though in 1841 he allowed numbers to increase to 362. This limitation was now withdrawn, and numbers climbed steadily to nearly 500, with a consequent over-

[1] A. G. Butler, later the first Headmaster of Haileybury.

crowding of Boarding Houses and the necessity of providing extra masters, a thing that was difficult since, as G. G. Bradley[1] noted, the system of payment was inequitable, 'enriching the older masters, but leaving no funds for increase of staff'.[2] There was concern for the possible effects of this overcrowding on the health of the boys, and in 1843 the Trustees found it necessary to make an order that a sickroom should be provided in every Boarding House, and four years later empowered Tait to make such extra charges as might be necessary for providing a proper sanatorium.

Tait himself was rapidly busy with improvements. In his first year we find the Trustees reimbursing £102 6s. 6d. which he had laid out on gas pipes for the use of the schools. The next year the School architect, Mr. Hussey, was asked to provide plans for additional studies in School House, and this work was completed by Richard Over in 1845 at a cost of £376 11s. 10d. The following year Hussey was again at work, first inspecting the School House for dry rot, which has been a periodic feature of the School buildings, and drawing up plans for better ventilation in the Chapel; then submitting plans for a library and museum (now the Arnold Library) to be erected over the existing Writing School at a cost of £2000. But in 1846 Tait had to report that subscriptions were unlikely to exceed £1500, and Hussey's plans had to be modified.

It was probably concern for health which caused two other improvements. The first was the draining and filling in of the moat round the Island, which had been a feature of the grounds since the Pond Close had been acquired in 1749, and which had

[1] Later Master of Marlborough.

[2] See 'Note on the Payment of Masters' Salaries (1862)' at the end of chapter.

been the scene of the last stand of the Great School Rebellion in 1797. Today the very name of the Island is being gradually superseded by the more prosaic the 'Mound'. The other was the purchase (for £750) and demolition of some insanitary cottages west of the School, which at the request of the boys were replaced by a fives court.

A good deal of attention was paid to the Chapel. The Trustees sanctioned the outlay of £30 on communion plate in 1844, and in 1848 a committee was set up to supervise the erection of a new transept in memory of the Rev. A. Grenfell and the Rev. C. Mayor, for which the masters undertook to raise £5000. On the condition that this sum was realised, the Trustees agreed to provide a further £200—a comparatively small contribution, but one dictated by the existing condition of the School finances. They were not always ungenerous; three years earlier they had ordered a repayment to the assistant masters of £25 'for the expense of additional cloth for mourning in the School Chapel on the occasion of Dr. Arnold's decease'.

On Tait's relations with the boys in the School evidence is a little mixed. At first he must have seemed rather remote; he left the School House very much to themselves, rarely interfering, taking, apparently, little interest in out-of-school activities, yet, according to Arthur Butler, observant and acquainted with what was going on—and if the occasion arose, 'striking in with a master hand'. He seldom punished. The story is well known of the boy who had been gated, but broke out and was discovered riding on a circus elephant; the escapade earned him no more than a severe reprimand, ending with: 'and remember, I won't be disobeyed, even for an elephant'. But when he did punish, he seems to have done so vigorously. 'There has been a great row

here about drinking', wrote Charles Dickins in an undated
letter to his sister.

> Two fellows have been sent away, three coached, one to have
> no more half-holidays all the half, four put down one form,
> and one put down out of the Sixth into the Fifth, that is two
> forms, but he is going to leave in consequence. Tait says he
> won't let him, but he says he will and won't come into School.
> Altogether there is an awful row, which is capital good fun.[1]

In his dealings with the boys, and indeed in much else in the
School, Tait was greatly helped by his wife, Catherine, a
daughter of Archdeacon Spooner of Elmdon, who took the
liveliest interest in all that was going on, entertained boys, the
young ones to tea and 'tall youths of the Sixth Form' to dinner,
and even made herself responsible for the School accounts, the
complexities of which she seems to have mastered completely.
Tait was respected in the School; she seems to have inspired
affection.

In February 1848 the Headmaster was struck down by
rheumatic fever, and early in March the doctors despaired of his
life. On Ash Wednesday, 8 March, he was hourly expected to
die, and dictated a letter of farewell to his VIth. The School
appears to have realised now the quality of the man they were
likely to lose, and the result was seen first in a curious incident
which occurred in April when Tait had turned the corner, but
was still very seriously ill. Whether or not the boys had been
touched by the revolutionary fever that was at this time sweeping
through Europe, upsetting thrones and governments in almost
every country except Great Britain, there was something very

---

[1] Quotation from boys' letters in this and the following chapters are from a collection in the Temple Reading Room at Rugby.

near to a revolution in the School against 'the Thirty Tyrants of the VIth'. It is not known who organised it, but lists were drawn up assigning two, three or four assailants to each member of the VIth, and the signal for the uprising was to be given at 9.30 a.m. in the Quadrangle. Security, however, was poor, and the news reached the intended victims through a friend of one of them in Price's House (now Bradley). As a result they appeared, all thirty of them, in the Quadrangle just as the rebels were assembling. There might still have been a considerable riot had not the sudden realisation spread, apparently spontaneously, through the throng that the noise involved might have a serious effect on the sick Headmaster; and by the time a master, Bradley, appeared on the scene, tempers had cooled and he was able to disperse the assembly peaceably. Indeed the incident ended in good-humoured laughter when he chased through the cloisters a fifteen-year-old who had shown an inclination to disobey. When, in June, Tait appeared for the first time on the Close, very weak still, but recovered, cricket stopped and he received such an ovation as few headmasters can have experienced from their pupils. Thereafter he was the object of increasing popularity, and when he left Rugby for the last time the boys took the horses out of his carriage and dragged it to the station. 'Wasn't it a queer way of showing respect?' said one of them. 'It was as if you were glad to be rid of him.' 'But how', said another, 'shall we ever get on without him?'

Unlike his predecessor, Tait did not often enter publicly into the debates, particularly over religion, that were raging in the country. He seems to have found his Rugby work sufficient to tax his powers to the utmost. He was, in fact, a tremendous worker, rising in time to prepare his day's lectures before early school at 7 a.m., and seldom retiring before midnight. Twice, however, we find him coming vigorously into public argument. The first was in 1845, when the publication of W. G. Ward's *Ideal for a Christian Church* caused such an outcry that the Convocation of Oxford decided to annul his degrees and to propose the imposition of a stricter religious test at the university. The first of these measures Tait approved as essential, although Ward was one of his oldest friends; against the second he made a vigorous protest, in a published pamphlet. 'There is no need', he wrote, 'of our narrowing the limits of the Church of England because some among us wish to make it too wide.' The pamphlet was influential, and was probably largely responsible for the defeat of the measure when the Proctors exercised their constitutional right of veto in Convocation. It was one of the rare occasions when the phrase '*Nobis Procuratoribus non placet*' has been heard in that body.

Tait's second emergence into the public view occurred shortly before he left Rugby and concerned the School more closely. One of his assistant masters, Henry Highton, had published a book which incurred the displeasure of the *Guardian*,[1] whose anonymous reviewer warned the public against the character of the religious teaching at Rugby. He claimed that the School had become 'a refuge of heresy and latitudinarianism' and that 'the spirit now paramount in the place is that of a sectarian and a freethinker'. To this attack Tait made a trenchantly vigorous reply.

> I ought not lightly to allow this great place of religious education to be vilified [he wrote to the Editor]. As to the words

[1] A Church of England periodical.

'sectarian' and 'latitudinarian', and even 'heretic' . . . I believe that coming from you they will be rightly understood by the public to mean simply that the person to whom these epithets are applied differs from your particular views in interpreting the formularies of the Church of England, though he may be supported in his interpretation by the authority of many of the wisest and most pious of those whom the Church delights to honour.[1]

And he described the terms in which the article was couched as being 'as direct as it usually suits the purpose of an anonymous calumniator to employ'. But the *Guardian* was unrepentant. In a further article, the writer, while professing the highest regard for Tait himself, declared that

> the opinions of some of his fellow-workers are of the laxest kind . . . 'Germanism' . . . 'Carlylism' . . . 'Cobdenism' . . . Is there any political or religious theory on the so-called liberal side which might not find its supporters there? . . . not that Dr. Tait is a freethinker any more than Dr. Arnold was a freethinker . . . but because the tendency of a system of education conducted by either of them is to a false and irreligious liberality.[2]

Perhaps it is not surprising that the body of Anglican country gentlemen who were the Trustees of Rugby School appointed a man of known conservative views as Tait's successor.

After his illness, which left him with impaired health for the rest of his life, Tait found the work at Rugby progressively beyond his powers, and it was with relief that in the autumn of

---

[1] R. T. Davidson and W. Benham, *Archibald Campbell Tait,* vol. I, p. 152.
[2] Ibid., pp. 153–4.

1849 he accepted Lord John Russell's offer of the Deanery of Carlisle. But one further event must be recorded. In that year the Headmaster was troubled by a persistent offensive smell in his study, the origin of which he could not trace. This prompted him to take advantage of Edwin Chadwick's Public Health Act of the previous year, and it was through his initiative that government inspectors were invited to make a report on the sanitary condition of the town of Rugby—including the School. Their report makes remarkable reading. They began with the School, where the origin of the offensive smell was discovered to be a house-drain near the wall, laid without mortar, whose contents 'found their way up the wall by capillary attraction'. The rest of the School drains, with a very shallow fall, converged on the south-west and led, by a most inadequate culvert, to an outfall at a crowded court in the Dunchurch Road where they fell into an open ditch. Conditions in the rest of the town were horrifying.

> Gravel [said the inspectors] is, as is well known, reputed to be an excellent filter. It certainly had need to be so, for all the wells in the town are within fifty feet, and the majority of them within five to ten feet of a cess-pool. The state of things which cannot but exist in the undrained, water-logged soil below can be imagined. Nevertheless the gravel does its work well and although, here and there, some fastidious person may now and then fancy a taste and not like to drink the water, the wells are by no means generally tainted, or at least the taint appears only at intervals or if the water be kept. It would be difficult to find a more perfect test of the efficiency of natural filtration, for it is physically demonstrable that the cess-pools do feed the wells, and in many cases, it cannot but be that the

fluid thrown into the cess-pool in the morning is pumped from
the well at night.[1]

In such conditions did our predecessors of only a century ago
exist. The Trustees, at the special meeting called in November
1849 to consider Tait's resignation, made the offer of one hundred guineas to the local board as a premium to the engineer
who provided the best overall plan for the drainage and
sewerage of Rugby town; but their concern seems to have cooled,
for six months later the offer was withdrawn.

Tait's influence on Rugby produced no spectacular changes,
as did Arnold's. Such changes as came were progressive and
gradual. Like Arnold he made the Chapel the central point in
the School and used the pulpit for what he regarded as the most
important part of his instruction. 'Dr. Tait preaches very impressive sermons', wrote the young James Lee Warner to his mother
in 1849. Arnold's system had tended to create, in his senior boys
at any rate, an exaggerated moral earnestness, and there was a
danger of Rugby turning out prigs. Of this danger Tait appeared
to be aware, and he countered it by administering doses of cold
water where it seemed to be needed. With a good deal of tact
and humour—of his sense of humour there is evidence on all
sides—without altering the system and without injuring discipline, he gradually introduced a more natural relation between
the VIth and the rest of the School. In this his success was not
complete; as will be seen, some bullying continued and there
were cases of indiscipline. But at the time of his resignation the
School was noted for what Arthur Butler called its 'high tone
and discipline', and it was no mere formality that caused the

[1] *Report to the Board of Health* (H.M.S.O., 1849).

R.S.A.—3

Trustees to record that Dr. Tait had maintained and increased the great reputation that the School had achieved under his predecessor.

On 3 April 1850 William Adams wrote to his sister Sarah: 'Tait is going to leave us in a few days now. Then we shall have the *pleasure* of seeing Gouldburn [*sic*] for I believe from all accounts he is a very mild fellow.' The 'mild fellow' already had a considerable reputation. From Eton he had gone, in 1834, as a Scholar to Balliol, the fifth Etonian in succession to win this distinction (it is interesting to note that in the decade 1830–9 Eton and Rugby provided twelve out of the twenty Balliol Scholars). His short-sightedness debarred him from athletic pursuits, but he acquired a considerable reputation as a humorist and was an accomplished mimic. During his Oxford period he held strong evangelical views—unlike his great friends Stanley and Lake, who at the time were followers of Newman—and although the Puritan element in his evangelicalism became modified during his service as chaplain to Bishop Wilberforce from 1847 to 1850, his authority in religious matters remained throughout his life the Bible, and he was a conservative by instinct, disliking liberalism in Church or State. He took a first in Classics in 1839, and in 1841 was elected a Fellow of Merton, where he resisted the Tractarianism that was then strongly entrenched at that college. In 1842 he was ordained and became Vicar of Holywell, where his sermons gained him a wide reputation as a popular preacher.

It was undoubtedly Goulburn's known hostility to liberalism in religion which commended him to the Rugby Trustees. His only formidable rival in the election was W. C. Lake, a confessed disciple of Arnold, whose powerful independence of character and opinion was yet to show itself. The decision of the Trustees disappointed the liberals, particularly Stanley, who was, indeed, exasperated and expressed his feelings sharply to his friends and even to Goulburn himself. But Lake behaved charitably and the assistant masters at Rugby, still predomɩinantly Arnoldian in character, received the new Headmaster kindly.

These were a remarkable body of men. They included the brothers Charles and Thomas Evans, the former later to be Headmaster of King Edward's School, Birmingham, the latter ('Old Tom') Professor of Greek at Durham; Bonamy Price; G. G. Bradley, later Master of Marlborough and Dean of Westminster; Henry Highton, an early expert on the electric telegraph, later Principal of Cheltenham; and G. E. Lynch Cotton, later Master of Marlborough and Bishop of Calcutta— all distinguished classical scholars; J. C. Shairp, later to be Professor of Poetry at Oxford and Principal of St. Andrews; Charles Arnold, an authority on German literature and art; and R. B. Mayor, a mathematician principally, but one ready to tackle almost any other subject in moments of crisis—'Like a fireman's horse,' said Goulburn, 'even when not at work, in the stable with his harness on.' Many of the staff were of long standing and had served under Arnold; at least two of them had been appointed by Dr. Wooll—C. A. Anstey in 1819 and H. J. Buckoll in 1826. Both of these were Old Rugbeians, and the latter, apart from a few years as an undergraduate at Queen's College, Oxford, spent his whole life at Rugby, serving under six Headmasters until his death in 1871.

A staff which thus combined intellectual brilliance with

long service might well have proved a difficult team for a young man to manage, but although there were inevitably some dis-agreements, relations on the whole seem to have been cordial enough. Goulburn himself appointed only four masters during his eight years of headmastership, compared to sixteen appointed by his predecessor and twenty-seven by his successor. This reflects a period of declining numbers in the School. Where Tait had admitted 1158 boys, Goulburn, in approximately the same period, admitted only 740. In his first full year (1851) there were 148 entrants; by 1856 the number had dwindled to 82; and the School, which in 1851 had been 466 strong, was by 1857 only 316. This decline cannot be attributed to any falling off in academic standards, for Rugby continued to provide more than its fair share of scholars to both universities; indeed 1857 has been called the School's *annus mirabilis*, for in that year almost all the open awards at Oxford and Cambridge were won by Rugbeians. Nor were the less able boys neglected. Where Arnold and Tait had to some extent excluded or got rid of unpromising boys, Goulburn considered it the duty of a Public School to do its best for all types, and his personal *forte* lay in encouraging the dull boy, in 'heartening', as he put it, the one who was in difficulties.

The decline in the popularity of the School was almost cer-tainly due to Goulburn's conservative convictions, and to the moderate ritualism—it was no more—that he introduced into the Chapel services. The image of Rugby, created by Arnold and Tait, as a home of liberalism and broad-churchmanship, was what had brought support, and 'it was apparently impos-sible', said Berdmore Compton, 'that the School could flourish on distinctive Church principles'. Perhaps if Goulburn had stayed longer he might have succeeded in attracting support from the conservatives, and an upswing in numbers to 365 in his last year suggests that the tide was turning. But he was never completely happy as a schoolmaster, pining always for parochial work; he blamed himself for the falling numbers—he was keenly aware that it meant financial loss to his masters—and it was with relief that he resigned in 1858. Later he was to say that he had expected 'too much advance in holiness from schoolboys' and had been disappointed.

Of Goulburn's appointments to the staff, two deserve a special mention. Tait had advised the new Headmaster to take the first opportunity of appointing a close personal friend, and the advice was followed in 1851 when the Rev. Berdmore Compton came to the School as the first teacher of natural science as a regular subject—though a lowly one—in the curriculum. There had been virtually no science taught in the School since 1834.[1] Up to that date there had been a course of lectures every three years, beginning in 1776 when Adam Walker had delivered the first; he had been succeeded by his son D. F. Walker, who seems to have lectured successfully until 1834, when he complained that Dr. Arnold was obstructive. When he next came in 1837, Arnold appears to have made the course impossible by allowing the lectures only on half-holidays when other engagements made attendance at them impracticable for all but a very few, and Walker abandoned them in disgust. Arnold, it appears, while interested in science, disapproved of it as a school subject, fearing that it might cause

---

[1] Tait had, in August 1849, appointed William Sharp as a natural philosophy tutor, but he had left in December 1850, and little, if any, progress appears to have been made in the subject.

a decline in other studies and feeling that it could not provide the moral lessons that he looked for in all school subjects. Now the subject was to start again and, in spite of misgivings on the part of Trustees and Governing Body, was to develop with increasing and uninterrupted momentum. At their June meeting in 1856 the Trustees agreed in principle to Goulburn's and Compton's request for the provision of 'a room for the teaching of Natural Philosophy', though for expense on so novel a project they had to secure the consent of the Charity Commissioners; two months later Goulburn offered, at his own expense, to employ an architect to design a natural science school. And the following year orders for the erection of the school were given. By 1862 the Royal Commissioners found natural philosophy, principally chemistry and electricity, being taught as an alternative to modern languages to one set in each of the blocks above the Lower School, for two in-school lessons a week, in addition to a good deal of out-of-school work, and they recorded that the Trustees had 'with exemplary liberality built a Physical Science Lecture Room and Labora- tory and partly furnished both at a cost of over £1000 drawn from capital'. The subject was one of those accepted for School exhibitions, and already Rugbeians had gained first class honours at Oxford, Cambridge and Dublin.

The other of Goulburn's notable appointments was Edward White Benson, who stayed at Rugby for six years only, leaving in 1858 to be the first Master of Wellington College, and there- after successively Chancellor of Lincoln, Bishop of Truro and Archbishop of Canterbury. In spite of the comparative brevity of his mastership at Rugby, he had a considerable influence, and his advice was largely followed in the improvements carried out in the Chapel at this time. These included the building of a south transept in 1851 to balance that on the north, the removal of the flat ceiling—Arnold's 'old enemy'— to give an extra eighteen feet of height; the removal of the organ gallery, which had blocked the West window, and the rebuilding of the organ on the north side in 1855; and the erection of the ante-Chapel, the lower west wall of which (with the windows presented by Goulburn himself) is the only part of the old Chapel still standing. Much of the money for these improvements was subscribed by the boys in the School and by Old Rugbeians.

Goulburn was, indeed, very active in adding to School buildings and amenities. In 1851 the Trustees accepted his offer to build a new Boarding House at his own expense, and the following year leased to him, for ninety-nine years, one acre of the School field at £5 a year. On this plot there arose the House first occupied by C. T. Arnold, which is now known as School Field. The Trustees, however, refused his suggestion that the School should buy the Rev. E. N. Stanley's House in School Street. It was to be a good many years before the policy was adopted of School ownership of Boarding Houses.

Attention was paid, too, to the grounds, and in 1854 Goulburn presented a new field, which was added to the Close by the felling of trees, and was first used for cricket in 1856. Levelling was also carried out on the western side of the grounds, which made Pontines less marshy. The management of the grounds seems to have been left largely to the boys, though the Trustees would sometimes accept part of the expenses, as when in 1850 they ordered £20 to be paid 'to the account incurred by the boys in new turfing the cricket ground'.

The reigns of Tait and Goulburn form a kind of parenthesis between the tremendous vigour of the development under Arnold and under Temple. To the boys there can have seemed to be but little alteration in their way of life. The School year was still divided into two halves of eighteen weeks each, from February to June and August to December (though Goulburn took to accepting new boys in April and October as well as at the beginning of the half, and this remained the practice until the introduction of three terms in 1866). In the winter months boys rose (in theory) at 7 a.m. for breakfast at 7.30 and school at 8. In the summer they rose at 6.30 a.m. for an hour and a half's school before breakfast at 8.30. A whole school day would involve three lessons of an hour each in the morning and two in the afternoon. The bulk of the time was still spent on the Classics, and the method of teaching seems to have been uniform throughout the School—the 'calling up' of a few boys each lesson to construe prepared work. In the lower forms there was 'place-taking' at each lesson—the boy who failed went down below the one who corrected him—but in the XX and VIth this occurred only every few weeks. 'Calling up' was in no regular order, but Charles Evans, taking the Upper Vth, said that each boy would be 'set on', on an average, once every four lessons. Mathematics occupied three hours a week on the average, modern languages—French or German or both—two. Arnold, who believed in the form principle, had insisted on his classical masters themselves teaching these subjects to their forms—thereby illustrating, as the Commissioners later reported, 'the requirements of a man ready to do wonders himself and sanguine in his expectation of the zeal and versatility of others'. Tait had begun appointing specialists—R. B. Mayor for mathematics and some short-lived gentlemen, such as Dr. Trithen, Monsieur Bernays and Alexander Ross for modern languages—and had allowed his classical masters, if they so wished, to delegate their work to these. In addition to the in-school lessons a good deal of time was spent at tutorial work; Charles Evans, for instance, taught his form for fifteen lessons each week and spent twenty-one with tutorial sets as large as and much less homogeneous than his form. It was virtually a necessity for each boy to have a private tutor (for which there was a charge of ten guineas a year), and although in theory the parents chose their boys' tutors, the choice was limited by the fact that a Housemaster would inevitably be the tutor to every boy in his house.

Although Goulburn, with declining numbers, had been able to reduce forms to reasonable proportions, before and after his time they were, by modern standards, very large. In 1848, omitting writing, drawing and music masters, there were twelve assistants for 490 boys; by 1862 there were eighteen for 463. The Headmaster's VIth form always numbered over forty, the XX about thirty, forms of the rest of the Upper School, the Middle School and the Remove not much under forty, and the Lower School less than twenty. Earlier the position was even tighter. 'My form', wrote John Penrose to his son in 1846, 'has 64 [boys], which is no joke. A long lesson is much harder work than pulling in an Oxford race.'

One of the features of the teaching seems to have been the stress laid on learning by heart. The VIth had to commit to memory, as a half-year's stint, the Eleventh Book of Virgil's *Aeneid,* the Eleventh and Twelfth Satires of Juvenal, the Fourth Book of Lucretius and the Fourth Georgic of Virgil, at the rate of 60 lines a week, in addition to passages from the Bible. C. T. Arnold's half-year list for the Lower Vth is formidable: 400 lines of Virgil, 500 of Horace, 300 of Aeschylus, 400 of English poets (Scott, Wordsworth or Tennyson), and in addition a choice of 400 of Milton or Shakespeare, 600 of Scott or Tennyson, 500 of Horace's *Odes,* 300 of a Greek play, 300 of Homer or 300 of Virgil.

Written work took the form of 'copies'. The VIth, each half, had to produce as composition 10 copies of Latin verse (of about 30 lines each), 20 of Latin prose and 8 of English prose; as translation 35 in-school and 5 out-of-school Latin copies, 20 in school and 10 out-of-school Greek. In addition 20 English essays were exacted, but below the Upper School no original composition of any kind was attempted. History, both ancient and modern, and geography were taught by form-masters. For mathematics, modern languages and natural philosophy the blocks were divided into sets, and numbers were much smaller than in the forms.

That the methods used produced results there can be no doubt. In Classics particularly the record is impressive. In the ten years 1852–62, Rugbeians won at Oxford 35 Firsts in Moderations and 22 in Greats; 3 Ireland and 3 Hertford scholarships; 2 Latin Verse, 1 Newdigate, 1 Sacred Poem, 1 Latin Essay, 2 Arnold Historical and 2 Denyer Theological Essay prizes; 19 College Fellowships, 41 open scholarships and 7 Exhibitions; at Cambridge 6 Firsts in Classics and 1 in Natural Science; a Craven, a David, a Porson and a Bell scholarship; a Camden Latin Verse, a Greek Epigram, a Greek Ode and a Moral Philosophy prize; 2 Chancellor's Medals, 13 Fellowships, and 18 open scholarships. This list, the Commissioners reported in 1864 'evinces the Teaching of the *Literae Humaniores* (at Rugby) to be absolutely unsurpassed—its training in exact scholarship to stand within the first rank and its practice of composition not to disentitle it to a very honourable position among the Public Schools'. In mathematics too there was success; the same ten years saw twelve Rugbeians as Wranglers at Cambridge and five securing Firsts at Oxford, where two mathematics scholarships were also won.

Discipline in School was strict, but not, it appears, inhuman. L. F. Burrows, one of Goulburn's appointments, said that his method with his Upper Middle Form was 'to keep absolute silence and try to make the lesson lively'. Assistant masters usually punished by giving impositions; sometimes they would lock up a boy in solitary confinement for the afternoon to get on with his work, and in cases of 'gross and frequent inattention in class' they might administer half a dozen blows with a cane on the hand. The Headmaster alone used the birch, and floggings do not appear to have averaged in this period more than eight a year; and there was seldom more than one expul-sion, though requests to parents to remove their sons were probably more frequent.

It was the praepostors who were responsible for the more general discipline of the School; their duty was 'to put down ill practices of every kind such as the frequenting of public houses, turbulent conduct, drinking and smoking'. Their sanction was the cane, administered sometimes with considerable severity across the shoulders. There was an appeal allowed by the victim to the Headmaster, but as there is no recorded instance of his reversing the judgment of the VIth it is hardly surprising that such appeals were rare.

For the younger boys there was fagging, which was the lot of everyone until he reached the dignity of the XX or became a 'swell', a distinction usually achieved by proved athletic prowess of one kind or another. Fagging could take such diverse forms as cooking, making tea or carrying hot water for the VIth—one fag giving evidence before the Royal Commission in 1862 complained that the storage cistern in School House was not large enough and that he was frequently punished for bringing water at too low a temperature—standing in goal at football or fielding at cricket. These last two were very unpopular. 'There is one horrid regulation,' wrote James Lee Warner in 1849, 'namely to fag at cricket for any Sixth fellow and pick up the ball which has given me a great dislike for it.' But it had one beneficial result perhaps, for in the Royal Commission's report in 1864 we find the remark that 'fagging at games seems almost to have resolved itself into a peculiar method of making physical education compulsory'.

At a time when so much of the running of affairs was left, without much interference, to the VIth, it was inevitable that there should be abuses. Bullying of the cruder sort described in *Tom Brown* seems to have been uncommon, but there were other kinds. 'I have got on quite well with bullying,' wrote Lee Warner, 'except their coming into my study pulling all my books about and preventing my learning by asking me to repeat the most horrid words, by pretending to know such things as boys ought not to know. I am sure I should like to know what I am to do.' But a fortnight later he says that 'bullying is almost at an end' and goes on to speak of other disadvantages of being small. 'Sunday was a wretched cold day, and yet I could not get near the fire; the large fellows keep it all to themselves.'

He mentions some other practices. 'Stealing here is not uncommon and they alter the 8th commandment to "Thou shalt steal nothing except . . .". 'They don't mind getting drunk or swearing.' 'I must do Dr. Tait the credit to say the boys' sins are not overlooked by him, but swearing and vile language are but too frequent although prayers are said in private by some.'

He got on badly at the School House 'Lamb-Singing' too, of which his account is worth quoting in full:

All the fellows assembled in the hall and the old fellows by the fire; the Sixth fellows then came down and an urchin followed them, bringing down two jugs in which were a handful of salt which had been boiled down in this water. Whilst the fellows were singing the second fellow in the House was stirring it with a tallow candle. My turn came; I ascended the table and held the candle stick in my hand and began some song which I had learnt an hour previous. 'Tune' was re-echoed, but to no effect. I, alas, doomed, descended. When all had done, those who had to drink came up to the table when a *brimmer* was presented, muddy water crammed with salt just liquid. Taking the potion I drank it to the dregs, and then speech was gone for an hour, my throat as if it had been skinned, and I could not drink the tea which is always given after. I was dreadfully sick and then drank 8 cups of tea, 4 mugs of milk and water and as many of water. After this they were afraid to give me any more, and then I went to bed dreadfully weak. One fellow is now staying out from the effect, and I am far from well.

This was in November 1849. At the same singing William Adams came off better. 'I have got on very well with the singing,' he wrote home, 'and have not drunk once, but it is a shame to make fellows drink for they are ill for two or three days afterwards.'

But life was by no means all misery. Though work was hard —'we are obliged to keep up till ten o'clock till one's eyes can scarcely keep open' (Lee Warner again)—there was a good deal of spare time; always there was an hour before dinner and an hour afterwards for cricket 'ends'[1] or puntabout or even rounders, as F. S. Parkin tells us in February of 1858. And on the long half-holidays those who were not playing cricket or football could escape into a countryside not yet built up, with their fishing-rods or their illegal shotguns, could go 'leaping' or join in the runs when the hares carrying bags of 'scent' were given ten minutes' start (to this day the Captain of running is the Holder of Bigside Bags); in the summer there was bathing in the Avon at Sleath's and in the season, for a few, an occasional run with foxhounds on foot or on a hired hunter or one kept surreptitiously at a livery stable. And there was plenty to do indoors. For the intellectual there was the Debating Society, started 1845, or the excitement of producing one of the many ephemeral School or House magazines, such as the *Rugby Miscellany* of 1845, which produced ten numbers; or the *Rugbaean*, which was started by T. W. Jex-Blake in 1850 and ran through twenty numbers before its death in 1852; or its successor the *New Rugbeian*, of 1858, which ran to three whole volumes of 26 numbers to 1861—1000 printed pages with some distinguished contributions; or the *Crescent* of Arnold's House. (1850–2). For the less thoughtful there was always cooking to be done or amateur science—or perhaps the two combined: 'Please send some book of chemical experiments', wrote F. S. Parkin, 'and some eatables as Browne and I are chemicalising together.' Food, not the House food, but what could be sent

---

[1] An 'end' is the Rugby term for a net.

from home, was a matter of constant importance. 'Would you tell Mamma', wrote William Adams to his sister, 'that I would like only a half ham, for I think it would get dry. As for marmalade it is a pity to send it for you know what fellows are when they are at school.' And a few years later, under Temple, D. B. Maclaren writes: 'I like everything here except the beer which is frightful. Do you think I might have porter in bottles?'

To list all the Rugbeians of this period who distinguished themselves would be impossible.[1] In all the stirring events of the time, the Crimean War, the Indian Mutiny, the Sikh, Burmese, Chinese, Afghan wars, the rapid developments in Africa, Australia and Canada, men educated at Rugby took a part. Three who entered under Tait (R. R. Glyn, G. G. Clowes and J. P. Winter) followed Cardigan in the charge of the Light Brigade at Balaclava; two (H. S. Wilmot and R. C. W. R. Mitford) won the Victoria Cross during the Mutiny. In politics and diplomacy G. J. Goschen became First Lord of the Admiralty and H. G. Wolff, in the course of a distinguished career, Ambassador at Madrid. In letters, C. L. Dodgson ('Lewis Carroll') made his entirely individual contribution to literature; in music there was Herbert Oakeley; in scholarship and philosophy, Henry and Arthur Sidgwick, S. N. Hodgeson and T. H. Green; in theology, A. B. Webb (Bishop of Bloemfontein and of Grahamstown and later Dean of Salisbury) and Henry Wace (Bampton Lecturer and Principal of King's College, London); in education, a High Master of St. Paul's (F. W. Walker) and Headmasters of Rugby (T. W.

---

[1] A remarkably comprehensive list is given in W. H. D. Rouse's *A History of Rugby School,* pp. 278–89.

Jex-Blake), Haileybury (A. G. Butler), University College School (H. W. Eve), Bedford Modern School (R. B. Poole), and Newcastle, Staffordshire, High School (F. E. Kitchener), as well as a Principal of Presidency College, Calcutta (C. H. Tawney) and a very large number of university dons. And the names of those who distinguished themselves on the field of sport are legion. The record is enough to suggest that, if the reigns of Tait and Goulburn represent a sort of parenthesis in the history of Rugby School, it is a parenthesis full of serious purpose and of vigorous life.

Note on the Payment of Masters' Salaries (1862)

The method of deciding masters' salaries was extremely complicated and depended to a large extent on the number of boys in the School. Only a minor part was paid directly by the Trustees from the Foundation—to the Headmaster £113 6s. 8d., to the seven senior classical masters and to the senior mathe- matical master £120 each, to the writing master £50 and to the drawing master £20.

The residue was made up:

1. From School fees, which were £16 5s. 6d. a year. This sum was divided as follows:

(a) £4 4s. per boy to the Headmaster. From this he paid £1 for every boy over fifty to his senior composition master, £100 to his junior composition master and £125 to his modern languages master.

(b) £7 7s. per boy to the seven senior classical masters, i.e. £1 1s. each, up to the maximum given by 320 boys.

(c) £1 11s. 6d. per boy to three senior mathematical masters, 10s. 6d. each, but two of them limited to £240.

(d) £1 1s. per boy to two modern languages masters, which, with the £125 provided by the Headmaster, was divided between them by agreement.

(e) From the remaining £2 2s., 12s. per boy went to one of the seven classical masters as master of the Lower School, to a maximum of £192; 15s. per boy to each of two additional classical masters up to a maximum of £240.

(f) The excess was termed the 'Reserve Fund' and was used to pay £240 to each of two additional classical masters; £360 to a master teaching Classics and mathematics; and an additional £300 to the junior composition master.

Any residue was at the disposal of masters for School pur-poses.

2. Private tuition. This was almost essential for all boys below the VIth and above the Lower School, and cost £10 10s. a year for classical tutors. Five of the seven senior classical masters were allowed to take pupils, limited in theory to fifty each. The senior mathematical master also took pupils at the same fee, and the senior modern languages master at £6 6s.

3. Profits on Boarding Houses, and entrance fees.

4. Fellowships: two of £200 and three of £100 were held until the Royal Commission's Report, after which no more were awarded.

On this basis, in the year of the Commission's evidence, the Headmaster received £2967 0s. 8d. (£113 6s. 8d. stipend,

£1332 12s. fees, £1277 10s. profits from Boarding Houses, £243 12s. entrance fees). A senior classical master with a Boarding House received £1617 6s. 6d.; one without a House £870 5s.; the lowest received £340. Mathematical masters averaged £881 18s., modern languages masters £760 12s.

The masters voluntarily taxed themselves to the extent of £500 a year to provide entrance scholarships, and provided generous contributions to School building funds. With the then value of the pound and income tax at 7d., perhaps they could afford to.

2

'Granite on Fire'

FREDERICK TEMPLE, 1858–69

For a man of any intellectual quality, the middle of the nine-teenth century was a tremendously exciting time to be alive. In 1851 the Great Exhibition had given visual demonstration to the gathering momentum of scientific and technical advance that was already revolutionising the old ways of life; the year after Temple came to Rugby, Darwin published his *Origin of Species*, striking, so it seemed to conservative opinion, at the eternal verities that formed the very foundation of Christian civilisation; and two years later the attention of the educated nation was anxiously focused on the great debate between T. H. Huxley and Bishop Wilberforce on the nature of man's origins. Discoveries in astronomy, in geology, in physics, in medicine appeared to be casting doubt on truths that had for centuries been accepted without question, and where many worthy men, clinging to what seemed the only stable and satis-factory basis of their lives, put up the shutters against the impli-cations of scientific revelation, others, the vigorous-minded and progressive, strove to harmonise the newly discovered truths, which their reason would not allow them to deny, with what was best and most useful in the old. Macaulay was the accepted prophet who taught that history was an ordered progress towards the betterment of man's condition, and Tennyson, in his 'Morte d'Arthur', had sung that

> God fulfils Himself in many ways,
> Lest one good custom should corrupt the world.

'Of all decades in our history,' says G. M. Young, 'a wise man would choose the eighteen-fifties to be young in.'[1]

In the microcosm of a great school, the intellectual ferment that was seething in the country found a reflection. For nine years Rugby had been guided by a man whose ways of thought were conservative, and it had appeared, in a sense, to mark time. Now it was to feel the impact of one no less pious, but whose dynamic vigour seemed to be inspired by the essential spirit of the new age, a man who had lived through the stormy period of the death of Tractarianism and had developed the con-viction that readiness to accept constant growth in doctrine was essential to religion, and indeed to man's healthy development. 'In change only,' he said, 'in perpetual progress, can truth be sought.'

There was need of but little debate among the Trustees as to who should be invited to succeed Goulburn at Rugby. Frederick Temple stood out from among the other candidates as incom-parably the most suitable. As long ago as 1849, when he was only twenty-eight years old, he had been urged by Tait to apply, but at that time he had recently undertaken the direction of the experimental training college for elementary-school teachers at Kneller Hall, and did not feel free to abandon work only just

---

[1] G. M. Young, *Victorian England: Portrait of an Age* (O.U.P., 1937).

started, though he confessed that the Rugby headmastership was 'the post on earth which he would most like to fill'. Now Kneller Hall was closed and he was to have his chance.

Frederick Temple was born in 1821 in the Ionian Islands, where his father, Major Octavius Temple, was the British Resident. His family returned home when Frederick was three years old, and settled at Axon in Cornwall, where the boy was taught by the vicar until January 1834, when he entered Blundell's School. It was here that he learnt the habit of hard work—and independent work—which remained with him for the rest of his life. 'We were not made merely to listen to a teacher,' he said many years later, 'but to learn . . . there is a real and special value in throwing a boy on his own resources, and allowing him to learn.' Blundell's taught him the value of the principle, which he applied at Rugby, of giving boys the opportunity of learning—or of neglecting to do so—on their own.

In 1839 he went as Blundell's Scholar to Balliol. The amount of the scholarship was not enough to keep him and his start at Oxford was made possible only by an anonymous gift of £50, almost certainly from Sir Thomas Acland, who had recognised his quality; all his time at Oxford he was very poor and never spent more than £80–£90 in a year. He worked with tremendous energy, rising at 3 or 4 a.m., working, with a break for Chapel, until 3 p.m., and then again from 6.30 or 7 p.m. until 10.30. The result was a double First in Classics and Mathematics, but he had also found time to read a good deal of history and biological science, and later he was to master the elements of chemistry and physics and to teach in the laboratory at Kneller Hall. He remained at Balliol, as Fellow and Tutor, from 1842 to 1848, when his interest in teachers and training colleges led him to become a member of the Committee of the Council on Education, examiner in the Education Office and Principal of Kneller Hall.

But his activity was by no means all intellectual. He enjoyed football and cricket and was, like so many of his contemporaries, a great walker. He confessed to having walked, on one occasion while on holiday in Wales, eighteen miles in three hours before breakfast; and while he was an undergraduate, hearing that Arnold wished to meet him, he shouldered a knapsack and walked the forty-eight miles from Oxford to Rugby in the day; he was quite ready to do the return journey the following day, but Arnold liked him and kept him at Rugby for a while. He also had a boyish love of climbing trees, and the story, which went round the School shortly after his arrival at Rugby, that the Headmaster had climbed all the elms in the Close, was not without foundation, as he himself admitted.

The contrast between the outgoing and the incoming Head-master could hardly have been greater. Henry Lee Warner, younger brother of the timid new boy quoted in the last chapter, saw the two together in the School House shortly before Goul-burn's departure, 'the one dignified, sweet-voiced, cassocked, almost pompous; the other with a wide shirt-front, a rasping voice and an elastic spring as he bounded up the stairs; what a contrast! a contrast almost entirely unfavourable to my young mind'. Goulburn could never have committed the appalling solecism of which Temple was guilty when, arriving in Rugby for the first time as Headmaster, he shocked the middle-class susceptibilities of the inhabitants by walking up from the station, wearing a swallow-tailed coat and carrying his own bag.

This was not the kind of behaviour to which they were accustomed in the Headmaster of Rugby School. Yet this was the
man who was to fulfil the prophecy of R. R. W. Lingen that,
if Temple were appointed to Rugby, it 'would mark an epoch
in the public education of this country not less notable than
that which followed the appointment of Dr. Arnold'.

Doubts there may have been at the start, but it was a matter
of only a few weeks before Temple had the whole School
completely in his hand, and for the next eleven years it is
difficult to find within the Rugby community (elsewhere it was
different) any note of opposition. Even that day-to-day criticism
of the Headmaster, almost universal in Schools, which was once
described by another Headmaster as 'inevitable if you have a
lively minded staff'—even this seems to have been stilled.
Rapidly the whole school, masters and boys alike, found that
they had to do with a man who was completely impartial,
scrupulously fair and rock-firm; one whose tremendous vigour
and enthusiasm were infectious, who was prepared to discuss
his ideas—masters were encouraged to air their views on projected changes—but who took his own decisions; a man who, if
he demanded the highest standards of industry, would push no
one half so far as he was prepared to push himself. He had a
genius for persuasion: F. E. Kitchener has described the
masters' meeting at which he persuaded his staff to agree to a
readjustment of salaries to the detriment of the senior masters
because it would be more equitable; they came away not really
knowing why they had agreed, but convinced that the decision
was right. So complete was Temple's mastery that, at the height
of the storm over *Essays and Reviews,* a boy[1] wrote home to a

[1] R. W. Hanbury.

worried parent: 'Temple's all right, but if he turns Mahommedan, the whole School will turn Mahommedan too.'

The new Headmaster was not a great classicist—stories were
soon current at the universities about 'Temple's rough-and-
ready scholars'—but he was a great teacher and a supremely great
schoolmaster. He managed, in class, 'to create an impression of
ease in the task while carefully disentangling the difficulties'.
He induced an atmosphere of cheerfulness and serenity in work
and engendered a lively interest. 'His hearers', said one who was
taught by him, 'stood on the threshold of life and were made to
feel that life was worth living'.[1] He insisted on no very strict
discipline and was impatient of those who demanded too high
an academic standard from less able boys. 'All your questions
are too hard,' he said to an over-zealous young master. 'Why do
you frighten your boys so?' Above all he was in the line of
progress, though he still regarded Classics as the essential foundation of a true education. Mathematics he looked on as an
admirable discipline in precision of thought and science as
cultivating, in some sense, a love of order and beauty; but
Classics, he said, 'touches the human part of our nature' and
trains a man to understand and deal with his fellow men.[2] And
so his lessons to the VIth were never allowed 'to degenerate
into grammatical hair-splitting', but became an education in
humanity. 'It was because he was so great a man', said H. G.
Hart, 'that he exercised such power as a teacher.'[3]

There were two outstanding events, each in its own way por-

[1] Henry Lee Warner.
[2] Answers to the Public Schools Commission. Quoted by F. E. Kitchener in
Frederick Temple, vol. I, p. 169.
[3] Ibid., p. 165.

tending change, during Temple's period as Headmaster—the Royal Commission on Public Schools, formed in 1861, which made its Report in 1864 and which bore fruit in the Public Schools Act of 1868; and the tercentenary of the School in 1867. But Temple could not wait to initiate reform, and much of the evidence given to the Royal Commissioners bears on changes that he had already made. It is therefore at his reforms that we shall first look.

The first problem arose owing to the increase in numbers that had already begun, as we have seen, under his predecessor; this rapidly became an unmanageable flood, and in 1862 Temple told the Commissioners: 'I refuse twice as many [non-Foundationers] as I take, because I have not room. I have three times as many applications as I can take into the school.'[1] Although this situation had the advantage of enabling Temple to make superannuation a reality and thereby get rid of unsuitable boys, and, a few years later, of requiring new boys to pass an entrance examination, it underlined the urgent necessity of increased strength in the teaching staff and of providing new schools— both of which demanded money. One of the results of the adjustment of salaries already referred to, reducing the income of the classical masters, had been to increase the difficulty of securing first-class men. 'I noticed', Temple wrote in 1862, 'that three years ago I had only to ask a man to come, and he came. This year I asked four men to come, and they declined, on the ground that the money was not enough.'[2] Moreover he wanted non-classical set-masters of a calibre equal to those who taught the forms, and men who would, in the eyes of the boys, be on an equal footing with them. This last point had probably

[1] P.S.C. Evidence. Ibid., p. 203.   [2] P.S.C. Minutes. Ibid., p. 188.

been already secured, for Robert Mayor in mathematics and Philip Bowden Smith in modern languages had already estab-lished the status of the 'by-subjects'. That Rugby was singular in this respect is clear from the tone of surprise in which the Commissioners commented on the situation. But Temple wanted much more:

> A boy ought not to be ignorant of this earth on which God has placed him, and ought, therefore, to be well acquainted with geography. He ought not to walk in the fields in total ignorance of what is growing under his very eyes, and he ought, therefore, to learn botany. There is hardly an occupation in which he can be employed where he will not find chemistry of use to him.[1]

And so we find Temple bombarding the Trustees with demands for more masters and more schools for them to operate in. Among his classical appointments were T. W. Jex-Blake, A. G. Butler, John Percival, A. W. Potts, J. S. Phillpots, F. E. Kitchener, James Robertson and R. W. Taylor, all later to be headmasters; for mathematics and natural science came J. M. Wilson, later Headmaster of Clifton, and Charles Elsee; for modern languages J. W. J. Vecqueray. And among the many other distinguished appointments—Moberly, Hutchinson, Arthur Sidgwick—perhaps we must single out Robert White-law, one of the most remarkable schoolmasters of all time. Of him more will be heard.

New schools were essential, and money was tight, but Temple was insistent, and in September 1858 the Trustees, 'it appearing that the study of Natural Science had been fairly established in the School by a trial of eight years', gave a definite order for the

---

[1] P.S.C. Answers. Ibid., p. 197.

erection of a school for this purpose to the design of George Gilbert Scott. More was needed. In 1861 Temple wrote: 'We are much pinched for want of room . . . the Headmaster's hayloft has been converted into a school-room and we rent another in the Town Hall.'[1] In 1864 the Trustees acceded to his suggestion that a house should be bought for extra schools, for which purpose the masters were prepared to subscribe £500, and agreed to an outlay of £2000. But this represented little more than a palliative. The answer was to come in the building of the New Quadrangle, which was the contribution of the masters to the Rugby tercentenary. In April 1867 the Trustees considered a letter from Temple informing them that the masters had raised £5000 towards new building and asking for permission to have plans prepared. Four months later he was urging the desirability of purchasing houses at the north-west corner of the School property, and told them that he and the assistant masters had agreed to buy the property for £3500 and would re-sell it to the School for £1800, 'the Domus fund for the School being responsible for the remainder'. To this the Trustees replied that 'they feel bound to record their sense of the great liberality of the Headmaster and assistant masters in so largely contributing to the new schools. They regret however that the state of the School funds will not admit of their contributing thereout to the expense of erecting such schools.' Temple was not deterred; he approached William Butterfield— to whom, in the face of great opposition, he remained thereafter obstinately faithful—and on 16 May 1868 the Trustees held a special meeting at Curzon House in South Audley Street to consider the plans submitted. They received a shock.

[1] P.S.C. Answers. Ibid., p. 189.

After the Masters' generosity [they minuted] the Trustees feel some delicacy in expressing any opinion or criticism of the plans now submitted to them. They however venture to state that they are unanimous in wishing greater congruity at least in colour with the old buildings, and they beg to know whether the Masters generally would acquiesce in their unanimous feeling on the subject so far as to allow the walls and roofs to be built of the same description of brick and slating as their present buildings, and the copings to be of the same kind of stone.[1]

But Temple was adamant. A week later 'The Trustees, while adhering to their unanimous opinion on the incongruity of the style of the proposed buildings, will not press their objections against the wish of those who have so liberally subscribed to the fund for their erection'—but no additional charges were to be thrown on the Trustees' funds.

So those who had the final responsibility went down fighting against the men whom they employed; Butterfield was in the saddle now and for many years to come—the Chapel, New Big School, the gymnasium, the Temple Reading Room and Art Museum are his work; his influence is everywhere and Rugby is as it is. But Temple got his schools, though they were not in use until the time of his successor.

That the reforms carried out in the period of Temple's head-mastership were his own work is abundantly clear. One of his early difficulties arose from the fact that, under his predecessor, the Housemasters had become largely independent—Kitchener refers to them as an *imperium in imperio*—and that the intellectual stimulus of the School had been provided by the tutors rather than the Headmaster; Thomas and Charles Evans, E. W.

[1] Rugby Trustee Order Books.

Benson, G. G. Bradley and Robert Mayor were the most powerful influences in the School. Temple just reassumed authority,
without any fuss and without arousing resentment or opposition;
it is a measure of the greatness of the man. His own views were
made to prevail, and what those views were is preserved for us
in the evidence placed in writing before the Royal Commission
and in the oral evidence given to the Commissioners when they
visited Rugby in 1862 and to the House of Lords Select Committee, which sat on the Public Schools Bill in 1865. The
investigation was in minute detail, as appears from the papers
preserved in the Public Record Office, and involved the masters
in a good deal of work, since each one had to make a return of
what he taught and how he taught it each lesson of the week,
the books he used, the time spent on each and the method of
using them. The Rugby masters were perhaps slow in sending
in their returns, but Temple was prepared to defend them.
'Now I will deliver my soul', he wrote in April 1862 to Professor Montague Bernard, Secretary of the Commission, 'of a
long, loud, savage growl at you. Have you no consideration for
busy men that you only give us seven days to send you back the
proofs? But we could easily do it if you had only the bowels to
send us down a copy each. If you only knew the gnashing of
teeth which you cause us.' And, asking for twenty copies, 'If
you decline for no reason, we shall turn crusty and decline to
give you any more evidence, oral or written. Bow-wow-wow.'
And in December of the same year a scribbled note: 'My dear
Bernard—once upon a time there was a man called Juan
Fernando who made the great discovery that no man can do
more than he can do—Yours ever, F. Temple.' In August of
that year there had been a request for details of Housemasters'

profits. 'I will do what I can to please the Commissioners,' wrote Temple, 'but it is by no means easy to bring *this* matter to book, and I have doubts.'

But in the end all was done, and as a result our detailed know-ledge of the School and its workings is greater for this period than for any other, and a broad ray of light is shed on Temple's objectives and his achievements. Helped by the Commission's Report—and one cannot avoid the conclusion that much in the Report merely reflected his own forceful arguments—he was able, from 1864, to make natural science a compulsory subject for all boys below the Upper School, with chemistry, geology, botany and some physics the main subjects (he had a personal interest in botany, which needed, anyway, very little specialised equipment); he introduced English language and literature as form subjects throughout the School, the literature coinciding with the period of history being studied; he introduced a 'cycle' system of ancient, modern and biblical history, each to be taught throughout the School at the same time to avoid overlapping through boys changing forms; he started the system of alternate preparation and lesson, which lasted for over half a century. And he gave tremendous encouragement to music. The Com-missioners had advised that music or drawing should be made compulsory at some stage for every boy; Temple was unable to secure the agreement of the Trustees to so revolutionary a move, but he doubled the teaching power and provided accommodation for both. (The New Quadrangle had schools for music and for drawing.) In 1865 J. L. Tupper was appointed for drawing, and Otto Goldschmidt, a professor and later Vice-Principal of the Royal Academy of Music, was engaged as general adviser and examiner in music. He was the husband of Jenny Lind, who came and sang to the School one Sunday morning in March 1862 and enthralled, among others, the sixteen-year-old Alic Tosswill, who had already fired the shot that won the 1861 Ashburton Shield. As a result of a memorandum by Goldschmidt, boys were encouraged to join the Chapel choir, to learn to read music and to play instruments, even class singing was introduced, and the first School concert took place in June 1865, when 'Zadok the Priest' was performed. L. H. Walker, the organist appointed by Arnold in 1840, was rapidly in disagreement with Goldschmidt and tendered his resignation in 1867. He tried to withdraw it, but the Trustees would not accept the withdrawal after hearing Temple's case, and he left with a chip on his shoulder; years later, writing to Mrs. Hayman to condole with her on her husband's death, he spoke in vitriolic terms of Temple as a 'worldly, evil and unjust man . . . that scheming man, the great Archbishop [who] has done nothing but mischief all through his life'. Walker is the only one among Temple's staff of whom there is a record of a serious disagree-ment. His departure left the way open for the appointment of Edwin Edwards and Andreas Petterson, under whom the School music flourished and biennial School concerts became the rule. But perhaps there were, even in those days, ulterior motives for joining the choir. 'I have joined the Choir of Rugby School', wrote D. B. Maclaren in September 1868 (that same Maclaren who wanted porter in bottles), 'which is quite a new idea in my line. It saves me, however, three hundred lines of English poetry at the end of the term.'

It was not only in the schoolroom that Temple was a refor-mer. His boundless energy touched every facet of School life. He was a believer in games, not only as a potent factor in moulding human character, but for themselves, and he patently enjoyed his walk round the Close on every half-holiday. But he was no respecter of useless tradition. In his first year he abolished, except, in deference to Old Rugbeian opinion, for three formal occasions, 'standing in goal', which by his time had become a mere farce, with the 'no caps' even attempting to attach fire-crackers to the garments of the players; and a year or two later he abolished intentional hacking at football. Whatever Old Rugbeians may have thought, in the School itself there was vir-tually no opposition to these measures. Indeed the announce-ment of the second was greeted with a cheer. He seems to have had a genius for putting across a new rule; his method was to expound his case and end with a curt injunction. Thus, in for-bidding fireworks, he began: 'I never could see why you should remember, remember the 5th of November' and ended 'You are not to do it!' This, too, raised a cheer, and an American visitor who heard him remarked: 'That man is the biggest demagogue I have heard in England.'

But, though he believed in games, he would not allow exag-gerated athleticism. Once when an athlete 'swell' was reported to him for neglecting his work, Temple sent for him 'accident-ally' at a time when a big match was about to begin. The boy found the Headmaster immersed in correspondence, and stood in the study, casting anxious eyes through the window at the Close, for a full hour, until no-side was called. Temple then looked up. 'Now you may go,' he said, and no other punish-ment was needed. 'Of course, Temple's a beast,' said another victim, 'but he's a just beast.' The VIth remained in charge of games and the Close, levying taxes, with the Headmaster's sanction, for expenses, and the Head of the School remained

Frederick Temple

Temple's staff, 1860

1. J. W. J. Vecqueray
2. Rev. C. Evans
3. Rev. C. E. Moberley
4. Rev. Frederick Temple
5. T. W. Jex-Blake
6. Rev. C. T. Arnold

7. Rev. C. Elsee
8. Rev. P. Bowden Smith
9. E. A. Scott
10. Rev. J. Percival
11. Rev. H. J. Buckoll
12. Rev. C. A. Anstey

13. Rev. R. B. Mayor
14. Rev. L. F. Burrows
15. Rev. C. B. Hutchinson
16. Rev. A. G. Butler
17. J. M. Wilson
18. Rev. T. S. Evans

ex officio captain of football. It is interesting to find the Commis¬ sioners commending this arrangement as one which prevented any rivalry to intellectual eminence.

In a real sense Temple regarded the Close and the Chapel as complementary and working together. He was inclined to regard too much religious zeal in the young as unhealthy, and his sermons, short and unpolished, were of a kind the boys appreciated. But perhaps he was best remembered for the talks he gave to those who had been confirmed on the Saturday evening before there was to be a communion service, which at this time occurred on only three Sundays each term, as a part of matins. The boys would come into Chapel straight from the football field, in their games clothes. 'No one who did not then hear him', said Arthur Butler, 'can judge of what he was in his power over boys.'

Of course Temple had his difficulties, practical ones such as the disastrous fire at Smythies' House (Cotton) in 1860, which entirely destroyed the house, when the School fire¬engine be¬ haved much better than the town machine, which, so H. E. C. Beaver told his parents, 'was in shocking repair, the hose bursting and the engine requiring to be stopped every 2 or 3 minutes'. Beaver was where he should not have been—on the roof trying to direct water on the flames until the tiles became too hot to touch. He ends his graphic account: 'Everything in the fellows' studies is burnt . . . but I believe the House and furniture are insured almost to their full value.'

A much more serious difficulty arose early in Temple's reign over the publication in 1860 of *Essays and Reviews*. This was a volume of essays by independent contributors, none knowing what the others were writing, on questions of theology and doctrine. Temple's, on 'The Education of the World', was the first in the book and was considered unobjectionable, but the views put forward by some other contributors roused a howl of rage from the orthodox and caused the Bishops in Convocation to condemn the book as a whole. Temple as a result, for having allowed himself to be connected with the volume, came under considerable suspicion, and there was a degree of uneasiness among the parents of Rugby boys and among the Trustees, which, in our own days, is a little difficult to understand. Temple himself was deeply distressed. He was honestly convinced that the views put forward in the book were views which needed airing. 'The book', he said, 'contains opinions which had long been lurking in corners; it was time they were dragged to light and faced.' But, though he had expected 'a good deal of worry from panic-stricken parents', he had not foreseen the effect that his connection with the volume would have on the boys. 'I think I made a blunder in one respect and in one alone. I ought not to have done anything which would encourage those boys to plunge into critical speculations before their time.' He was not a man given by nature to self-defence, but on this occasion he set himself to put things right with both masters and boys. 'I would warn you', he said to his VIth, 'against two things, against entering on the speculations concerned in that book in a light or cursory way, and against supposing that I agree with all that is said in that book. I am sure you know me too well to suppose this for an instant.' He knew that it would be fruitless to forbid them to read it. And to the masters, at a special meeting, he gave a full account of the origins of the book, of his attitude towards the views it held and of what he was doing about it in the School. To the world in general he would make no self-defence, but he was persuaded, much against his will, to allow his sermons to be printed, unamended, as a kind of antidote. They had little effect, except, perhaps, among Rugby parents, and the storm simmered for some years and broke out anew when the news was published of his appointment to the See of Exeter.

There remained the Trustees. They had been seriously alarmed. Arnold, Tait and now Temple, all had come under public attack for their supposed unorthodox views in religious matters. A special meeting was called on 19 April 1861 to consider the matter and a somewhat stern letter to the Headmaster was drafted.

> The Trustees do not think themselves called upon to offer any opinion on matters of religious controversy connected with the objections made to some parts of that volume, as tending to impair the reverence due to the Holy Scriptures. But they cannot be blind to the fact that such objections are entertained by the highest Ecclesiastical authorities. The Trustees have occasion to believe that Dr. Temple has made some statements to persons officially connected with the School, and to pupils, with respect to the appearance of his name and writings in connection with the volume in question, and would feel much obliged if Dr. Temple would furnish them with the substance of those statements. . . . They are unwilling to remain uninformed of any statements which Dr. Temple may have thought fit to make . . . on a subject which has elicited comment of so grave a character and which might affect the best interests of the School.[1]

Temple's reply was factual and straightforward. Boys had

[1] Rugby Trustee Order Books.

been discouraged from reading the book; no harm had been done to the School—it was still full and there had been, in spite of the national outcry, only three withdrawals. The Trustees professed themselves satisfied, but ordered Temple never again to allow his name to be associated with 'speculations of a questionable religious character, ascribing it to inadvertence that it has so appeared in the present instance'.

And so the storm blew over, as far as the School was concerned, and the proceedings of the Trustees reverted to such pressing matters as the inadvisability of siting a new water-closet in School House too near to the housemaids' closet, the necessity of providing scholarships that would meet the competition of Eton and Winchester for able boys, the raising of tuition fees to meet the needs of a larger staff, and of boarding fees to avoid the necessity of charging extra for tea and sugar, study fires and candles. And from 1864 the business of fighting or implementing the recommendations of the Public Schools Commission became a matter of urgency.

The Commissioners had pressed the desirability of abandoning the School's local responsibilities and transferring the funds used for free education to the provision of scholarships for open competition. The townsfolk, naturally enough, were horrified at this proposal; they had already suffered, since Arnold's day, from the practice of not admitting boys to Rugby until after their twelfth birthday—which meant that the education required to prepare a boy for entry could no longer be had free. Temple was, in principle, in favour of open scholarships, which he thought would be of general benefit; but he saw the force of the arguments of the people of Rugby. And it was his idea that a middle course might be found in the creation of a Lower

School, where a semi-classical and commercial education would be available and from which the abler boys might pass by exhibition to Rugby School proper. This scheme commended itself neither to the Commissioners nor to the townsfolk, but the Act of 1868 made it possible, and Lawrence Sheriff School was the result.

On 26 June 1867 a notable gathering assembled at Rugby to listen to speeches and to celebrate the three-hundredth birthday of the School. The proceedings began at 11 a.m. with a service in Chapel and a sermon by the Headmaster, followed by ceremonial lunches at School House and elsewhere. Then, at 3 p.m., the company moved to Big School, 'crowded to incon-venience', where Temple had with him on the platform A. C. Tait, by now Bishop of London, A. P. Stanley, Dean of Westminster, John Percival, Headmaster of Clifton; C. J. Vaughan, lately Headmaster of Harrow, the Rt. Hon. G. J. Goschen, and a number of others. Among the formidable list of honours read out there was the achievement of Alfred Bar-ratt, the Balliol Scholar who had secured five Firsts, in Modera-tions, Final Classics, Mathematics, Law and Modern History; he was later to be Secretary to the Universities Commission in 1880. They listened to speeches in Latin and Greek, and to A. W. Rowden reading his Queen's Medal Essay on the suitable title 'Varieties of Greatness in Great Rulers'. And the boys heard with delight a request by the Rev. W. Holbeche to the Trustees for an extra week's holiday.

In the evening Dean Stanley took the chair at a dinner, attended by about two hundred, in the Town Hall, where a gallery had been specially erected, surmounted by a star of bayonets, to accommodate the ladies. Here the guests, with unwearied enthusiasm, sat through ten toasts—nineteen speeches in all, for, though the loyal toast took little time, each of the others required a proposer and a responder, and 'Past and Present Masters' was replied to by both Temple and Bradley. 'The Church', in those days, had to come immediately after 'the Queen'; then followed 'Floreat Rugbeia', proposed by Stanley. He had been, he said, at the Third Cataract of the Nile, 'and rejoiced to see how large a proportion of Rugby names were carved on the rock which marked the southern extremity of European travel'. One is tempted to wonder if, perhaps, some of the unpopularity of Temple's successor was due to his attempt to check this Rugby habit. Two lead tablets exist still on inner walls of the New Quadrangle calling on boys to refrain from defacing the buildings; they are signed 'H. Hayman'.

The speeches continued and were such as one would expect on an occasion of this sort. Temple, in replying for the masters, said that the School 'seems to move along because it has inherited from past days a strength with which the Headmaster can do very little more then stand, as it were, at the head of its motion'. With Temple, this was probably not just affected modesty, but a few years were to prove how wrong he was. Towards the end of the evening Sir J. M. Stewart raised a cheer, in proposing 'the Games and the Rifle Corps', when he remarked that he saw behind him the XI who had won the Marlborough match. They had indeed, most convincingly, by six wickets. It must have been something of a relief when the last toast was reached, 'the Ladies', proposed by the Rev. W. H. Benn and replied to—since ladies were not then expected to do such things—most gracefully by Arthur Sidgwick.

And so the great day ended, and Rugby set out on its fourth century, as strong as it had ever been and with as high a repute.

Two other lasting things that came out of the tercentenary year must be briefly alluded to. The first is the *Meteor*, the first issue of which appeared on 7 February 1867. Its stated object was 'To hand down to posterity a short chronicle of what was daily passing around us.' 'On glancing at this paper', wrote the editor, 'you will immediately exclaim, "How long will it last?"' And indeed the quality of the earlier numbers was not such as to suggest that it would have a longer life than any other of the ephemeral periodicals which had appeared from time to time during the century. They were full of longwinded articles and letters of criticism, particularly of the unwieldy character of Bigside Levée,[1] then composed of all the five forms of the Upper School; or alarm at the decline in the Rifle Corps, reduced in number from its original 120 to 30. But a real record of School events was included, and gradually, as the articles and letters became fewer, the paper settled down to its true function of providing a complete chronicle, if a dull one, of what was going on. It is a pity, perhaps, that 'news', as opposed to official events, has altogether dropped out. The description, for instance, in the first number, of a fall of snow which brought 'its inevitable lout row' is entertaining. And 'lout rows', a junior form of the Town and Gown riots at the universities, were quite a feature of Rugby life. Alic Tosswill described in 1862 how a fall of snow 'caused a snowballing row with the louts. We licked them on the whole, though now and then they managed to get hold of a fellow and smashed his hat in, etc. I got the back of my head slightly cut

---

[1] The body that controlled the School games.

open by a ball, which no doubt had a stone in it, after having chased some louts, and whilst returning in a dignified way at a walk.' But such events gradually became rarer and perhaps copy of this type for the *Meteor* was harder to come by as time went on and class snobbery became less pronounced.

There also emerged from the tercentenary year the Rugby School Natural History Society, with F. E. Kitchener as its first president and G. B. Longstaff of Wilson's (Whitelaw) as secretary. From the first it received a great deal of official encouragement. Among the masters, J. M. Wilson—who had himself been ordered by Temple to 'learn some botany' in order to teach it—Arthur Sidgwick, C. E. Moberly and Charles Elsee were firm supporters, and others who helped by giving lectures or advice were Dr. Clement Dukes and Matthew Bloxam. One of the foundation members was F. C. Selous, who kept an illegal gun at a local farm and who was to make his name as naturalist, explorer and big-game hunter in South Africa. His portrait hangs today in Speech Room. The new society was popular and gradually extended the range of its activities, until today it arranges for a great many of those occupations, not all of them strictly 'Natural History', which are not covered by School curriculum or organised games.

During his last two years as Headmaster, there was no falling off in Temple's activity. In 1868 we find him getting the sanction of the Trustees for yet more building—this time a gymnasium. And he was tremendously vigorous in his reaction to the proposals of the Public Schools Bill. One of the directions for the composition of the new Governing Body, which was to replace the Trustees, was that four men should be appointed to it for their eminence in literature and science, and that the

Governors should be given a more detailed control over the Headmaster. To both of these he objected strongly.

> The Headmaster of a School like this [he wrote] ought to be a man better capable of working it well, and better able to initiate improvements than anyone else that can be found for the post. If a mistake has been made (in the selection of Headmaster) . . . the worst that can happen is that the School will languish a little, and that improvements will be delayed, until the time comes for electing another Headmaster. But this is a very minor evil in comparison with hampering all Headmasters by subjecting them to constant interference. For this reason I cannot concur in the recommendation to elect four Trustees eminent in literature or science. . . . What the School needs in the Trustees is good sense and knowledge of the world. The four gentlemen elected for their eminence in literature or science would be perpetually tempted to justify their election by doing what the Headmaster ought to do, and, if he is fit for his post, can do better than anyone else. They would often be tempted to push the interests of their own particular study to the detriment of general education. They would be almost certain to encourage an amount of interference, which, if it hastened or even introduced improvements at the time, would purchase them at the dear price of diminishing the Headmaster's sense of responsibility and freedom of action. I am confident that the School would lose much more than it gained.[1]

One can hardly doubt that he was right; but he was to forget much of what he had then said when he was himself a Governor and Hayman was the Headmaster of Rugby School.

But the dynamic, the 'granite on fire', was not the only side to

[1] P.S.C. Reports. Quoted by F. E. Kitchener in *Frederick Temple*, vol. I, pp. 192–3.

Temple's character. There was a simplicity in his home life—
where his sister (also a person of remarkable character) ruled
over the domestic arrangements—that appealed to masters and
boys alike. Temple was always good company. He had a
tremendous sense of fun and a real good-hearted kindliness.
When Mrs. Haslam, the widowed mother of four Rugbeians,
fell ill and had to go abroad, he wrote to her at once: 'I presume
I may take it for granted that your four sons will look upon
School House as their home for next Christmas and will come
here for any time that is not taken up with invitations elsewhere.
It will give me real pleasure to see them.' Arthur Haslam did in
fact spend a holiday in the Lakes with the Temples in 1866, and
when his sister Sophie heard that this was to happen, she wrote,
full of envy of his good fortune: 'Dr. Temple's company would
make a coal-cellar a pleasant sojourn, but Temple and the
Lakes together . . . !' He appealed to the young. Young masters,
to whom he gave meticulous training in their duties, even
teaching specimen lessons for their benefit, enjoyed the enter-
tainment in School House, where an example of simplicity and
frugality helped them not to make foolish use of an income, in
many cases, well above their needs. And Temple's own great
generosity encouraged them to be generous.

To the boys Temple became something of a hero, and there
seems little doubt that the School under him was a happy and
efficient place. But they remained eternally boys, and many of
the remarks in their letters might easily have been written a
century later. Thus F. S. Parkin wrote in February 1860, 'They
are thinking I believe of setting up a rifle corps or something of
the sort in the School',[1] and, six months later: 'Am I to go into

[1] The Rifle Corps, started in 1860 in connection with the volunteer movement

the rifle corps as I have plenty to do during the day without anything else and it will only be an additional trouble and expense.' Current events touched them, and their reaction was sometimes as cheerfully irreverent as it might be today. 'Are you going to sport a black band on your hat for the Prince Con-sort?' wrote Parkin to his father in December of 1861. 'Most of our fellows are, I believe. They say there is to be no more hunting for a month in consequence [of the Prince's death] which I don't believe, as it would be rather too much of a good joke for the pocket of the Master of Hounds. We are to have no School concert or House grub this term for the Prince's death.' The learned and thoughtful might attend meetings of the Debating Society, and argue that 'It is the duty of England to give up Gibraltar', but for the mass there was probably more interest in purely parochial matters: the shifting by Batley,[2] in 1865, of a full-grown elm some ninety feet to make room for extension to the Chapel 'which was done by running beams, along a tramway of planks, on wood and metal rollers. Two crabs, with ropes, chains and pulleys were employed to draw the heavy mass—tree, roots, soil and framework—to its new site.' But the actual moving was done in the very early morning before the School was up. The tree came into leaf the next year. Or the accident in School House, in 1866, when one of the weights of the clock fell into the Hall and broke the janitor's

resulting from the war scare of 1859, is the subject of a monograph, *A History of the First Hundred Years of the Rugby School Corps, 1860–1960* (1962), by Lt.-Col. H. J. Harris. The present writer has thought it unnecessary to go over again ground already so thoroughly covered.

[2] Batley's name is still to be seen on the brick shed at the north end of Caldecott's, where he had a market garden.

feet. Or the damage caused to the house man at Hutchinson's by the bursting of a bottle of porter which he was opening 'while preparing dinner for the young gentlemen'. Or, if they had to look abroad, the news that Tommy Wills (Evans [Bradley] 1851) had introduced cricket to the Australian Aborigines and had produced from among them a team which had beaten all the local XIs in the Hamilton district. And within the grounds there was plenty of interest those last two years of Temple, as the site was cleared and foundations were laid and the walls began to go up for the new buildings.

John Percival, many years later, when he was Bishop of Hereford, wrote:

> . . . I have never yet seen a school which was perfect even within the reasonable limits of attainable perfection. . . . I cannot say that Rugby, as I remember it . . . was a perfect school. It was a fine, strong, healthy, rough and vigorous, self-centred, and completely self-confident society. We felt that we were breath-ing the strong and wholesome air which makes strong, brave and efficient Englishmen; and . . . I think we were right in the main.[1]

To the School the end came with startling suddenness. Temple and Rugby seemed to have become inseparably iden-tified. True, from 1865 to 1868 he had been a member of the Secondary Schools Commission, and had had frequently to be away in London (indeed, he wrote one of the sections of that Commission's report in one uninterrupted session of thirty-six hours), but his management of the School was affected not at all except that A. W. Potts took a few of his VIth lessons. The

[1] Letter quoted by F. E. Kitchener in *Frederick Temple,* vol. i, p. 222.

School did not know that he was being pressed to go elsewhere
and that in July of 1869 he had refused Gladstone's offer of the
Deanery of Durham; so that when, in September of that year,
the news came that he had accepted the Bishopric of Exeter, the
shock to Rugby was profound. The shock to the nation was, in
another sense, as great; the whole controversy over *Essays and
Reviews* was reopened, and a movement was started to oppose
the election of the new bishop. An advertisement was circulated from a committee-room in Cockspur Street:

> The Earl of Shaftesbury and the Rev. Dr. Pusey having con-
> sented to act in unison in using every effort to prevent the
> scandal to the Church caused by the Premier's nomination of
> Dr. Temple, clergymen and laymen willing to support their
> brethren in the Diocese of Exeter are requested to communicate
> without delay with the secretaries.[1]

This is not the place to describe the stormy events of Temple's
election and consecration. At Rugby his time drew all too
swiftly to an end; his last Chapel, crowded with Old Rugbeians,
where he preached his last sermon as Headmaster, described by
Thomas Hughes, who heard it, provided a tense scene, and the
last concert a few days later, when he said a less formal farewell
to the School was an occasion of deep emotion.

Meanwhile the Trustees, to whom the news had not been
quite so unexpected, were seeking a successor. At a special
meeting called at Rugby on 20 November 1869, from a powerful field of candidates, which included Theodore Walrond and
John Percival, in an ill-starred moment they selected Henry
Hayman.

[1] Quoted by E. G. Sandford in *Frederick Temple*, vol. I, p. 281.

3

Calamity

HENRY HAYMAN, 1870–4

The sad story of Henry Hayman has never been fully told. 'The time has not yet come', wrote H. C. Bradby in 1900, 'when the details of the trouble can be sketched without offence.' W. H. D. Rouse mentions him only in connection with the new buildings that were opened during his time, and other printed accounts, such as those by J. M. Wilson and C. R. Evers, are, in the absence of full evidence, very heavily biased against the Headmaster. Nor is it easy, even after nearly a century, to give a balanced judgment, since it has proved, so far, impossible to find a coherent statement of the case for the Governing Body, though the defence of Henry Hayman is available in minute detail. Frederick Temple, who was undoubtedly the moving spirit of the attack, was not, as has already been stated, given to explanation or defence of his actions. 'The Bishop of Exeter', he wrote on 20 January 1873 to one who wished to bring new evidence on Hayman's behalf, 'has the honour to acknowledge the receipt of Mr. Stuart Russell's letter of this morning's date. Mr. Stuart Russell will hardly expect the Bishop of Exeter to answer questions until he has shown his right to put them.' And this was his attitude throughout. The best that a historian can

do, in the absence of fresh evidence, is to give a brief chronological account of the events as they emerge from the minutes of the
Trustees and Governing Body, from contemporary newspapers
and correspondence, and from the transcript of the Chancery
case in 1874. Even this bare recital provides a story that is
remarkable enough.

Henry Hayman was born in 1823. He was educated at
Merchant Taylors' School and went as Scholar to St. John's
College, Oxford, where he took second class Honours in
Classics and Mathematics and was elected to a Fellowship. He
became an assistant master at Charterhouse in 1852, and went
on to be Headmaster successively of St. Olave's School, South-
wark, 1855–9, of Cheltenham Grammar School, 1859–68, and
of Bradfield College, 1868–9. Why the Trustees decided to
appoint him, 'a good double second', as Temple contemp-
tuously described him, with a commendable, but not outstanding, record, it is, indeed, a little difficult to understand.
The opposition was so formidable. Theodore Walrond, who
was Temple's personal recommendation, was a Rugbeian who
had also taught at Rugby and whose academic record was distinguished; he was at this time Secretary to the Civil Service
Commission. John Percival, with a brilliant double First in
both Mathematics and Classics, who had also been a Rugby
master, had already made a very great name for himself as the
first Headmaster of Clifton. And there were others whose
qualifications seemed to be superior to Hayman's. At the time
it was widely believed that he was appointed as a known conservative and high-churchman to counteract the influence of
recent liberal and latitudinarian Headmasters. This was denied
by the Trustees themselves, but it was a theory widely can-

vassed in the Press, the *Spectator*, on 29 November 1869, referring to the election baldly as 'a conservative reprisal'. There was probably truth in the letter written to *The Times* much later, on 5 January 1874, by 'A Trustee of Rugby School' (almost certainly the Earl of Warwick),[1] categorically denying that Hayman was appointed for his conservatism; the Trustees knew only, he said, that his politics were 'negative'. But he affirmed that Hayman's character as 'a good Churchman, free from any particular high or low tendencies' had been influential. 'How far this qualification on his part', the writer went on, 'may have been the cause of the formidable conspiracy deliberately organised against him from the first day he set foot in Rugby, it is not for me to say.'

Whatever their reasons, the Trustees did appoint him, and there was immediately an outburst of indignation almost as great, though from a different section of the population, as that which attended the announcement of Temple's elevation to the See of Exeter. 'To all who look with hope and interest to the future of the greatest school in England', wrote the *Spectator*,[2] the election would be 'a profound disappointment'. 'We cannot but think', said the *Daily News*,[3] 'that Rugby may justly resent the importation of a stranger who can point to no higher antecedents than having been the almost unknown master of third-rate grammar schools . . . an insult to its past, its present and its future.' The Press, local and national, took sides. The *Rugby Advertiser,* in correspondence and comment, on the whole favoured Hayman; so did *John Bull,* the *Cheltenham Examiner* and, more powerfully, the *Standard*.[4] The *Morning*

---

[1] *The Times* has no record of the writer's identity.
[2] 29 November 1869.   [3] 30 November 1869   [4] 4 December 1869.

Henry Hayman

E. A. Scott

Post[1] pointed out that Temple had been successful at Rugby after failing dismally at Kneller Hall. The *Pall Mall Gazette* started by being judiciously critical, but by 13 December was saying that, if the Trustees persisted, 'Rugby may be ruined, if only for a time', and five days later asked, 'Is it true or is it not, that St. Andrew's College, Bradfield, has materially fallen off under his care? That he has provoked a rebellion in the College by violent and very injudicious severity to one of the oldest of the pr[a]epostors.' (On which Hayman's comment was: 'Altogether false.') *The Times*[2] came out solidly against the new Headmaster, attacking the Trustees as an 'irresponsible body'— though *The Times* later was to change its tune. The *Globe,* on 20 December, attacked the *Spectator* as 'a radical Mrs. Grundy', and *Public Opinion* on 18 December pointed out that Temple and Hayman were in some sense parallel cases, since Temple was 'greatly distrusted by the Church of which he has been made a bishop', and yet would not answer criticisms; why then should Hayman do so?

If the Press uproar had been all, it might have been possible for Hayman to follow Goulburn's later advice to 'reply to the newspapers by dignified silence'. But the trouble came rapidly much nearer home. It was not until ten days before the election that Hayman had decided to become a candidate, and there had been no time to secure and have printed a complete set of new testimonials. He had therefore used in his application some which had been written for him when he was a candidate for other posts. On this fact the dissidents rapidly seized. The point was first raised by the *Spectator*. Hayman's testimonials, they wrote, 'must have been of a very high order to have beaten

[1] 17 December 1869.   [2] E.g. 14 December.

those of Walrond, recommended by the Archbishops of York and Canterbury, the Bishop of Chester, the Deans of West⁄minster and Durham, Dr. Temple, Dr. Scott of Baliol [*sic*] and Professor Jowett'. And it was at Hayman's testimonials that his future assistant staff first looked.

On 27 November 1869 Hayman received a visit at Bradfield from A. W. Potts, who had recently been appointed the first Headmaster of Fettes. He brought with him a memorandum, signed by the complete assistant staff of Rugby except the Rev. L. F. Burrows, protesting against the circumstances of Hay⁄man's election. This is so remarkable a document to have been addressed by assistant masters to their future chief that it deserves extensive quotation. It expressed

the grief and anxiety which the Assistant Masters cannot help feeling in reference to some of the facts connected with your election as Headmaster.

1. Your candidature has violated some of the most cherished traditions of the place [because] you have not received testi⁄monials from any of those who for years past have been the most active and well⁄known lovers of the School away from Rugby . . .

2. Absence of testimony from your own former pupils or the masters who have worked under you . . .

3. We cannot discover that you have the strongly tenable moral position which may in some cases justify men in assum⁄ing a prominent post in spite of a strong public feeling against them . . .

We have only in the last few days, and that with considerable difficulty, obtained a sight of your printed testimonials—a fact which will, we trust, exonerate us from the charge of incon⁄

siderateness in having made our remonstrance only at this late period.[1]

They objected to the use of old testimonials.

The differences between Rugby on the one hand and King's College School, St. Olave's and Cheltenham Grammar School on the other, are not so few or so slight that fitness for the duties of one implies fitness for those of the other. . . . We submit that there was the strongest presumption beforehand that if you had applied to some of the writers for Rugby testimonials, you would not have obtained them. As they stand, they plainly do not express the opinion of those who have given them that you are fit for the post of Headmaster here. . . . There never has been a Headmaster here in the memory of living man who has come here with at all this kind of support . . . it is of no use our attempting to disguise from you our conviction that the position of the School has been already imperilled by your departure from established customs. . . . We say that the man who asks us to work with and under him frankly and cordially ought himself to begin his career with nothing which seemed ambiguous or questionable as to the means by which he obtained his post.[2]

This was a poor start, but Hayman thought that he would be able to overcome the opposition. He decided to make no written answer, but on 3 December, at Temple's invitation, he went with his wife on a three-day visit to Rugby, on the last day of which Temple assembled the assistant staff to hear the new Headmaster in person. He gave them his own explanation of the character of his testimonials and begged them not to judge him without a

[1] Chancery transcript, 1874-H-42, filed 18 February 1874.
[2] Ibid.

trial. But there was a disturbing coldness and lack of response; J. M. Wilson sat grimly taking notes of the proceedings, and Hayman, feeling that he had got nowhere with them, returned to the Headmaster's study, where he asked Temple to use his influence with his masters to persuade them to co-operate. On this Temple rounded on him, told him that he considered the appointment a disastrous mistake, that Hayman ought to with-draw, and that it was his, Temple's, duty to write to the Trustees to give them his opinion. Hayman thereupon left the study and went upstairs to tell his wife, who was preparing for lunch, what had occurred. She seems to have been a lady of spirit, for she immediately put on her bonnet, a cab was summoned, and the pair left School House to spend their few remaining hours in Rugby under the more hospitable roof of Mr. Burrows.

Temple was as good as his word. He wrote to the Trustees pointing out that Hayman, at the age of forty-five, had made no impression as a schoolmaster, 'though some as a laborious scholar', and that his use of testimonials was 'an act liable to very grave censure'.

> The plain truth is that he is quite incompetent to perform some of the most important duties of the place. . . . He has the ability implied in a clear perception of his own purposes, much power of expression, and extraordinary strength of will. But in true insight into character, which alone will enable a man to deal justly with the older boys, or to govern able and high-minded men, he is absolutely deficient. The result is certain: as far as mere strength goes towards good government he will govern the School. But his government of the VIth will assuredly fail, and he will never get men of high mark to work under him. . . . The staff will inevitably deteriorate . . . the moral tone and the

discipline will sink, and the confidence of the parents will be justly withdrawn. It would be natural that, on leaving, I should recommend my successor to the parents who consult me confidentially, but as an honest man I am unable to do so. I can only be silent, and silence in such cases is condemnation.[1]

Shortly afterwards the assistant masters sent their own memorial on the subject to the Trustees, and Dr. G. G. Bradley wrote to them stating that his testimonial to Hayman, admittedly a 'general purpose' one, had been written in 1866 and was not intended for a Rugby application. On 20 December Bradley followed this up with a letter to *The Times* stating that he had written to the Chairman of the Trustees about the testimonial, but not saying in what sense. On the same day the Trustees met, having refused to hear Temple orally on behalf of the assistant masters, and entirely exonerated Hayman, professing themselves completely satisfied with the circumstances of his application and the new Headmaster entirely blameless in his use of testimonials. But they made no censure of the action of the masters.

All this had occurred before Hayman even reached Rugby. In January 1870 he moved to School House and took up his duties, and for some months an uneasy peace prevailed. By July Hayman was able to report that the new schools were in use, and the Trustees made a grant of £100 towards the £500 required for desks and other equipment. In that month Hayman and C. T. Arnold attended a Trustee meeting to report on the proposed rebuilding of the Chapel, which was estimated to cost £8620, of which £8500 had been subscribed. The Trustees gave sanction for the work to start, but 'without expressing any opinion of the architectural character of the plans submitted'.

[1] Chancery transcript.

They had lost none of their dislike of Butterfield's style. They were busy, too, protesting against the statute constituting the new Governing Body under the Public Schools Act, took Counsel's opinion and retained Sir Rowndell Palmer to press a petition to the Privy Council on the subject, objecting particularly to the proposed virtual disappearance of local men on the new Body, and to the omission of a clause requiring all Governors to be members of the Church of England.

But at Rugby, though there was overt peace, there was neither cordiality nor comfort. Only a fortnight after term started a question of discipline arose and a praepostor wrote to Temple at Exeter to ask his advice; he received an answer that made no reference to the Headmaster's authority. Some masters were also in correspondence with Temple, Old Rugbeians spread the views of masters among the boys, and at House suppers there were, in several instances, 'Three cheers for the Bishop of Exeter'. There was no mutiny, but Hayman came increasingly to feel that, among his staff, he could rely only on Burrows, his friend of long standing, and William Sargent, who had replaced Potts. In particular he felt that he could not trust his two School House tutors, E. A. Scott and James Robertson. That he had some reason for uneasiness appears from the fact that in February 1870 an attempt had been made by the masters to get a question asked in the House of Commons about the Trustees' decision of 20 December in the matter of Hayman's testimonials; this attempt had been led by Scott and Robertson. By the autumn the position had become intolerable and on 10 November Hayman wrote to the Trustees telling them that he had failed to secure the loyalty of the two men and that he proposed to remove them from their position of tutors in School

House and to try to persuade them to resign their masterships. It was not within his power to dismiss Scott, who, as a 'Foundation master' (i.e. receiving a salary from the Foundation), could be dismissed only by the Trustees, but at their meeting on 5 December, they gave their 'full approval' to the dismissal from tutorships and promised their 'full consideration' of the possible dismissal of Scott if Hayman should require it. He did require it, but by the time the Trustees met, on 16 January 1871, to consider the matter, they had received letters from, among others, Robertson, E. W. Benson, Potts, Jex-Blake and Percival in support of Scott, and they decided to summon him and the Headmaster to a meeting to resolve their differences. This occurred on 24 February and, after hearing both men, separately and together, the Trustees refused to concur in the dismissal.

This was the first round in a duel which was to last for three years, but it rapidly drew in other men and attracted the notice of a wider public, and Hayman's failure to secure co-operation from staff or boys bedevilled the situation. How far it was his fault and how far due to subversive action by his enemies—and he seems to have been an adept at making them—it is difficult to say. But by 1871 the whole miserable business was having a damaging effect on the reputation of the School. This is reflected in a sharp fall in numbers. In 1870 Hayman had accepted 146 new boys, ten more than Temple in his last year; in 1871 the number fell to 115; and in the following two years to 101 and 72. The financial problem caused by this decline had its effect on the progress of the quarrel, as will be seen.

At their next meeting, on 25 March 1871, the Trustees had to deal with letters from unsatisfied parents. A. S. Field, guardian in England of an American boy, P. M. Westfeldt, wrote indignantly at the removal of his ward from the School and sent copies of his correspondence with Hayman; Mr. J. C. Bolton wrote complaining that his son's authority as a VIth had not been supported by the Headmaster; and the Head of the School, W. J. Arnold, wrote about a rebellion in School House against the VIth. In all these matters the Trustees, after hearing Hayman's comments, gave him their support. And at this meeting they actually gave their agreement, in principle, to his repeated requests for the dismissal of Scott, but, for a technical reason, decided to postpone the formal notice to an adjourned meeting in five days' time. When this took place, their Clerk explained that under an old Act of Parliament (17 Geo. III (1777)) the Trustees could not dismiss a master except at the General Annual Meeting. The decision was therefore rescinded, and it was decided to meet at Rugby on 11 April to consider the state of the School. All interested parties, including the Head of the School, were to be informed. At this meeting, when Mr. Bolton had been examined in the Head-master's presence and various statements read—it was decided after all not to question the VIth—and Hayman's comments heard, the Trustees issued an important minute:

> They are of the opinion that the irregularities complained of are not such as to call for any special interference on their part, or to cause alarm to the parents of the boys, being of a character which must at times be expected in a large school . . . they feel it now their duty, in justice to the Headmaster, to impress upon the Undermasters generally the necessity, for the good of the School, of giving to the Headmaster not only a nominal but a cordial support.[1]

[1] Trustee Order Books.

This minute was, by order of the Trustees, published in *The Times* three days later.

Round Two, one would have thought, to Hayman. But when the General Annual Meeting took place on 24 June at the School and the Headmaster again requested the dismissal of Scott, the request was finally refused. Perhaps the Trustees had been nettled by more indignant letters from parents whom Hayman had not allowed to choose tutors for their sons, though they so far supported him as to issue a statement that parents of School House boys had no right to choose tutors not approved by the Headmaster.

The next stage in the quarrel concerned the constitution of the new Governing Body, which, under the Public Schools Act, was to replace the Trustees in December 1871. Three of the existing Trustee Body were elected to it (the Earl of Warwick, Philpott, Bishop of Worcester, and Charles Adderley) and the Trustees also elected Charles Newdigate Newdegate and the Marquis of Hertford. But the election of Temple by London University, of G. G. Bradley by Oxford and of W. H. Bateson ('Bull' Bateson), Master of St. John's, by Cambridge, all known to be very hostile to Hayman, caused him great uneasiness, and he wrote to protest vigorously against Temple's appointment. A further member was to be elected by 'the Headmaster and Undermasters'. Hayman held this to mean that the Headmaster must agree with a majority of the assistant masters on a representative; the others insisted that the Head-master should have only one vote among the rest. In the event the assistant masters voted for Sir Robert Lingen, the Head-master taking no part in the election and, in spite of Hayman's protests, Lingen took his place among the Governors. The

Body was now nicely balanced. The three old Trustees and their two nominees were at first usually prepared to support the Headmaster; of the others, five were usually hostile, and the Bishop of Worcester, as Chairman, had several times to use his casting vote.

Towards the end of 1871 a new trouble arose. Burrows resigned his house, and Hayman nominated W. C. Green, an appointment of his own who had only in the previous January joined the staff, to replace him. This, naturally, aroused a storm and, on 29 January 1872, Scott and nine other assistant masters wrote to the Governing Body protesting that Houses should go by seniority; they enclosed as evidence the letter written by Temple to Lee Warner[1] on his appointment, a letter which Hayman had not previously seen. The Headmaster, in his defence, claimed the right of discretion under the Public Schools Act, though 'I should doubtless under ordinary circumstances be disposed to show all due deference to seniority of standing when coupled with loyal and cordial support for myself.' A further letter from the ten, with a copy to the Headmaster, went on 7 February. 'No previous intimation of any dissatisfaction with our services', they said, 'has ever been given to any of us by the Headmaster . . . our anxiety has always been to co-operate loyally.' The Governing Body, on 9 February, told Hayman to make no appointment for the moment, but three days later he wrote to say that the appointment was already made. 'Any Headmaster', he added, 'might reasonably wish that there should be at least one House beside his own where he might feel confident that his influence would have full opportunity to

---

[1] Henry Lee Warner, a boy in the School 1854-60, was appointed to the staff in 1864 and served till 1885.

prevail.' To show that the action was not without precedent he enclosed a letter from Goulburn, who stated that he had himself passed over a senior master in appointing to a House. Goulburn had, in fact, forgotten the exact circumstances and wrote a second letter contradicting the first; this second letter Hayman did not forward to the Governors, but a copy had gone to C. T. Arnold, who sent it to the Chairman, Philpott, and the fact of Hayman's apparent duplicity made an enemy of the Bishop of Worcester. In the event the Governors, in spite of a protest by Temple, Lingen, Bateson and one other, decided on this occasion not to interfere with the appointment of Green; 'at the same time the Governing Body refrain from expressing any approval of the exercise of the Headmaster's discretion in this particular instance'. This confidential minute appeared verbatim in the Rugby Press a week later. They then instructed Hayman to make no further changes or 'departure from Rugby customs' pending the passing of the Rugby statutes, then in course of formulation.

From this time on, the personal quarrel between Hayman and Scott took the centre of the stage and began to work up a crescendo of bitterness. Early in January 1872 Scott claimed to have been misreported in the account given in the local Press of a speech he made at a workmen's dinner held on 22 December to celebrate the completion of the gymnasium, in which he seemed, by the report, to have made complimentary remarks about the Headmaster. 'I cannot but feel', he wrote to the Chair man, 'that the words attributed to me might cause you surprise, which I should be glad to remove', and he asked the Editor of the *Rugby Advertiser* to correct the report. The Editor, who had himself written the report, wrote indignantly to protest against this charge of inaccuracy and offered to produce the shorthand manuscript, which he had kept. This episode caused those who did not like him to question Scott's honesty; 'Scott is a liar' was chalked on a number of walls in Rugby, but the Governing Body refused to investigate 'charges of untruthfulness in a Foundation master'. He had in that same month applied to Hayman for liberty to take pupils[1] once more, claiming that he had done nothing to forfeit the Headmaster's confidence. 'I cannot admit this,' wrote Hayman. 'If you had felt a corres/ ponding confidence to that which you would like to have shown to you, you would not have said, or left unsaid, or both together, what according to your own statement you did say or leave unsaid on 22nd December last.' Thereupon Scott appealed to the Governing Body, and there followed a series of letters and meetings, which culminated in July in a direct order to Hayman that Scott should again be allowed to take pupils, as he had been suffering, by his own computation, 'an average annual loss of £463 3. 1.' during his suspension from tutorship. To this order Hayman gave a grudging consent, but reiterated his lack of confidence; his reply was considered unsatisfactory by the Governing Body, who held that Hayman had no grounds for his suspicion, and ordered that Scott should without delay be restored to his full position.

Hayman next made a grave mistake, though he possibly made it in good faith. On the advice of Tait, Bishop of London, and of Haig Brown, Headmaster of Charterhouse, he wrote to Scott giving particulars of his grounds for lack of confidence and asking for an explanation. The grounds proved to be of the flimsiest nature, concerned largely with some letters received by

---

[1] To 'take pupils' was to act as private tutor. See note on masters' salaries, pp. 36–38.

a brother-in-law of Scott, which Hayman assumed to have been written by Scott himself, containing derogatory remarks about the Headmaster, which had led to widespread gossip away from Rugby. Instead of giving any explanation, Scott sent Hayman's statement to the Governing Body, who chose to regard it as a 'charge' and demanded that Hayman should either substantiate it or make a full retraction. This was on 23 October 1872, and a full report of the Governing Body's decision appeared shortly afterwards in the *Rugby Advertiser* and some national newspapers. On 12 November Hayman withdrew his statement, while protesting against the way the matter had been handled. But meanwhile the Governors had had further correspondence from Scott, who had been investigating Hayman's very shaky evidence. As a result Hayman (this time accompanied by Counsel, who was not, however, called) was summoned to another meeting on 30 November. Here, after considering the matter, the Governing Body issued a minute of which the following is the most important part:

> They desire to express their conviction that the course taken throughout by Dr. Hayman in dealing with Mr. Scott has not been marked by that spirit of justice which the circumstances of the case required. They regret that the charges . . . which have been shown to rest on no foundation, have been withdrawn only on compulsion, and that no apology has been offered . . . for the serious evil occasioned to Mr. Scott or for the heavy pecuniary loss inflicted on him. If Dr. Hayman is not prepared to act in future in a spirit of cordial good will towards Mr. Scott, the Governing Body think it is due to the interests of the School that he should lose no time in retiring from the office of Headmaster.[1]

[1] Minutes of the Governing Body.

Of portions of this, Hayman and Scott were sent copies.

The parts of this minute most damaging to Hayman appeared in the *Echo* of 2 December, the *Daily News* of the 3rd, and the *Standard* of the 6th, and from this time any proceedings of the Governing Body damaging to the Headmaster found their way into the Press, and a newspaper battle on the case again began to work up. *The Times* had, as long before as 6 March 1871, carried a leader entitled 'The Civil War at Rugby'. Now the *Globe*, on 12 December 1872, wrote:

> As the Governing Body, whether through carelessness or design, have allowed their censure to reach the columns of a newspaper, and given rise to the publication of a great deal of evidence exclusively on one side, the least they can do . . . is to give from the minutes of their meetings an account of the matter which the public can understand.

John Bull, on the 14th, published a stricture on the impropriety of the Governing Body's publication of a minute of censure. 'An M.P.' wrote in the *Daily News* of the 19th: 'The Governing Body has shown that want of "wrist" which is characteristic of "bodies" and makes one long sometimes for one hour of the despotism of personal government.' On the 26th *The Times* published a complete collection of the correspondence between Hayman, Scott and others connected with the case, and a leader highly critical of the assistant masters, but critical also of Hayman's methods. The *Standard*, on the 27th, supported Hayman: 'His resignation under present circumstances would be a further encouragement to mutinous behaviour. . . . The plain truth of the matter is, that the Assistant Masters desired to overrule the nomination of Dr. Hayman and impose their own choice upon the Governors. Foiled in this, they conspired together to make the place too hot to hold him.' The *Pall Mall Gazette* of the same date called for Hayman's resignation. 'The truth is', declared the *Spectator* of the 28th, 'there never was a man more wholly unfitted for the Mastership of Rugby than its present chief.' And so it went on—these are but a few from hundreds of references—until, on 10 March 1873, the *Daily Post* could declare that the quarrel was 'almost a national difficulty'.

There is no direct evidence of who was responsible for the divulgence of confidential matter to the Press. As early as April 1872 the Earl of Warwick had protested at the reporting of the Governing Body's proceedings in newspapers, and with the publication of the minute of 30 November he and the Marquis of Hertford entered a vigorous protest, which caused the Chairman to make a ruling that only by authority could any proceedings of the Governors be made public. But Temple and Bateson declared that 'they considered themselves free to state to anyone anything they pleased and would not be bound by any vote to fetter them', and Temple is reported to have said that 'he would like to see anyone who could stop his mouth'. There seems little doubt that it was these two who were principally to blame.

It looked by now as if, whatever the rights of the matter, Hayman's position was becoming untenable, but he clung on. On 8 January 1873 he extended an olive branch to Scott: 'I have withdrawn the whole of the statement I sent to you in August . . . it is my earnest desire to act in a spirit of cordial good will and I sincerely hope to find the same reciprocated.' Scott replied on the 13th that he 'must refer to the judgment of the Governing Body whether your letter contains all that I had a right to expect. In any case it will be and always has been my earnest desire, so long as I continue to be an Assistant Master, to dis-charge faithfully my duties to the School and to yourself as Headmaster.' The following day Hayman wrote again: 'I am sincerely disposed to regard the whole matter as at an end and to let bygones be bygones. I exceedingly regret any annoyance to which you have been subjected'; to which Scott answered, 'Having referred the matter to the Governing Body, I do not feel at liberty to take it out of their hands.'

When they met on 15 January the Governing Body professed themselves not satisfied with Hayman's letters. A motion for his dismissal was defeated only by the casting vote of the Chairman, and they minuted that 'the position of Dr. Hayman and the School is so seriously compromised that they must consider whether Dr. Hayman should not be requested to retire from the Headmastership'. The whole matter was deferred to another meeting on 23 January. This was the first day of term and Hayman wrote pleading that it was impossible for him to be present, asking to be represented by Counsel and declaring himself ready to make such further action towards Scott as the Governors might wish. He had received from Dr. J. D. Collis, who had already advised complete submission, a telegram, which ran: 'I think ample retractation due consequently com-pensation due to be settled by an arbitrator . . . full, warm letter of cordial co-operation ought to go to Scott else *Actum est de te omnino.*' And so he sent such a letter, one of unqualified with-drawal and apology, on 4 February. On the following day he attended for a Governing Body meeting at the Westminster Palace Hotel; for three hours he was kept waiting, and then the Clerk came out and read to him the following minute: 'The

Governing Body are of opinion that the letter from Dr. Hayman to Mr. Scott is satisfactory, but they deeply regret that such a compliance with their minute of 30th of November, 1872, has been delayed until it has lost its value. . . . They feel it to be their duty . . . to consider the question whether Dr. Hayman should not now be recommended to retire from the Headmaster-ship.' Finally, at a meeting on 25 February, at which Hayman, attended by Counsel, was allowed to be present, a motion was passed, again only by a casting vote, that 'no further proceedings be taken in the matter of Mr. Scott's appeal' and the Governing Body conceded—after two years, and too late—the right of the Headmaster, under the Public Schools Act, to dismiss assistant masters. Another motion, proposed by Bateson and Lingen,[1] that Hayman should be recommended to resign, and that if he did not do so he should be dismissed, was defeated, but a resolution was passed that he should find some means of honourable retirement by his own act.

And so, although even after this the Governing Body found themselves asked to consider enormously long, printed docu-ments that Hayman produced in his own justification, the great quarrel with Scott came officially to an end.

Meanwhile at Rugby the numbers were steadily dropping, and it became necessary to reduce the staff. At the end of the summer term of 1873, two junior masters, both Hayman's appointments, were dismissed, and he intended next to get rid of a junior mathematics and natural science master. But the Governing Body had issued a new financial schedule, which

---

[1] The Chancery transcript states that Temple was the mover, but the Minutes of the Governing Body make it clear that this was not so.

could not be adhered to without reducing the numbers of senior classical masters as well, and on 22 September 1873 notices of dismissal were sent to Arthur Sidgwick ('the only single man' was Hayman's excuse) and C. J. E. Smith. Immediately these two and thirteen other masters, led by C. T. Arnold, protested to the Governing Body, who again found themselves the centre of a storm. The senior masters claimed that, by Temple's terms of employment, it was guaranteed that, if dismissals became necessary, they should be in order of juniority; William Sargent, W. C. Green and Edward Armstrong wrote in defence of the junior masters; the Rev. Clarence Hilton of Faversham and George Dixon, M.P., of Birmingham wrote protesting violently against the dismissal of Sidgwick. Hayman himself wrote, analysing the financial schedules and suggesting that, if they were modified, the dismissal of Sidgwick could be avoided. The letters of protest, but not Hayman's analysis, were considered at a meeting on 29 October, when a letter was sent to Hayman stating that the dismissals constituted 'a departure from the customs of the School'. Hayman reacted with a long apologia, sent to each Governor on 14 November, asserting the right of the Headmaster to decide the composition of his staff. On the 19th he was heard by the Governing Body. He took his stand on the Report of the Public Schools Commission and challenged them to find in this or in any other document a scheme for the order of retirement of masters. To this challenge there was no reply. He claimed that necessity for the notice given to Sidgwick was imposed on him by the Governing Body themselves through their financial schedules. But it was all to no purpose, and the Governing Body resolved that

Dr. Hayman, in giving notice of dismissal to Mr. Arthur Sidgwick and the Rev. C. J. E. Smith, has not acted in accordance with the undertaking given by him . . . to observe the usages and customs of the School. The Governing Body feel that, under existing circumstances, they must give effect to the intimation conveyed to Dr. Hayman in the Chairman's letter of Feby. 25 1873: they accordingly require him to place his resignation in the hands of the clerks, on or before Wednesday, Decr. 23rd to take effect at Easter next.[1]

But Hayman considered that, by resigning, he would put himself in the wrong. He asked to be heard again, but was refused. On 18 December he wrote to the Chairman refusing to resign. On the following day at a meeting of the Governing Body, it was moved by the Lord-Lieutenant of Warwickshire and seconded by Sir George Rickards that

upon a review of the administration of the School from the time that the Governing Body came into office to the present time, they are of opinion that Dr. Hayman is not a fit and proper person to hold the position of Headmaster of Rugby School, and that it is for the interests of the School that he should cease to hold that office . . . that Dr. Hayman be removed from his office of Headmaster, such removal to take effect from 7th Day of April next.[2]

To this motion there was no dissentient voice. The Earl of Warwick was not present, and at their next meeting the Governing Body recorded his resignation.

The rest is not long to tell. Hayman was down, but not out.

---

[1] Minutes of the Governing Body.   [2] Ibid.

On 14 January 1874 the Governors were considering a letter expressing his intention of taking legal action and 'moving the Queen's Bench for a mandamus to stay the proceedings of the Governing Body'. They also received a memorial from 'Dr. Collis of Stratford-on-Avon and 344 others' in favour of the Headmaster. They refused, however, to hear him again and affixed their seal to the formal order for his dismissal. In the event Hayman, after taking legal advice, decided to proceed by way of a Bill of Complaint in Chancery, denying the right of the Governing Body, under the Public Schools Act, to dismiss him without giving a cause. Shortly before the case came up Temple and Bradley, acting for the Governing Body, came in with a demurrer, denying the right of Chancery to decide the case, and it was the demurrer, not the case proper, that was heard. As a result, no detailed defence of the Governing Body's position emerged, since, on a technical point of law, the demurrer, after a six days' hearing, was upheld on 24 March, though the Vice-Chancellor, Sir R. Malins, who tried the case, refused to award costs to the Governing Body, and delivered himself of several severe strictures on them, saying that he 'never saw conduct which more strongly required explanation', and that he 'believed that Dr. Hayman would have succeeded in the management of the School if he had been given a chance, but that he had not'. In his *obiter dicta* he commented severely on the conduct of Temple and Bradley in allowing themselves to be elected to the Governing Body and on their treatment of Hayman. The defeated Headmaster received hundreds of letters of sympathy (all of which he kept), including one from Gladstone, and contributions from sympathisers on a sufficient scale to pay, largely, the costs of the case.

On 28 March 1874 *The Times* printed a long letter from Hay-man.

> After an argument of six days duration, the Court of Chancery decided that it could not interfere with a sentence of dismissal which was repugnant to justice but had the force of law. I shall not attempt to appeal against that decision. Enough has transpired in the course of the trial amply to vindicate my character and conduct, both as a Headmaster and a gentleman, from the aspersions which have been freely cast upon them. The vindication would have included the exposure of the machinations of my opponents, if they had had the man-liness to join issue upon the facts of the case instead of sheltering themselves under the forms of law, and would have revealed a course of official tyranny which has no parallel within living memory. . . . My own personal injury I am content to leave to the sense of justice of my countrymen.

In May he was presented by Disraeli (who was careful to say that the action was no indication of his feelings about the justice of Hayman's case) with the lucrative living of Aldingham, in the Furness District of Lancashire; and thither he departed into oblivion. But not quite. In 1891, at the instance of a rather disreputable relation of his wife, he allowed himself to be put, as chairman, on the board of the 'Canadian Pacific Colonisa-tion Company', the prospectus of which turned out to be fraudulent. Two cases resulted from this, both lost by Hayman, in the course of which Mr. Justice Kekewich spoke of his 'dis-graceful carelessness. . . . He had no reasonable grounds for believing the statement to be true, and he had the means of knowledge that it was false.' Poor man; in public affairs, he seems to have been accident-prone. He died, still at Aldingham, in 1904.

'He was a scholar and a gentleman', the *Chronicle* had said. 'Had he been a low Churchman and a liberal, he would have remained at Rugby.' This was not the opinion of most of Hayman's colleagues. Among the snatches of satirical humour with which the masters of the day seasoned their dissatisfaction, a quip has been preserved: 'If a Headmaster can't teach and can't preach and can't organise, he ought to be either a scholar or a gentleman.' One senses in this the acid wit of J. M. Wilson, who was throughout among the most strenuous opponents of the Headmaster. But one must not suppose that the ordinary life of the School did not, during these black years, go on. Wilson in his *Autobiography*, written many years later when his memory for detail was not always accurate, claimed that the disagreement between Headmaster and assistants was carefully veiled from the boys, and that they knew nothing about it. This can surely not have been the case. It is impossible to believe that, at the time when the Prussians were besieging Paris and setting up the German Empire, when the Commune rebellion was taking place, when Livingstone was opening up Africa and diamonds were being discovered at Kimberley, when Gladstone and Disraeli were conducting their duel for political control, when all this was going on in England and the world, that no boy ever opened a newspaper. They could follow the progress of the dispute in the national Press or, nearer home, in the columns of the *Rugby Advertiser*.

But they did not need to read it in the papers; the thing must have been patent in the School. On one occasion at least, at the

height of the Scott quarrel, Hayman locked Scott out of his
school to prevent him taking his pupils; whereupon the boys
went in through the windows, took out the desks by the same
route, and Scott 'held his form' on the Close. Nor were other
masters always careful. As early as April 1870 James Robertson
was guilty of an unguarded phrase when reprimanding a boy.
'If I were on speaking terms with the Headmaster,' he said (or
'on better terms', or 'on terms of greater intimacy': the exact
phrase is uncertain), 'I would send you for punishment.' This
came to Hayman's ears and an uncomfortable interview for
Robertson followed. He thought he had cleared the matter up
and that it was finished, but Hayman, with that irritating habit
of his of pursuing an imagined fault to the bitter end, followed
up the interview with a letter a couple of days later. 'I. Do you
or do you not admit having used words to the effect imputed?
2. Do you wish, assuming the answer to I. to be in the affir-
mative, to express any retractation of these, I do not of course
mean to the boy, but to myself as charged with the discipline
which I think they tended to damage, or any regret for having
used them?' 'I could not but suppose', wrote Robertson in
answer, 'that my conversation with you on Tuesday night had
laid the matter to rest.'

Discipline, indeed, seems not to have been good, and des-
criptions in the School House Fasti[1] of occasions when boys
climbed on the roof while the Headmaster was entertaining
guests to dinner to drop squibs and fire-crackers down his draw-
ing-room chimney cannot be without some foundation. Hayman seems to have had a pernickety strictness in small matters
far removed from the broad and humane tolerance with which

[1] Records of the House kept by and reserved for senior boys.

Temple had ruled the school, which irritated boys and masters alike and tended to provoke opposition. 'One of the most difficult problems presented to all who are in authority', wrote J. M. Wilson, 'is: How much ought I not to know and see.' Hayman wanted to know and see everything.

It could have been such a great period in the history of Rugby. Outward signs of the School's growth made their appearance one after another; the new schools, the gift of the masters, were opened in 1870, and at last there was ample space for teaching; in October 1872 the new, enlarged Chapel—as yet without its tower and with Hakewill's West end marrying perhaps not very happily with Butterfield's taller florid nave, transepts and chancel—was consecrated, in the presence of a distinguished congregation, by the Bishop of Worcester. The gymnasium was completed by the end of 1871, and Goulburn sold to the Trustees in 1872, for £6000, 'the interest which he possessed in the house in School Field', which became the first of the Boarding Houses, apart from School House, actually owned by the School. The Governing Body refused, however, an offer by J. M. Wilson in 1873 to sell or lease his House to the School, though they accepted with gratitude his offer of an 8¼-inch refracting telescope, together with an observatory to house it. This instrument, made by Alvan Clarke in America, had been owned by the Rev. H. E. Lowe of Atherstone. It was G. M. Seabroke, who had been in Wilson's House, 1863–5, who introduced him to Lowe in 1871 and enabled him to buy telescope and observatory for £450. And it is the same instrument, through which splendid work has been done, particularly on double-star measurements, which is housed in the Temple Observatory today.

This, too, is the period during which the complete reorganisation was made in the constitution of the School. As a result of the Public Schools Act of 1868 and the Rugby School statute, approved by the Queen in Council on 9 August 1871, the old body of Trustees ceased to have any control over the School. They continued in existence to manage the property of the Rugby Charity, but the School itself was vested in a new Governing Body, which now took over complete control of the administration. The Lord-Lieutenant of Warwickshire was a member *ex officio*, the universities of Oxford, Cambridge and London, the Royal Society, the Lord Chancellor and the masters of the School nominated a member each, and the Trustees, in the first instance, appointed the remainder; later the Governing Body filled vacancies by co-optation. To this body was paid the income of the Charity after expenses had been deducted. It was their duty to appoint the Headmaster; and, though the rights of existing assistant masters were safeguarded, the old complicated method of salary payment disappeared and was replaced by a regular scale, paid by the Governing Body. This allowed to fifteen senior masters £500 a year (£600 if they had no House) with an additional capitation fee of £1 for each boy in the School over the number of 300 to a maximum of 500; and to the remainder £450 a year. The old division between 'Foundation masters' and others finally disappeared, and the Headmaster was now at liberty to dismiss any master, though in all cases he was required to give his reasons to the Governing Body.

The rights of the inhabitants of Rugby and Brownsover to get free education for their sons were radically changed. Those who had been living within five miles of the School before 31 July 1868 were still entitled to send their sons to the School, 'if of good character and able to read English and capable of being taught the first elements of Grammar'. These were the 'Old Foundationers', whose number would gradually diminish. Their place was to be taken by twelve major Foundationers, who would be educated free and twenty-four minor Founda-tioners who would pay half-fees. To these new arrangements there was a good deal of local resistance; the Governing Body received on 28 February 1872 a memorial from a public meeting at Rugby praying that the right of sending day boys should be preserved, and begging also for the establishment of a 'Middle Class' school from which boys might pass into the 'Head School'; and on 19 July there came a petition asking that there should be no alteration in the Foundation, but that any surplus finance should be applied to a 'Second School' to serve the demands of the neighbourhood. On the same date C. M. Caldecott, leading a deputation of nineteen Rugby citizens, entered a series of objections against the proposed Rugby Statutes. But the Governing Body, fortified by the Commission's Report, went ahead, and the change was made. There was at the time a good deal of bitterness about it; in fact the 1868 Act has been called 'an Act of Confiscation'.[1] But on 26 July 1872 the decision was definitely made by the Governors to found a 'Subordinate School, suited to the education of the Middle Classes', which was 'to provide instruction and qualify boys for admission to the Higher School', and the Trustees were asked to appropriate, from their accumulated funds, a sufficient sum for the purpose.[2]

---

[1] F. Betts, *Rugby School. A Reconstructed History from the Foundationers' Standpoint.* A collection of articles from the *Rugby Advertiser*, 1924.

[2] See below, pp. 108–11.

There was no striking change in curriculum or teaching methods during Hayman's time, but there were indications that changes were coming. In February 1872 we find him putting before the Governing Body a scheme for 'bifurcation' in the Upper School into classical and modern sides and five months later urging them to write nothing into the Regulations that might make such a division impossible. The Governors were interested, and although a year later they postponed a decision on the matter until Statutes and Regulations had been finally settled, it was to be not long before the division was made and Classics abandoned the overridingly dominant position they had held since the School was founded. Hayman also, as appears from his comments on the draft regulations, wanted to make either music or art a compulsory subject in a boy's first two terms, but, like Temple, he could not move the Governors in that direction.

Academic standards during Hayman's time remained high, and although some of the successes may have represented a carry-over from Temple and much credit must be given to the assistant masters, some at least of the quality must be ascribed to the Headmaster. There were nearly thirty scholarships and exhibitions from among his pupils, and as many Firsts at the universities; and perhaps one must single out C. A. James, who, besides winning a Scholarship at Balliol and a double First, also ran away with the Hertford, the Ireland, the Craven and the Eldon scholarships as well as the Latin Verse prize; and at Cambridge H. F. Wilson, a Scholar of Trinity, who took a First in the Classical Tripos and won the Senior Bell Scholarship and the Chancellor's Medal.

For the boys, life at School was much the same as before. They noted, in their House records, the resignation of Mr.

Buckoll, who 'has been a master for forty-five years and was nominated by Dr. Wooll', but were more interested in the House matches or 'House leaping' and entered occasional spicy comments such as: 'Violent lout-rows occurred this term (Summer 1871). Knuckle-dusters, revolvers and life-preservers were the order of the day.'[1] Like the youth of all generations they seemed to shrug off the troubles of their seniors, and it was the masters to whom it seemed that a great weight had lifted when the summer term of 1874 brought with it a new Head-master; not the man whom some of them (C. T. Arnold and J. M. Wilson in particular) would have chosen, but at least one whom they knew and one whose long connection with Rugby made him acceptable.

Comic Literature resulting from the Hayman Case

It was perhaps natural that the Hayman case should give rise to a certain amount of comic literature. This included an anonymous 'tragedy' entitled *The Fall of Haman*, 'Appropriate for School Theatricals', in which Temple appears as 'Temenus' and Scott as 'Mordecai'. It was printed at the offices of the *Yorkshire Post* and sold at sixpence.

The following parody, also anonymous, is preserved in 'The Rugby Album'.

[1] Ye Annals of Evans'.

Ye veritable Ballad of
'Who killed poor Hayman'

Who killed poor Hayman?
I, said *Froddy*[1]
With my Governing Body,
I killed poor Hayman.

Who saw him die?
I, said *Lee Warner*,
From my little corner,
I saw him die.

How did he die?
I know, said old *Green*,
For I witnessed the scene,
I know how he died.

Who caught his blood?
I, answered *Mason*,
With my little basin,
I caught his blood.

Who helped the disaster?
I, said *Mons. Vec.*,[2]
I wrung his neck
And helped the disaster.

Who'll dig his grave?
Not I, said *Neville*,[3]
He may go to the devil,
I won't dig his grave.

[1] Frederick Temple.   [2] J. W. J. Vecqueray.   [3] Neville Hutchinson.

Then who will dig his grave?
Not I, answered *Plug*,[1]
It's already dug,
I won't dig his grave.

Who'll toll the bell?
I, roared *the Bull*,[2]
Because I can pull,
I'll toll the bell.

Who'll make his shroud?
I, answered *Kitch*,[3]
Because I can stitch,
I'll make his shroud.

Who'll go to the funeral?
I, said old *Moberly*,
Calmly and soberly,
I'll go to the funeral.

Who'll be chief mourner?
I, said old *Taylor*,
I'm a capital wailer,
So I'll be chief mourner.

Who'll bear his coffin?
Not I, answered *Scott*,
I'd sooner be shot
Than I'd bear his coffin.

[1] C. T. Arnold.   [2] C. Elsee.   [3] F. E. Kitchener.

Who'll read the service?
Not I, said '*Old Beak*'[1]
Unless it's my week,
I won't read the service.

Who'll be the clerk?
Not I, answered *Jim*[2]
I can't sing a hymn,
So I won't be the clerk.

Who'll shed some tears?
Not I, said the '*Swede*',[3]
My mind's too relieved
For me to shed tears.

Who'll play the organ?
I, answered *Edwards*,
If it's before I go bedwards,
I'll play the organ.

Who thinks him ill-treated?
Not I, answered *Whitelaw*,
For I know the right law,
I don't think him ill-treated.

Who feels his death?
I, said old *Bradley*,
Though not very sadly,
I feel his death.

---

[1] C. B. Hutchinson. [2] J. M. Wilson. [3] Andreas Petterson.

Who cheeked him most?
I, answered '*Carlo*'[1]
But didn't he 'snarl ho',
I cheeked him most.

Who'll write his epitaph?
I, said old '*Hodge*',[2]
I'm up to a dodge,
So I'll write his epitaph.

Who'll tell the sad story?
I, said the *School Marshal*,[3]
For I'm quite impartial,
So I'll tell the sad story.

Who'll be his successor?
I, said *Jex-Blake,*
And I'll be wide awake
When I'm his successor.

[1] C. J. Smith.   [2] P. Bowden Smith.   [3] G. E. Patey.

'The Story of Hayman'

Arthur Sidgwick hauls Hayman up, while Burrows climbs the pole to try to cut him down. Temple watches from a window of School House, Scott rushes on from the right to see the fun, and Moberly, Philip Bowden Smith, Anstey and C. T. Arnold from the left. J. M. Wilson looks on sardonically on the extreme left and Whitelaw holds the testimonials in the foreground, while the music master, Taylor, plays a fanfare. The winged head of Thomas Arnold observes the scene from above.

T. W. Jex-Blake

4

Recovery

THOMAS WILLIAM JEX-BLAKE, 1874–87
JOHN PERCIVAL, 1887–95

T. W. Jex-Blake was born in 1832 and came of a Norfolk family, though his father had settled on the south coast. It was almost by chance that he became a Rugbeian. He was sent at the age of eight to 'Mr. Guest's school at Brighton; good prep^y for Eton, with good connection',[1] where, so he tells us, his companions were young members of the aristocracy—Lords Calthorpe, Gough, Somerset, Bangor—and where the best teacher was Edward Bradley, a brother of G. G. Bradley. They must have been a rough lot of boys, for on 1 July 1840 Jex-Blake had his right arm broken 'being twisted round by it on the ground by Gough and Calthorpe. Arm badly set by Badcock, a mere apothecary: but when Lawrence, a very good surgeon, said it must be broken again and reset, I howled so that they forbore. The arm has an awkward lump and is somewhat shortened, but thoroughly effective.'[2] In the spring of 1844 there appeared Stanley's *Life of Arnold* 'wh. so deeply impressed

---

[1] T. W. Jex-Blake, 'Rough Notes for an Autobiography' (manuscript).
[2] Ibid.

my Father—who told me that he had no idea that any public School attempted to act on the X^(an) ideal—that my name was put down on the list of G. E. L. Cotton; and at the shortest of notice, a fortnight of holiday, I went Aug. 13 to Rugby at $12\frac{1}{2}$'.[1] Here, he tells us, he was very idle at first, spending a whole year in the Lower Vth, and wasting a great deal of time until he reached the VIth, which he enjoyed greatly. He was one of a distinguished generation; his particular friends were J. F. Bright, later Master of University College, Oxford; John Cordery, whose sister he later married; Miles MacInnes; G. J. Goschen; Godfrey Lushington, later Permanent Under Secretary of State at the Home Office; Edward Parry, later Bishop of Dover; and J. H. Bridges. These formed an intellectual group who started a Literary Society and edited the *Rugbaean*. But Jex-Blake was also not undistinguished athletically; though 'too small for foot-ball' at first—he played bat-fives instead when he could get a court—he became a reasonable cricketer, playing for the XI in 1851, though not at Lord's, and was a considerable runner, winning the Crick[2] in 1851 and running on Bigside Hare and Hounds 1847–50. He also ran quite frequently with the Pytchley, Atherstone and Warwickshire hunts.

In 1851 Jex-Blake beat Goschen to a scholarship at University College. Goschen 'always beat me at school, but his strongest points, History & Philosophy, we were barely examined in'.[3] At Oxford he was again thrown into a stimulating society, and came much under the influence of Goldwin Smith, with whom he went for long Sunday walks. He seems to have

---

[1] Jex-Blake, 'Rough Notes for an Autobiography.'
[2] The annual cross-country race, originally to Crick and back.
[3] Jex-Blake, 'Rough Notes for an Autobiography.'

thrown himself with zest into university life, joining an essay society, riding a good deal on a chestnut mare, which 'taught me to ride, with many falls at fences—my fault, not hers', attending debates at the Union, but not speaking—'mauvaise honte prevented'—and entering for various university prizes without success, though he was *proxime accessit* for the Hertford and was mentioned for the Ireland. He finished with a double First in Classics and was elected to a Fellowship at Queen's, which he had to abandon when he married Hetty Cordery in 1857.

Jex-Blake was doubtful what profession to take up until Cotton invited him to Marlborough to teach the Lower Bench; this he did until 1857, when Temple asked him to come to Rugby, and the following year to succeed G. G. Bradley, who had been appointed Master of Marlborough, in his Boarding House, 'the best in Rugby: and so it remained all my time, admittedly'.[1] He remained at Rugby until 1868 when he was appointed Principal of Cheltenham College, a post which he occupied with distinction and success until 1874.

The only other serious candidate for the Rugby headmaster-ship was John Percival, who was strongly supported by Temple, and who had already been a candidate in 1869. This fact told against Percival. 'It was felt', Temple wrote to him, 'that to elect a man now instead of Hayman, to whom Hayman had been preferred some years ago, was a kind of slap to the Trus-tees. This I had not at all foreseen.' It must also have been felt that a man who combined known moderation with proved administrative ability was what, at the moment, Rugby needed

---

[1] Ibid. Temple appears to have had no scruple in putting a junior master into a House over the heads of others of long standing.

rather than one of Percival's fiery energy. The voting at the election was close, 7 to 5. There were some among the masters who were bitterly disappointed, C. T. Arnold and J. M. Wilson in particular; but for most of them the relief of having got rid of Hayman made them willing to accept one who was at least a Rugbeian through and through. Their feelings were expressed by C. T. Arnold in a letter to Percival on 19 February 1874.

> . . . Jex-Blake having been elected it becomes the duty of every one who cares for Rugby at all to be unanimous in forgetting this last four years of dark trial, and especially for all working here to allow no feeling of any kind to interfere for one moment with his spirit of self forgetfulness and devotion to work, with eyes fixed on the future as the only hope of forgetting a miserable past. Neither you nor Jex-Blake, nor any one else can know the blackness of that time as I know it. . . . All that can be done is to bury it and let no thought rest on it.[1]

On 26 April Robert Whitelaw, now after eight years at Rugby established as a very great teacher of the XX, wrote in lighter vein to his friend E. M. Oakeley at Clifton.

> We were new-born yesterday. . . . There are no bad smells lingering in the S.H. . . . I wonder if the G.B. paid for the chloride of lime. More probably it was decided by the casting vote of the Chairman that Jex should pay for it himself. . . . We shall get on: perhaps none the worse for our buffeting. Time and the Agagite have taught us many things. Study the 30th Psalm, ye prosperous ones, and say not in your hearts: Percival will never be removed. Not even the great Conservative

---

[1] W. Temple, *Life of Bishop Percival*, pp. 48–49.

Reaction is an inevitable and eternal fact. When he does go, may you fare better than we did in the day of our adversity.[1]

It was to a school dimmed in reputation and depleted in numbers that Jex-Blake succeeded in April 1874, but with his urbane rule public confidence was rapidly restored and numbers at once began to rise. In his first two terms he accepted 106 new boys, in the following year 153, and the School settled down to an average of about 425, at which it remained fairly steadily until a slight decline set in during Jex-Blake's last three years, when it dropped for a while below 400.

By February 1875 the Governing Body was considering the question of maximum numbers and deferring their decision until Dr. George Wilson, Medical Officer of Health for mid-Warwickshire, had inspected the sanitary condition of all the Boarding Houses. This he had done by the time the Governors met in December, and some Housemasters (Bowden Smith, Hutchinson, Elsee, Wilson and Green, as well as the Headmaster) were instructed to carry out his recommendations, which included the installation of a filtration plant for the use of town water in School House, by the end of the summer holidays 1876; there was then to be a further inspection, and no licence for a Boarding House was to be issued to anyone who had failed to carry out the recommendations. This new concern with the interior economy of the Houses was not very welcome to the Housemasters; they owned their Houses and were responsible for expenses involved in the suggested improvements. Two of them, indeed—Bonamy Price and Anstey—made an attempt to sell their Houses to the School, and the Governing Body was,

---

[1] David papers, in possession of Mrs. David.

this time, not uninterested in the proposition, but refused in June 1876, because they could not get the Charity Commissioners to agree to the sale of Trust stock which would be necessary.

The increased concern of parents, and through them of the Governing Body, with the conditions in which the boys lived is reflected in a good deal of the activity of this period. Jex-Blake wanted an isolation block and Butterfield designed a 'fever cottage', which was erected by John Parnell for £984; £220 was sanctioned for the provision of a 'Dressing-room and sponge-baths' in Arnold's House, and his rent was increased to cover the cost; in 1880 the Governing Body ordered that 'to prevent the boys drinking the water from the pump standing on the site of the old stables, the handle be taken off and only used when necessary'. Generally there was an increased awareness of the necessity for hygienic conditions in the School.

New building and improvements continued unchecked, and Butterfield was kept busy. He was asked in 1875 to design a new storey for School House to accommodate Jex-Blake's growing family (in the end two sons and nine daughters); the same year Butterfield designed the swimming-bath, which was one of the Headmaster's gifts to the School and which remained in use until the opening of the present 'Tosh'. In 1877 the Governors accepted his plans for the Temple Reading Room, Art Museum and Curator's house, the necessity for which was pressed on them by Jex-Blake. Plans were submitted in 1882 for the 'completion' of the Chapel rebuilding, and, as a House annalist recorded, 'a new spire, "of no great length" was put on'. The following year the decision was made to purchase, for £3200, W. C. Green's house, tenanted at the time by W. G. Michell, and to use the site for the erection of a new Big School. For this Jex-Blake assured the Governors that they would be put to no expense beyond the actual purchase of the house.

Jex-Blake had an abiding interest in art and a firm belief in its educational value. To the Art Museum his gifts were generous 'in the hope', as he said, 'that leisure hours would be given by many boys to a delightful form of culture often too little thought of at home and school, and with the conviction that some few boys would draw great enjoyment, lifelong interest and a new faculty from it'. At least some boys were apprecia-tive. 'On June 24', writes the keeper of the Annals of Evans' in 1879, 'was opened at Rugby the first Art Museum possessed by any school in England, with a Reading Room (bearing Dr. Temple's name) in the same building. It was stocked for the first two months with a loan collection of great value, to which the Kensington Museum contributed largely.' To this new department came T. M. Lindsay in March 1880 as Art Master and Curator, to replace Tupper, who had died the previous September.

Lindsay was one of a number of distinguished appointments made by Jex-Blake. Some of them left Rugby for important posts elsewhere—G. L. Bennett, to headmasterships at Ply-mouth and Sutton Valence; Henry Whitehead, later Bishop of Madras; C. H. Hodges, headmaster successively of two Aus-tralian schools; F. B. Westcott, Headmaster of Sherborne; others, such as A. E. Donkin, Linnaeus Cumming ('Puff' Cumming to generations of Rugbeians), W. G. Michell, C. G. Steel, W. P. Brooke (father of Rupert), George Stallard, W. H. Payne-Smith and W. N. ('Spitter') Wilson stayed on, and their names are inseparably connected with Rugby. And in his last year Jex-Blake appointed Basil Johnson, one of the most stimulating of music masters, who knew what boys could sing and succeeded in making them do it. These, with those who remained of Temple's appointments and a further brilliant group brought in by Percival, formed the core of a teaching staff second to none in England, who saw the School with an undimmed academic reputation out of the nineteenth and well into the twentieth century.

The period of Jex-Blake saw the foundation of the 'Sub-ordinate School of Lawrence Sheriff' and much of the business of the Governing Body, from December 1875 onwards, was concerned with its establishment. Lawrence Sheriff School—the 'hateful name: The Subordinate School', as H. V. White-house, its second Headmaster called it, was dropped many years ago—has a proud and distinguished history of its own, which does not belong to these pages; but in so far as it was an attempt to provide for local boys the education that Lawrence Sheriffe had intended for them, at a time when it was increasingly difficult for them to have it at Rugby School, and when, be it said, the Governing Body was more interested in the boarding character of the School than in its local responsibilities, the facts of the foundation need to be recorded.

It is quite clear that the original method of offering free education at the School for the sons of all Rugby residents could not have been continued. Rugby School, whether the residents liked it or not, was no longer just a local grammar school, and had not been so since, at least, the time of Henry Holyoake's headmastership (1688–1731). Its reputation had attracted to Rugby many who settled in the town purely to enjoy the benefit of a first-class, free education for their sons up to university level. The type of education provided, largely classical, was not the kind needed by many of the residents, whose sons would be destined not for the universities, but for agriculture or com/ merce. And, whether or not the intent of the pious founder had been neglected, there could clearly be no going back to the con/ ditions of the sixteenth and early seventeenth centuries. If the Public Schools Commissioners had had their way, there would have been a clean break of the Trust, the Foundationers would have disappeared and the funds thereby released would have been used to provide open scholarships; Rugby School would have entirely lost its local character and connection. To this Temple, though a believer in the principle of open scholarships, was not prepared to agree. He, and with him a large number of the intelligent citizens of the town, saw the necessity of providing education of a rather different sort to serve local needs, and that the answer lay in the creation of a second school. And it was this view which, as we have seen, was accepted by the Govern/ ing Body in 1872.

In December 1875 the decision was made to purchase, for £2520, six acres of the rectory glebe as a site for the new school; a committee, of which Temple was the most influential mem/ ber, was set up to deal with the business and 'Mr. Clarke of 13, Halford Place, Oxford St., London' was asked to prepare plans. Three months later there was still disagreement as to what form the school was to take; was it to be purely a day school or was there to be provision for boarders? Clarke was eventually instructed to submit plans for a school with class/ rooms for 150 boys, costing not more than £3000, and alter/ native plans for a Master's house without boarders and for one with provision for forty boarders. By June 1876 the decision was made against boarders, Clarke's plans were accepted, and a month later he was getting to work on drainage and the new building was out to tender. But the Governing Body must have realised very soon that their estimate of the cost of the work was unrealistic, for the tender eventually accepted was that of Claridge of Banbury for £7280; and even this had, a month later, to be raised by £400, since Claridge had made a major error in estimating, and the final figure was £7754.

Early in 1878 the buildings were complete and Jex-Blake was advertising for a Headmaster. His choice was a happy one, and H. T. Rhoades, who had been a boy at Rugby under Tait, opened the School on 27 May of that year. He was to receive a salary based on capitation fees (minimum £200), which could never have risen to £500 until an adjustment was made in 1881; he was to appoint two assistants at £150 and £100, and 'help' for modern languages, vocal music, drawing and drill, which together must not exceed £100. When numbers in the school rose to 80, he was empowered to appoint a third assistant at £120. One-fifth of the Rugby School Trust income was allocated to the new school, and its Headmaster was responsible for the financial administration, acting as his own bursar and collecting fees.[1] Boys who had attended this school for a minimum of two years might compete for one of the twelve major or twenty-four minor Foundationerships at Rugby School, and it was through this side door that those who had settled in Rugby for the sake of their sons' education were still sometimes able to have it almost free.

---

[1] Fees were charged at first at the rate of eight to ten guineas a year according to age. A petition was received by the Governing Body, in August 1885, from Richard Over and forty-six other inhabitants of Rugby that they should be reduced to the same as Foundationers' fees, four to five guineas. They were in fact reduced to £6 to £7 10s.

It was inevitable that, for the first year or two, there should be a deficit in the new school's finances, and this was paid, not always with a very good grace,[1] by the Governing Body. But it decreased annually as the school filled up. Until 1906 the Headmaster of Rugby School had the main responsibility for the new foundation, but in that year a proper Board of Governors was set up, on which, *ex officio*, he had a place. And from this time the school developed to its present position of one of the leading Secondary Schools of the Midlands.

It is probable that Jex-Blake regarded his work with the new school as a part of his outside interests, together with his concern for the rebuilding of the parish church and of the old chapel at Brownsover. Within the main school there was plenty doing. The New Quadrangle was completed in 1885, though the funds for the purpose were not entirely adequate and the Headmaster was authorised to contribute £250 from the Lecture Fund. In the same year Butterfield submitted his plans for the New Big School and the Governing Body, in accepting them, authorised what must surely be one of the ugliest buildings of its kind in the country. (Later, Rupert Brooke was to speak of 'a wonderful beauty in the air which makes New Big School almost bearable'.) Speeches and the School concert were held there for the first time in 1886, and a House annalist informs us that, as the whole School were able to be present, 'the chorus of the *Floreat* was tremendous'. In 1885, too, Caldecott's Piece was added to the grounds as a new cricket field, and the Governing Body voted £200 towards its purchase, to which they added another £900 the following year.

In the general running of the School the only reform Jex-

[1] They called it a 'grant in aid'.

Blake appears to have made was the introduction of 'Hall Prep.' for the lower forms in every House. In some Houses this had already been in force in an unofficial fashion, the House-master or tutor spending a part of each evening in the House Hall to ensure conditions in which work could be done and to prevent the gatherings of senior boys, which had caused anxiety to several Headmasters. Now the principle became official and it came to stay.

But Jex-Blake was not a firm Headmaster. Probably he was what was needed for a year or two after his predecessor, but when the turmoil over Hayman's dismissal died down and the difficult years began to slip into a forgotten past, something much more vigorous was needed than the leadership provided by the new Headmaster. At first, when the prime necessity was to increase numbers, it was difficult for him to expel or to implement strictly the rules about superannuation, and this laxness became a habit. He was a mild and benevolent man, very popular with the boys, and he hated rows. Discipline had become slack under Hayman, and there is no doubt that there were a good many boys in the School who, either for academic or for moral reasons, would have been better out of it. The result was that, though numbers increased, there was a decline in the tone of the place and the Headmaster did little to arrest it. 'He would never flog,' wrote J. M. Wilson (had that shortened right arm with the awkward lump anything to do with it?), 'so that there was no punishment between 500 lines and expulsion, and he would not expel; and he had no moral or religious weight with the boys. "Wash your dirty linen at home, Wilson," was often said to me.' He disliked issuing firm orders to the School as a whole, always preferring a conditional suggestion to a categorical imperative, and the boys, though they liked him, felt little, if any, awe and, on the whole, went their own way. The result was inevitable; though there was no evident falling off in the top academic standards—eighty of those who entered under Jex-Blake won open awards at the university and over forty (including both G. F. and H. C. Bradby) won Firsts—the School as a whole became slack and the public image of Rugby as a vigorous go-ahead School again gradually became dimmed; and from the summer of 1884 numbers were again declining, not disastrously, as under Hayman, but sufficiently to cause uneasiness to the Governing Body. They were therefore not very much distressed when in 1886 he tendered his resignation to become Rector of Alvechurch, whence he was to move, in 1891, to the Deanery of Wells.

But this decline was towards the end, and Jex-Blake cannot just be written off as a failure. For one thing, if for nothing else, Rugby has reason to be grateful to him. In 1917 A. E. Donkin spoke of him to a meeting of Old Rugbeians: 'All who remember the time when he came there', he said, 'can never forget what he did for Rugby at the time of her greatest need, and at a time, I may add, when no other man could have done what he did to restore the School to its proper place in the hearts of Old Rugbeians, and to put it right in the eyes of all others.' Let this be the final judgment on him.

For twelve years Rugby School had been ambling along comfortably on a loose rein. Now, suddenly, it was to be pulled in tight and to feel the whiplash. 'Percival', wrote T. E. Brown, poet and Clifton Housemaster, to J. M. Wilson in 1879, 'was like an inspired, demonic conductor of an orchestra. He has

lashed us into Bacchic fury—wind and strings and voices—
forte, forte, fortissimo. At the end of term we sink back on our
seats and mop our foreheads and pant. He is divine; but we
want rest.'[1] This was the man whom the Trustees had passed
over in 1869 and the Governing Body in 1874, and whom they
now, with one voice, invited to come to Rugby. They asked for
no other application; they interviewed no other candidate. He
was the one man in England who, they were convinced, could
restore the School to its former greatness, and they simply wrote
and asked him to come; and, by return of post,[2] he accepted.

John Percival was one of those remarkable nineteenth-century
characters, like Professor Joseph Wright, who by sheer ability,
indomitable industry and unwavering faith rose from very
humble beginnings to great eminence. His father was a West-
morland farmer, a 'Statesman' owning his own land, and a
notable wrestler. His early education was at local village schools
at Winton and Hackthorpe, but in 1846 at the age of twelve, he
began attending Appleby Grammar School, to which he
walked the five or six miles in brass-sided clogs, or rode at a
great pace on a chestnut cob. At the grammar school he proved
a great worker, and this, combined with the splendid teaching
of the Headmaster, John Richardson, brought him a Scholarship at Queen's College, Oxford, in 1856. Here his life included
little but uninterrupted labour; he took first class honours in
Classical and Mathematical Moderations, and again in the final
examination of both those subjects; and it was when he was
taking the final examination of the History School that his

[1] Quoted in W. Temple, *Life of Bishop Percival*, p. 57.
[2] The Bishop of Worcester's letter of invitation was dated 17 November 1886;
Percival's letter of acceptance the 18th.

health broke down; he had completed two papers only and had reached first-class standard in both. It was thought at the time that he would never again be able to work, but a winter (1858/9) with friends at Pau restored him and in 1860 Temple appointed him to Rugby.

At Rugby, during that first short stay, probably only Temple recognised his quality, though his other colleagues seem to have been aware that he was in some way different from them. He made no intimate friends. 'He was always agreeable to meet,' said J. M. Wilson, 'not at all unsociable. But he stood alone.' The only anecdote that has come down from that period is that he was severely reprimanded by Patey, the School Marshal, for giving boys beer when he entertained them to breakfast. It is a measure of Temple's insight that when, in 1862, Charles Evans withdrew at the last minute from the headmastership of Clifton to which he had been appointed, it was Percival whom Temple recommended for the post. And the history of the opening and development of Clifton College is the history of the first great period of Percival's career. There he drove himself —and his staff—almost beyond his powers, and it was with impaired health that in 1878 he moved to Oxford to become President of Trinity College. Here, though it was not in his nature to relax, the strain was not so great, and it was no worn-out or senile man who took over the headmastership of Rugby nine years later at the age of fifty-two.

From all sides the appointment was greeted with enthusiasm. 'You are the only man', wrote Henry Lee Warner, recently retired, 'that Rugby will welcome unitedly'—though he hoped that some of the staff would stay only long enough to welcome him. From Clifton H. G. Dakyns wrote delightedly:

As a Rugby man I dance about and am mad, and can only sing out (to the scandal of my more passive and more ultra-Cliftonian friends) *magnus ab integro saeculorum nascitur ordo*. . . . I do devoutly hope and expect and believe that another Rugby will ere long arise, and that you will not only have created one school at a time of life when some thought you too young, but at an age when some . . . may look upon you as too old, you will recreate another.[1]

And from all sides, though mostly with less exuberance, congratulations flowed in.

Percival had probably intended to apply reform gently and progressively; but the School he found when he took up his duties in April 1887 bore little resemblance, except in externals, to the one he had left in 1862, and he was deeply disappointed. He decided that there was no time to waste and began from his early months to make changes in all directions. Very rapidly he took the measure of the School, hardly less rapidly of individual boys. He found a School which he considered idle and one in which there was a good deal of evil—and he regarded idleness as immoral and hated evil with a single-minded intensity that made him frightening. In his second term he started exercising strictly the rules of superannuation, which Jex-Blake had feared, for the sake of numbers, to apply. In the spring of 1888 he expelled five boys, striking their names publicly from the list and delivering to the School a searing address, which left them smarting and frightened; and a number did not return next term who had not been due to leave. He startled the School by flogging a boy whose report indicated persistent idleness. Finding that athleticism had got out of hand, and that some unworthy

---

[1] Quoted in W. Temple, *Life of Bishop Percival*, pp. 95–96.

John Percival

G. F. Bradby

Robert Whitelaw

boys were gaining privileges and status which he thought undesirable, he abolished a number of minor games distinctions such as the braid worn round the cap by those who had been awarded their 'flannels'. The School was angry—but it was impressed; and it began, uncomfortably, to move. Ordinary idleness he attacked by insisting that masters should give test questions on paper at the beginning of a lesson—what G. F. Bradby called 'that bugbear alike of the educational idealist and of the idle boy'—and rapidly standards of industry began to rise. He was always about the place, always watching with what William Temple, who entered the School under him, described as 'an unerring eye for the unwholesome boy'. He watched them as they filed in and out of Chapel, he watched them on the Close, alert always for behaviour that he regarded as 'symptomatic', noting the House or the individual who offended. He insisted on his VIth carrying out their disciplinary duties, and was as emphatic to them as to any others when they appeared to be failing, for instance, to check foul language. He spoke to his new boys on the first day of each term and his departing shot of 'Eh—I shall be watching you every day of your lives' fell little short of the truth. He had no objection whatever to using fear as an element in discipline.

It was not only the improvement of the general tone and industry of the School at which Percival aimed; he was also determined to improve quality. He believed fully in Arnold's opinion that 'the first, second and third duty of a Headmaster is to get rid of unpromising material', but this was a purely negative injunction; it was important too to attract good entrants. To this end Percival increased the number and the value of scholarships. He could hope for little help in this from the Governing

Body, however sympathetic they might be; the School was not making enough profit even for necessary repairs and improvements (in 1889 Lord Leigh, heading the Committee for repairs, was instructed to pay attention to 'the very straitened condition of the finances of the Governing Body'). So Percival went first to the Old Rugbeians, raising subscriptions in memory of distinguished O.R.s such as the Earl of Derby and Theodore Walrond; and then to his masters, particularly the Housemasters, whom he persuaded to give generously.

His second reform in the direction of improved quality was to develop the scheme of 'bifurcation', which had been urged by Hayman and which JexBlake had begun in his last year; and the Upper School was now divided into classical and modern sides, with an Army Class as a subdivision of the latter. This new scheme required additional masters, and again Percival went to his staff. In July 1887 the Governing Body sanctioned the expenditure of £200 a year for effecting the new scheme, 'the present masters undertaking to tax themselves in a sum equal to that which may be contributed by the Governing Body'. It was clearly important that the new modern side should be well regarded in the School, and a ruling of the Governors in 1891 that not more than five (nor less than four) Boarding Houses should be held by classical masters is illuminating.

Percival's appointments to the staff were brilliant. He took little stock of 'experience', rather preferring young men straight from the university, whom he could train, and whom he could keep up to the mark with continual pinpricks—his 'little notes' were famous, concerning even the scent of tobacco on a pile of papers or a letter sent to him. The subsequent career of many whom he appointed was distinguished—George Smith, who shared the Upper Bench[1] with Percival, became Headmaster of Merchiston and Master of Dulwich; J. Lewis Paton, the Lower Bench master, became the greatest of all High Masters of Manchester Grammar School; Frank Fletcher went to Marlborough and to Charterhouse; R. Waterfield to Cheltenham; and A. A. David to Clifton and back to Rugby before becoming Bishop of St. Edmundsbury and Ipswich and then of Liverpool. And of those who remained at Rugby there lives in the memory and affection of Rugbeians (and of many others who read his books) G. F. Bradby as one of the greatest of them all.

There was further modification, too, in the salary scale. By the scheme adopted finally in 1894 the fifteen senior assistant masters received £500 a year, with an extra £100 for the seven who were not Housemasters; in addition, those who had held a House for not more than eight years were to have a capitation fee of 6s. 8d. for every boy in the School over 300 up to 500. Other masters on the regular staff received £450 a year; any others who became necessary were to be paid by arrangement with the Headmaster, to a maximum of £450. Boarding Houses could henceforth he held for fifteen years only, or until the age of sixty, which became the normal retirement age, though masters could be kept on for a further five years at a reduced salary. Percival had the reputation of being 'hard' in the matter of salaries; it was reported that, while at Clifton, he had once said: 'I don't believe in paying my assistant masters well.'

With a first-class staff, a new organisation and Percival's own driving force at the head, the School became by swift degrees an industrious, efficient and moral community. In spite of the early superannuations and expulsions, numbers began to rise. Jex-

[1] The Upper and Lower Benches are the upper and lower divisions of the VIth form.

Blake had handed over a School of 394 boys, taught by twenty-
three masters, including the Head. In the next five years average
numbers were 415, 435, 459, 482, 499 and when Percival
retired in 1895 there were over 500 and thirty-three masters.
This was without any doubt his own work. His control of the
School, masters and boys, was complete; his discipline, though
there was nothing mechanical about it and he made a distinction
between technical and moral offences, was absolute. Boys may
have laughed in his absence at his broad north-country accent,
or at the more extravagant manifestations of his narrow puritanism, but they obeyed him. And they never laughed at him to
his face. There was an occasion when, coming down to take
prayers in the School House Hall, he slipped on the stairs and
cascaded feet first into the presence of the House; the expression
on his face did not change and there was no hint of laughter
from his boys. Obedience may have rested, as William Temple
suggests, on respect as much as on fear, but there is no doubt
that they did fear him and more than one contemporary has
borne witness to the terror inspired by his wintry smile when
he was angry.

And so Percival restored Rugby's greatness. But he did not
create a happy School, and there is a reverse side to the coin
even of his efficiency. So intense was his moral earnestness and
passion for righteousness that he was unwilling to allow any
liberty. He feared it. He wanted to know what every boy was
doing each minute of the day; they were to be given a time-table
so detailed that there would be no time for them to get into evil
ways, and they were to be watched. The result was that,
though in the VIth there was a good deal of independent
thought and a remarkable amount of reading was done outside

prescribed work, elsewhere—and even there, to some extent—
there was a loss of initiative and a good deal of stereotyping.
'There is no way', said William Temple, perhaps inheriting the
opinion of his father, 'of teaching boys to work for themselves
except by giving them the chance to be idle: there is no way of
teaching boys to use time except by giving them the chance to
waste it.' This chance Percival was never ready to give. He was
a task-master who exacted the last ounce of work from his
pupils, and there was no place for the boy of unusual tastes.
Selous, if what J. M. Wilson says of him is true, would never
have lasted at Rugby under Percival.

Yet it would be a mistake to suppose that the School was
cowed—it is almost impossible, fortunately, to cow Public
School boys. If proof of this were needed, it can be found in the
pages of the *Sibyl*, whose first issue was published on 25 October
1890 and which is possibly the most distinguished (in its earlier
numbers at least) of all the 'private enterprise' magazines that the
School has produced. So thought no less an authority than
Frederick Harrison, who wrote to the editor, W. H. Draper,
saying that he had read all the first three numbers 'and it is
about the best school magazine I ever saw'. It lasted—though the
later issues were not very regular—for five years. In its pages are
to be found literary contributions, prose and verse, of some
merit and a great deal of very intelligent satire. When on 5
November 1892 a new boy, M. F. Heron, died in rather tragic
circumstances while out for a run, and Press criticism, which
reached even *The Times*, of conditions at Rugby School became
widespread, the *Sibyl* sprang to the School's defence. 'The
power', wrote the editor on 26 November, 'which the press
gives of making serious charges anonymously is one of its great

evils. Such anonymous correspondents would do well to remember the rhyme

> Anonymous letters, anonymous letters
> Are usually sent from inferiors to betters.'

In the next issue, of 15 December, he wrote:

Complaints are raised on our behalf which we should not dream of raising ourselves, and to which we should give no support . . . The following extract from one contemporary gives a most novel view of ourselves as some others see us. 'Rugby boys are driven to their games with a knotted cord; they frequently seek escape from their persecutors behind the forms of their class rooms, and beneath the beds of their dormitories.' What a pity the writer was not better acquainted with our rules! He might have added with telling emphasis, 'but to prevent even this escape the doors of both dormitory and class room are frequently locked'.

There follow a number of comic letters. 'The Mother of the Gracchi' writes '. . . my boys also told me, as a reason for not playing, that boys repeatedly died during the games, and that a man goes round with a barrow after every game to pick them up. This ought not to be.' And 'Lundener':

Dear Sir—

As I have never taken part in any manly exercise except bicycling, I feel particularly well fitted to instruct the public about the dangers of Rugby games. Yes sir, the Close is the scene of brutal atrocities. I have seen a stout fellow quite out of breath after a long game, and even panting. To an aesthetic nature, like mine, such sights are simply revolting.

The *Sibyl* also poked fun, mostly good humoured, at masters, particularly Headmasters, past and present. There must have existed a collection of headmagisterial *dicta,* from which excerpts were printed from time to time. Thus Goulburn ended an eloquent sermon on the text 'The smoking flax shall He not quench' with: 'My brethren, there is some chance for a boy even if he smokes.' Temple's accent was mocked: 'Bies, yer getting ruude; this must cease.' Hayman seems to have been famous for his long-windedness, as in 'You must not use periphrastic laxity of oratorical circumlocution in your composition', or his request to Patey, the School Marshal, 'Propound this interrogation to Mr. Bowden Smith and convey to me his response.' Jex-Blake is recorded as having said of the Marylebone match in 1879, 'They sent down three cricketers who weren't gentlemen, and four gentlemen who weren't cricketers.' Percival himself is more guardedly referred to, but he must have been easily recognisable in an article entitled 'Phantasmata' (2 June 1894), the dream of a schoolmaster in A.D. 1994: 'Eh—you haven't read the notes in your Horace, man, or you might get it into better English. This Philistinism shows that there's no tone in your work. . . . You don't seem to remember that there's a back-stairs way out of this form as well as a way up. I must have it, man; what are you looking like that for? Sit down, and let's hear somebody else.' There follow caricatures of a dozen masters, easy for contem-poraries to recognise, difficult to identify today—but it must surely be Whitelaw whose voice cried: 'Really, I think the standard of the form is worse than it has ever been, it is per-fectly sickening (here the owner seemed to be nearly weeping). *Cannot one* of you understand . . .?'

One gets an insight, too, into the day-to-day routine, as in 'An American view of Rugby' (11 June 1891): 'the 6.15 morning bell wakes us, but we don't want to get up. Then another bell rings at ten minutes off seven for five minutes. We've got to get in our places in chapel in that time to be "called over", and if we're too lazy to make it it means a "licking", that's all.' And so it goes on through the day. 'Every boy has got to join the games on half-holidays unless he's got good excuse. Sometimes we get off by shamming a sore foot and many other ways well known to us boys.' In the evening at nine o'clock 'they give us a light supper that don't make anybody dream. Then it's go to bed, and no fooling, or it means another licking, sure as fees and marshals.' It is interesting to find the Marshal referred to as a secret reporter of misconduct and the 'dread bearer of the summons "to the Doctor's chamber"'.

One also hears some of the current Rugby slang; there is a suggestion (24 October 1893) that a dictionary of Public School slang should be compiled. Some of the terms mentioned are still in use, for instance: '*Oil*—substantive; . . . describes any trick or device (not necessarily a mean one), by which you score something over your comrades or masters. Derivation obvious. —e.g.: "It's a beastly oil Smith's stopping out for that exam".' Others have, regrettably, fallen out; '*Tweak*—substantive; in very frequent use at Rugby; any stratagem whereby trouble is avoided. Hence *Tweaky* = full of stratagems.'

But the bulk of the *Sibyl* was original prose and verse, a good deal of it topical, much of it very good. It provides a mine of information about Percival's period and even contains photo-graphs of the famous 'below the knee' shorts.

One great and lasting reform that Percival carried out was in improving the status of 'the Town'. Among the most impor-tant pieces of work that he had done at Clifton was the creation of an organisation that would give to day boys as nearly as possible the same advantages as were afforded to boarders. At Rugby, when he came, there was little feeling of corporate identity among the day boys. From time to time they had organised a 'Town House' society or produced a magazine (the *Lion*), and there had been a time when they could provide a team at cricket or football that could challenge all comers. But they had no local habitation—they used the steps of Pepperday's shop or a cleaner's room (the 'Town' annalist calls it a stoke-hole) to leave their clothes before games—they had no tutor of their own, sharing the School House tutors, and for ten years before Percival took them in hand their corporate organisation seems to have collapsed and they were regarded with some contempt by the rest of the School.[1]

The first step in improving their condition was to organise them as, and to call them a 'House', and from 1888 they began playing House matches and using the Close. Next they had to have a tutor of their own, and J. L. Paton was appointed to that office in 1891. Percival could hardly have chosen better, and under Paton's vigorous management Town House gradually developed a sense of identity and self-respect, which was pre-served and developed by successive tutors until in 1901 it was decided to build on the Close a permanent Town Room, with a proper changing-room and a library, which was opened by Arthur Sidgwick, himself an old Town boy, in March 1902. This remained their abode until, after the Second World War, the old Kilbracken was adapted to serve the Town House more spaciously, and the old Town Room became the Bursary. In 1903 Donald Macaulay felt sufficient pride and interest in his

---

[1] This is made very clear by an article published in *Macmillan's Magazine* in March 1885, by 'An Ex-Day-Boy'.

House to undertake the compilation of a Town House register, which still exists. Percival saw only the beginning of this process, but his was the original initiative.

In some small matters Percival's puritanism led him to enactments that seem to us—and indeed seemed to the School then—surprising. There was, for instance, the dislike he took (or perhaps, as the School thought, it was Mrs. Percival's dislike) to the exposure of knees at football, and his order that all football shorts must be cut to reach below the knee. F. C. C. Wrigley (brother of H. C. Wrigley, in whose memory the Wrigley Cup was given), who must today (1966) be one of the very few survivors from Percival's time, describes how, when wearing a pair of illegally brief shorts, he met the Headmaster outside School House. He had a moment of acute anxiety, but on this occasion his explanation was accepted that the Rugby tailors had been flooded with several hundred pairs of shorts for lengthening, and that there was a time-lag of several weeks before his could be attended to. Loose shorts below the knee were, in any case, impossible for football, and the boys just turned them up. So Percival made a second order that they must all be fitted with elastic which would hold them firmly below the knee. But this was near the end of his time, and with a new Headmaster the rule was dropped. Less unreasonable, perhaps, was his dislike of the way in which boys wore their caps on the back of the head, leaving an untidy and, in Percival's view, an unsightly forelock free to the air at the front. 'You look like a coal heaver,' he said to a boy whom he found breaking his rule on the subject; and to his companion: 'Take him back to the House and comb his hair and put his cap on properly for him.'

But these were little matters, and in all essentials Percival was a very big man, a fact which the boys, through all their fear and sometimes dislike of him, came to realise. He himself was completely fearless and would never alter his convictions or compromise his principles to court popularity. He took the unpopular side in the dispute over the disestablishment of the Welsh Church, and in May 1894 provoked an outburst with a powerful letter to *The Times*, which caused a number of entries to Rugby to be withdrawn; shortly afterwards, when Lord Rosebery had won the Derby, he preached in Westminster Abbey a sermon denouncing gambling and lamenting a racing Prime Minister. And he always had an eye open for opportunities of service. It was through his initiative that in 1889 the Rugby School Mission was started, which adopted Arthur Walrond's Boys' Club in Notting Dale and founded a Club in Birmingham; and since then the Rugby Clubs have had a continuous and most useful history.

New Big School was complete when Percival took office, but he was responsible for raising the money to provide it with an organ. The only major building put up during his time was the new Boarding House, the necessity for which was recognised by the Governing Body in 1891, and which was opened by George Stallard two years later (Tudor House). There was a great deal of minor work done on the buildings. School House boys would have been pleased with a new heating installation which was to send 'hot water instead of hot air through the pipes'. Boys were, apparently, often cold in this period, but perhaps it was not always the fault of the arrangements for heating. 'Steel is a stupid,' wrote O. R. McMullen. 'Last Wednesday (I do not know if it was cold with you as it was with us) he made us write prose with four windows and the door open; my fingers got frightfully cold . . . we do not begin fires till the 20th of this month. I hope we do not all get frozen.' This was in November.

Boys would have been interested too in the application of modern inventions. A device to blow the Chapel organ 'by water' was installed in 1888—in Jex-Blake's time a 'gas engine' had been used for the purpose. And in 1892 the great decision was made to light the schools by electricity, since 'there would be no harm to eyesight if proper precautions were taken'. There were then no electric mains to draw on, and the change was made possible by the formation of the Rugby School Electric Lighting Company Ltd., in which Housemasters were the principal shareholders, and which at a cost of £1100 built a powerhouse near the gymnasium and wired the schools. The installation was not always very efficient. The engine produced a peculiar smell, not unlike pork, which caused the editors of the *Sibyl* to suggest that the southern end of the Close should in future be called 'New Pigside'; and the frequency of breakdowns on Sunday led to the belief that the smell of 'Dowson Gas' spoiled the incense in the Roman Catholic Church and that the engine was stopped in consequence. Compared to this, other work was minor—the provision of a new lavatory for School Field and a bathroom for the Curator of the Art Museum (it cost only £15), or the further levelling and draining of Pontines. More important, perhaps, was the division of the old Writing School, to provide a masters' common-room.

Two gifts to the School deserve a record; one was the Bloxam bequest of 'books, manuscripts, antiquities and paintings' in 1888; Percival was instructed to make a selection, but he could not move the Governors to provide a suitable place to house them. The books, a most valuable collection, still rest in locked cupboards in the present Lower Bench room[1], and other treasures were given to the Temple Reading Room and the Art Museum. The second was the 'Headmaster's Window', which was put in the Upper Bench school in 1889.

At the end of January 1895 Lord Rosebery, who seems to have been not too much offended by the sermon against gambling, offered Percival the See of Hereford, and after a week of hesitation he accepted it. It would be idle to pretend that to the boys and to many of the staff the news did not bring, with their sense of loss, a sense also of relief. The pace had been too hard for all but a very few. Even the elements seemed to recognise that something monumental was passing, for on 24 March 1895 a great gale swept over the Midlands, and Percival, waiting until the time came to go for the train that was to take him to London and his consecration, watched at his study window while seventeen great elms in the Close came crashing to the ground. He had himself blown like a whirlwind through the life of Rugby, and his work was done. He had brought discomfort and discontent for the idle and the self-satisfied, he had jerked a placid community into intense activity, he had subjected the School to a strain almost beyond bearing. But he had done what he had been put there to do, and, as William Temple said, he had 'inspired Rugby with an ideal of life in which service ranked higher than popularity and duty came before enjoyment'. More simply, writing of his successor to E. M. Oakeley in February 1895, Percival could say: 'If a good man

[1] Since this was written, the best of them have been moved to the rearranged Temple Reading Room.

comes, he will have a good time, as the School is in a good condition, with a rare set of young boys.'

Perhaps the last word may be with G. F. Bradby, who on 8 March 1922 wrote thus to F. T. Dallin[1] in Cairo about Percival: 'It was as a Headmaster that he really left his mark on his generation, and Clifton was his greatest achievement. . . . It always seems to me astonishing that, in his brief (and not particularly successful) apprenticeship here under Temple, he should have grasped so surely what are the things that really matter.' There follow some remarks about the Clifton period, then,

He was a man of very strong emotions—and he was mortally afraid of them; bottled them up and sealed the corks; and, even so, was afraid of the bottles bursting some day. His own will kept them in the bottle and kept *him* rather isolated. He hungered for intimacy and companionship—and feared it lest it should lead him from the path of duty. The touch of grave melancholy about him was the result of this conscious self-repression. He always liked people who talked to him naturally and without fear, e.g. Sam Slater.[2] A hard man, never; a fierce man, sometimes, because in punishing others he was also punishing himself, and you can't punish yourself calmly.

He had infinite patience with anybody who tried, and infinite sympathy with people who had had no chances; but *no* sympathy with people who had the chances but wouldn't take them. He understood boys extraordinarily well, but I don't think he understood undergraduates, and he did not influence them in the way he influenced boys. Boys lived more comfortably in the atmosphere that surrounded him than men. They

[1] Dallin had entered Donkin's House in May 1889.

[2] A contemporary of Dallin who was for three years in the cricket XI.

discarded more easily what was exaggeration, and assimilated more easily what was divine. It was as a spiritual influence that he counted most. And, as is generally the case, the people who came under that influence were mostly unconscious of it. . . . He was a great man, and when one has served under a great man, a little man does seem so deplorably little.[1]

So the great man passed on to the higher reaches of the Church, and Rugby drew a deep breath and wondered what new phenomenon the Governing Body would have in store for them.

[1] Manuscript letter at Rugby.

5

'The Bodger'

HERBERT ARMITAGE JAMES, 1895–1910

The identity has never been discovered of the original genius who first called H. A. James 'The Bodger' and thereby attached a generic nickname to the Headmaster of Rugby School. Attempts were made to vary the name to suit the more slender proportions of James's successor, and to call him 'The Bidger' or 'The Bidge'; but they were unsuccessful. Fifteen years of 'The Bodger' established the term, and 'The Bodger' he remains to this day.

James has been described by Maurice Collis.[1]

> In build stout, of average height and clumsy like a bear, he was dressed in black clerical clothes of traditional cut. A vast grey beard spread over his chest; his hair, very vigorous and thick, grew down his forehead. He looked out from behind his hair, immensely distant, an enigma, and as if distraught by the world's wrong.

'The Bodger' suited him.

Herbert Armitage James was the son of an evangelical preacher, who, as incumbent of St. Mary's Church, Kirkdale,

[1] *The Journey Outward.*

H. A. James

King Edward VII planting the 'King's Oak' after the opening of the Speech Room, 3 July 1909

was one of a group of Liverpool clergymen who carried out a crusade against Roman Catholicism. Later the elder James was Headmaster, for a year only, of Llandovery College and vicar of a parish near Huddersfield before moving, in 1857, to Panteg, near Pontypool. From here he sent his son Herbert to King Henry VIII's Grammar School, Abergavenny. The boy did well at school and won an open Scholarhip to Lincoln College, Oxford, in 1864. At Oxford he came under Mark Pattison and, according to his own account,[1] he was much influenced by E. E. Morris, an Old Rugbeian two years his senior, who was later to become Headmaster of Bedford County School and to make a name for himself in Australia as a headmaster and then a professor at Melbourne. James secured a double First in Classics, and in 1868 went as a temporary master to Marl-borough under G. G. Bradley. The following year he was elected to a Fellowship at St. John's College, Oxford, and while there was ordained. In 1875 he became Headmaster of Rossall, where he stayed eleven years, and then, after a three years' 'rest' as Dean of St. Asaph (1886–9), a post which he said he found tedious, he was appointed Principal of Cheltenham. Here he was proving so successful that when, later in 1890, he was appointed to, and accepted, the headmastership of Clifton, he received such strong representations from Governors, parents and even the boys themselves, that he withdrew his acceptance. Perhaps it would have been unjust to Cheltenham if, after little more than a year at the school, he had not done so. But when, not much over four years later, the Rugby opportunity occurred, Cheltenham could no longer hold him.

There was one interesting innovation in the method of

[1] Manuscript notes for autobiography.

appointment made in 1895. Previously a great deal of importance had been attached to a candidate's testimonials. Jex-Blake,
for instance, had submitted no fewer than ninety-four, which
added up to a booklet of eighty-six printed pages; and, as has
been seen, it was the alleged inadequacy of Hayman's testimonials which was made the first point of attack on him. But in
advertising for applications for the headmastership in 1895, the
Rugby Governing Body inserted the clause that 'no testimonials
will be required or received'; all they wanted was the names of
five referees. Perhaps it was the first public recognition of the
fact that open testimonials have, at the best, a very limited value.

The history of Rugby under James is one of almost unbroken
success. Percival had left him a brilliant staff and the reputation
of the School made it fairly easy to attract men of first-class
calibre when vacancies arose. Of his own appointments James
himself singled out as the outstanding ones Robert Prior, whom
he tempted from Cheltenham; F. J. Kittermaster, a Salopian
who had taught at Clifton and Uppingham; and C. P.
('Tiger') Hastings, whose pupils won over sixty History
Scholarships. The record of university success in the less than
fifteen years of James's headmastership is a really remarkable
one,[1] including twenty-three Balliol Scholarships and twenty-
one at Trinity College, Cambridge.

But it is doubtful if the credit for the success can go entirely
to James. He himself said that succeeding Percival meant
keeping a high standard instead of, as at Rossall and Cheltenham, creating one. 'The outstanding difference between Rugby
boys and those at my other schools', he wrote, 'was that they
read for themselves outside their form work. I recall one in my

---

[1] In all, 238 boys who were in the School under James won university awards.

own house who, being a science specialist, taught himself San-
scrit and was no mean Egyptologist. William Temple was, I
remember, reading Kant.' The habit of industry, driven into the
School by Percival, was lasting. B. B. Dickinson, who had
been Percival's first appointment, and who served also under
James, David and, for a short while, Vaughan, considered that
Percival was the only really great Headmaster of the four.
Writing to P. H. B. Lyon to congratulate him on his appointment in 1931, he said that 'the re-birth of Rugby after the
troubled Hayman days . . . and the negative period of Jex-
Blake . . . was entirely due to Percival—NOT to James, as some
people seemed to think'. There was certainly a remarkable
change in the relations between Headmaster and assistant
masters. At his first Masters' Meeting James made what some
held to be a grave mistake in saying, by way of introduction, 'I
know that I am but a rush-light compared with the brilliance
of my new colleagues.' Dickinson described the scene:

> It was most enlightening to a junior looker-on to see the
> expression on the faces of Whitelaw and others after this amaz-
> ing statement. James's ill-timed modesty had curious results
> later on. It positively made me blush to hear the way in which
> Whitelaw and others actually rated James for things that he
> had proposed. It was astonishing to me, after eight years of
> Percival, to see how the power of the Housemasters steadily
> increased, until practically they ruled the roost, especially in
> financial matters.

If this evidence stood alone, it could be treated with suspicion; Whitelaw, in any case, had acquired the habit of
opposition to the Headmaster under Hayman, and it remained
with him, as will be seen, to the end of his career. But support

for Dickinson's view comes from another source, perhaps one of those who did the 'rating'. Writing to David, now at Oxford, on 29 May 1900 G. F. Bradby said:

> J.P. was a man and the boys knew it: whatever he did they knew that he did it off his own bat and nobody would ever dream of his being worked from behind. Jimmy is a jellyfish and the boys know it. They aren't afraid of him: they don't mind his threats . . . and he can't even hurt them with a birch. Whenever he does take action they know he has been primed by one of these damned tutors. Grylls[1] gave me a list of the crimes imputed to me, and it included *all* the things I've most disapproved of which Jimmy has performed on the rare occasions when he has taken the bit between his teeth and charged . . . the truth is one has to perform a good many of the Housemaster's functions without the Housemaster's power. . . . With a jellyfish at the head of things, a weak Sixth and a gang of big bad fellows, those who try to keep things going will not have an easy time. . . . I dragged Jimmy from his drawingroom to tell him that unless he looked after things a little better, the House would go to pot, and left him a mass of helpless, frightened flesh, plaintively appealing to know what he was to do. . . . There is a certain grim humour in the situation which makes one the butt and washpot of boys whose bottoms one would be kicking if one did not hanker after their immortal apologies for souls—if I've fired off this epigram at you before, by any chance, don't tell me.[2]

Bradby was writing only about School House, where David had also been a tutor until the previous year. The two were at the time (later it was to change sadly) close friends and allowance

---

[1] H. B. Grylls, S.H. 1894-9.   [2] David papers.

must be made for friendly exaggeration. J. H. Simpson[1] gives a
very different picture of Whitelaw's House of his time (1897–
1902) and indeed of the School as a whole. But even the School
House matron, the famous 'Ma Mac', was unhappy about the
situation and was 'conscious of a great change'. She hoped that
it was due to her 'personal unpopularity'. James however seems
to have been largely unaware of the difficulties—or perhaps the
passage of time smoothed them out in his memory. In his
autobiographical notes, written when he was President of St.
John's, he says, 'The most remarkable feature of the School was
the disciplining work and influence of the VIth Form. It did
not depend on athletic excellence: to take only one instance,
W. Spens [afterwards scholar of King's and Master of C.C.C.,
Cambridge] without any sort of physical pre-eminence, made his
will law in the S.H. The Arnold tradition was still a living
force for good.' And he goes on to speak of 'the help given me
by that most efficient of matrons, Mrs. Macintyre, "Ma Mac" as
she was affectionately called, a woman of extraordinary loyalty
and high ideals'.

It is certain that some slackening of the authoritarian control
exercised by Percival was a necessity, and that, even if they
criticised him, the masters and the School as a whole felt considerable benefit from the looser rein on which the new Headmaster held them. Percival's insistence on continual tests and
examinations on paper had involved the masters in so much
laborious correction that, although it had imposed a much-
needed habit of industry, it had tended to dry up originality
and enthusiasm. James, by trusting his masters, and his heads
of department in particular, to manage their own affairs, and

[1] J. H. Simpson, *Schoolmaster's Harvest . . . 1894–1944.*

by a minimum of interference, gave scope to their individual methods and made possible the freedom of approach and the intelligent teaching that was responsible for the great academic success of the period.

By most of the boys 'The Bodger' seems to have been regarded as, in some sort, a giant—in spite of his short build—towering in stature above the other masters, a being of a different kind. Maurice Collis could hardly imagine even his Housemaster, John Collins, for whom he had a most reverent respect, talking to James as man to man. Few boys had more than one conversation with the Headmaster during their school career, and that was when he spoke individually to each candidate for confirmation; those who have left a record of this interview seem to have been impressed and agreeably surprised by an unexpected broadness and humanity in one who had been for them a distant and formidable figure. And the interview sometimes took a surprising course, as in the case of F. C. C. Wrigley.

> I received word to proceed to Mr. Whitelaw's study to see the Headmaster. He asked me my name and where I came from. I told him that my home was near Huddersfield in Yorkshire. He asked me if I knew anybody of the name of Armitage. I told him that Yorkshire was full of Armitages, but we were very friendly with some people of that name who lived in High Royd. 'How funny,' he said, 'because I am related to those people.' Well, we talked Armitage until my allotted time was up, when he said, 'Bless my life, I must go. Anyway be a good boy.' That was all the preparation I got from him, but it didn't matter as I got plenty from dear old Bob Whitelaw.

James was not one of those headmasters who thought it necessary to know his boys individually, and he often could not put a name even to senior boys of distinction. T. Howard Somervell, later a surgeon in India and a very distinguished mountaineer, describes how, at the end of his last term, when he had won a major scholarship in science, he went to say good⁄bye to the Headmaster. After the knock on the study door and the gruff 'Come in!' the conversation went roughly as follows:

JAMES: Well, what d' you want?
SOMERVELL: I've come to say good⁄bye, sir.
JAMES: Oh! What's your name?
SOMERVELL: Somervell, sir.
JAMES: Mm . . . What are you going to do now?
SOMERVELL: I'm going up to Cambridge, sir.
JAMES: Oh! Passed your Littlego?
SOMERVELL: No, sir. I've got a scholarship.
JAMES: Well, good⁄bye.

To this day Dr. Somervell holds that the Headmaster knew perfectly well that he was a Scholar, but because his subject was science refused to take any notice of it—until the time came for reading out the year's distinctions on Speech Day. Yet James did remember his old boys, and Maurice Collis, who while at School had spoken to him only once, at the time of his confir⁄ mation, tells of his surprise at receiving a letter five years later from the President of St. John's to congratulate him on gaining a First in the History school.

James was a man of many parts; some of his interests were known to the boys, others he kept dark. They knew, for instance, that he was a cricketer of some note, a round⁄arm break⁄bowler, who had played, during his vacations, for Mon⁄ mouthshire, and who had on one notable occasion, in 1869, taken eight Herefordshire wickets for 58 runs. They possibly knew that he and A. A. Bourne had bowled a whole side out for two runs (both off James) at Earl Shilton in 1872. Quite certainly they knew that he was a great philatelist, and it was a matter of some pride in the School that their Headmaster owned a 'British Guiana 4c. Blue on "sugar paper", coloured through' and the 'inverted swan' of Western Australia, and that he was one of the experts who contributed to Stanley Gibbons's *Stamp Issuing Countries*. Probably the masters knew more about his passion for foreign travel; every year from 1873 he went abroad, riding on mule or horseback through the then little known north of Greece with 'a capital dragoman known as Angelo', or exploring Algeria, visiting Biskra and Tunis or going to northern Italy or to Spain. It was said that his temper was always short at the beginning of term, since he rarely returned to Rugby until just before the boys and always found more correspondence than he could get through. Everyone knew, too, that he played golf as often as he could, and that he delighted in music, though his attempt to produce a school hymn-book that would include suitable hymns for every saint's day led to some bizarre results; his own composition for St. Matthias inspired G. F. Bradby to write a parody, to 'St. Lebbaeus'.[1] The best-known verses of the parody are

> Though his past is strange and dim,
> Mother Church and Father Jim
> Deem him worthy of a hymn.
>
> Therefore with the waking throstle
> Let us hail him an apostle
> As at Cheltenham or at Rossall.

[1] It is printed in full in C. R. Evers's *Rugby*.

But it was not only to hymn-writing that James turned his poetical talent, and probably few outside his immediate family and intimate friends knew that all his life he was a prolific writer of light verse. There is preserved in the Library at St. John's College, Oxford, a manuscript volume of his outpourings, which he entitled 'Ludicra—some original Nonsense Verses'. And nonsense they are. It was the period of the Limerick, a form that appears to have taken James's fancy, and he penned some hundreds of Limericks with topical or personal associations. There are several letters in verse, one of which, to a boy of ten years old who was unhappy at school and afraid of making his end-of-term journey by himself, begins:

> My dear little boy
> I mean to employ
> A minute or two
> In a letter to you.

On an occasion at Rugby when a minor indisposition kept him out of School, James whiled away some of the time by imagining, in verse, the reactions to his absence:

> 'The Doctor's ill,' round went the fateful word:
> In Close, School, House, at Hobley's it was heard.
> 'Woe!' cried the fags; 'the VIth will now enslave us.
> Who from their petty tyranny shall save us?'
> 'Woe!' cried the VIth, 'the fags will rule the roast,
> Put bombs in studies, poison on our toast!'
> 'Woe!' cried the Tutors, 'each one more address
> On Sunday eves. O powerful toil and stress!'

There follows an imaginary debate among boys and masters as to what the Doctor's malady may be, an exercise in rhyming ingenuity, with 'weasels' dragged in to rhyme with 'measles', and such couplets as

> my opinion right is
> An operation for appendicitis

until it is capped by:

> Then Poulton: 'let not this discussion vex ye:
> The real truth is, it is an apoplexy'.

Probably James sought refuge in writing doggerel from the difficulties he encountered, his heavier academic labours, his theological studies and the composition of his sermons. He does not seem to have been inspiring either as a teacher or as a preacher, though he had a superb speaking voice, and the School is said to have been electrified by the sound that emerged from the small body the first time he announced the hymn in Chapel. But he was certainly an outstanding 'character' at a time when 'characters' among schoolmasters were not as uncommon as they are today.

He had a number of 'characters' among his staff, too. There was W. P. ('Tooler') Brooke, who always brought his dog into school, where it sat throughout the lesson in the waste-paper basket, and who had the surprising habit of awarding marks from nought downwards instead of upwards; or Robert White-law, who used to invite boys in his House to accompany him for rides on his tricycle, a side-by-side double-saddled machine on which the guest was expected to do the greater part of the work. There was the corpulent Linnaeus Cumming—'Puff'—whose laboratory lessons tended to be uncontrolled riots, but who was regarded with such affection that, when he came to retire, some of his pupils had printed a little work entitled *The Puffin* in which a few of the more extravagant stories about him were told in very indifferent verse; its epilogue contains the lines

> Beloved at Rugby, this old chap
> So good and kind,
> When he has gone away a gap (!)
> Will leave behind.

Then there was W. N. Wilson, whose difficulty in controlling his saliva gave him the nickname 'Spitter', and whose attempts to overcome it led often to a sound which the boys standardised as 'ob'. The most famous remark imputed to him was 'Little boys should be (ob) seen and not heard'. There was E. L. D. Cole, a brilliant classicist—he succeeded Whitelaw in the XX later on—whose nose made him 'Beaky' from the moment of his arrival; he had a lisp, but he also had a sense of humour, for he is reported to have said on one occasion, 'S (pronounced *eth*) ith a nathty thibilant thound. I've had thome trouble with it mythelf; I don't know if anybody'th notithed it.' There was E. A. St. Hill, known to the boys as 'Holy' and to his colleagues as 'the Saint', and W. G. Michell ('Mike'), one of the most lovable men who have ever served on the Rugby staff. Every man in those days, when christian names were not so widely used, had his nickname: A. E. Donkin, for obvious reasons, was 'the Moke'; W. F. Stokes, enormously tall, thin and rigidly erect, was 'Poker'; the Rev. W. C. Mayne, though he dropped his first initial for all School purposes, remained 'Topos'; C. G. Steel, because of a probably undeserved reputation for creeping round his House in carpet-slippers, was 'Pussy'. Any Smith at that time was 'Piff', so Godfrey Bowden

Smith was 'Bow-Piff'; and Llewellyn Bullock, a clergyman with a vivid red beard, because of the way he pronounced the name of the deity, was "the man of Gud".

The boys might criticise and laugh at their masters, but it was a brilliant staff, and the School, in this bright evening of the Victorian era, experienced in some sort a golden age. There was very great pressure for entry; James had 520 boys and thirty-two regular assistant masters his first term, and numbers rose steadily until, in the last term of the century, he presided over a school of 586 boys. This was exceptional, and the average over the years from 1898 onwards was about 570; a slight decline towards the end perhaps gives some colour to Dickinson's opinion that for the last two or three years of James's régime 'the machine was slowly running down', but it more probably reflected the concern of the Governing Body with what they regarded as the overcrowded state of the School. At their General Annual Meeting in 1901 they fixed 540 as the maximum number of non-Foundationers, and this was to be reduced 'with due regard to vested interests' as opportunity arose. Six months later they went further; boarders were to be limited to 499, and non-Foundationer day boys to 13—which, with Foundationers, would have given an overall limit of 548—though the Headmaster was empowered at his discretion to admit nineteen more boarders and five more day boys. He evidently found himself compelled to do so, and the Governors accepted the situation in December 1902 by fixing maximum numbers in Boarding Houses at 84 for the School House and 54 for each of the rest, with small waiting houses holding 33 at the most. This, with those on the Foundation, gave a School of 585, which James exceeded only once.

The School might increase in numbers, but the expenses of the Governing Body increased even faster. There was capital expense of a substantial nature on essential improvements in School House, where new bathrooms were installed in 1898 and new dormitories built the following year, and on the enlargement of the Headmaster's house at Lawrence Sheriff School; more schools were needed in the main buildings, and the provision of a completely new building for the teaching of science was becoming urgent. Smaller matters such as the repair of the Chapel organ[1] in 1896 (nearly £280), levelling of the new playing fields at Benn's farm, which had been left to the School by an Old Rugbeian, in 1897 (£250), and improvement to the heating and ventilation of the schools in 1901 (nearly £300) proved a drain on income; and looming ahead was the problem of the purchase of Boarding Houses, which had now been adopted as definite policy. In August 1901 the accounts made it clear that the income of the School did not meet its expenditure, and Sir Arthur Godley was asked to prepare 'a scheme for augmentation of income'. His report in October inevitably recommended an increase of fees and in the following January a new scale was adopted, which brought payment for boarders up to £118 a year. This included £3 for a Reserve Fund, which could be applied to any purpose connected with Governing Body property; when it reached £1500, any excess was to be used for the purchase of Boarding Houses.

The most important new building during James's time was the rebuilding of the West end of the Chapel and the erection of the Temple Speech Room. A memorial fund had been

---

[1] The organ was perpetually causing expense. A 'Kinetic blower' was installed in 1907, and in 1909 the instrument had to be entirely rebuilt at a cost of about £1000.

opened for Philip Bowden Smith, who had been a boy in the School under Tait, had been appointed a master by Goulburn in 1852 and who died in 1895; the secretaries of the fund proposed that the Chapel should be enlarged in his memory, and as Butterfield was deemed to be too old at eighty-two to undertake the work, T. G. Jackson (later Sir Thomas Jackson) was asked to submit designs, which were accepted in June 1896. He is said to have obtained Butterfield's approval, but the general character of his work differs markedly from the earlier building, although the raising of the roof and the use of red brick gave more homogeneity than had been the case when Hakewill and Butterfield sat side by side. To this work the Governing Body subscribed £1000, though they refused eighteen months later to take any financial responsibility for the alteration of the cloister to give accommodation to the boys' hats. New windows for the enlarged Chapel were presented in 1898 by John Collins and the following year by Godfrey Bowden Smith, in memory of his mother; and in 1900 the great West window, from the Morris workshops, was offered (anonymously) by Leonard Eaton-Smith, who had left the School only seven years previously. It was unveiled in 1902. The enlarged Chapel was consecrated in 1898 by Frederick Temple, now Archbishop of Canterbury and Chairman of the Governing Body; and, apart from the stalls and canopies put in at the West end in 1903 in memory of J. W. J. Vecqueray and the internal renovation carried out in 1960 under the supervision of S. E. Dykes-Bower, it has remained substantially unchanged since then. Even some of the blank marble tablets put up by James's order in 1902—to facilitate the inscribing of memorials as need arose—remain blank to this day.

In 1903 Frederick Temple died, and it was decided that a

new Big School, capable of holding the increased numbers in the School, would form a suitable memorial for him. For some time there was dispute as to whether it would be better to employ the £6000, which it was proposed to raise from Temple's old pupils, for the enlargement of the existing New Big or to build something completely new. The South African War also seemed to require a memorial, and in 1904 a suggestion was even made that the two appeals should be combined and the building of an armoury and the enlargement of New Big School should be run together. The Governing Body was in some difficulty as they felt unable to contribute to the new building, though when, in 1905, the decision was finally made to erect a Speech Room, they offered to provide a site. The decision to create a building that was really big enough for the School and could also accommodate visitors on Speech Day—no one then foresaw that numbers would rise to over 700—meant, as James pointed out in his speech at the opening, that it was to be not merely a memorial to Temple, given by his old pupils, as had been the original intention, but an important accession, and a necessary one, to the buildings of the School, to which Rugbeians of all generations were asked to subscribe. They responded nobly, and by the spring of 1908 a House annalist could record that 'Speech Room is rising slowly and solemnly from the ground and has already attained the height of several feet'. The architect employed was again Thomas Jackson, and in July 1909, on an occasion when, according to the same annalist, 'the usual Speech Day ceremony was mercifully curtailed', King Edward VII, the first ruling monarch ever to visit the School, declared the building open and planted an oak-tree in the Close. The Head of the School, H. J. B. Clough, reading an address of welcome to the King, ventured 'to remind your Majesty that it is a kingly prerogative to command an addition to our hard-earned holidays. Should Your Majesty be pleased to exercise it on our behalf, it will be a kindness long to be gratefully remembered by the School.' After a whispered consultation with the Headmaster, His Majesty did, in fact, command an extra week. Rugby did rather well in this respect during James's time; the Governors had already sanctioned two extra days in 1898 because of distinctions won at Balliol, a week in 1902 to celebrate the coronation, an extra day to the Easter holidays in 1905, at the request of the Head of the School, for an exceptional list of honours at Oxford and Cambridge, and another at the request of Princess Henry of Battenberg, who visited Rugby in 1907.

Compared with Speech Room and the Chapel extension other building was minor, but not unimportant. The Town Room, or the Town Boys' Hall as the Governors called it, was opened in 1902. 'We hope', wrote a boarder, 'that it may prove useful, since it certainly is not pleasant to look upon.' The years have not mellowed it much, but it is not offensive and it certainly has proved useful. Even more significant in foreshadowing future development was the decision definitely made in July 1901 to build Science schools on the south-east corner of the Close, 'the precise position being determined so as to leave as much room as possible both for extensions and for the erection of a Physical Laboratory and possibly Music Rooms in the future'. And the internal accommodation was to be 'such as to allow for an increase in the present number of students without addition to the building'. So a beginning was made in the great block of buildings that became the Science Schools, though

Linnaeus ('Puff') Cumming

A. W. Lloyd's cartoon of the masters

From left to right: L. Cumming, E. L. D. Cole, W. P. Brooke, Dr. H. A. James, W. H. Payne-Smith, R. Whitelaw, G. Stallard

when the first part was completed in 1903 only the chemists left their old quarters in the New Quadrangle. The physicists had to make do until David's time with their rooms in the 'Tin Tabernacle' on the Hillmorton Road. In 1902 the Governing Body sanctioned the erection of six new schools, two for use as laboratories, in the New Quadrangle, but these were not built.

Science teaching must have been good, judging by the results, but equipment in the old buildings was necessarily poor and the subject attracted only a small minority of specialists. That Classics still dominated the scene is proved by the scale of marks laid down in 1900 for the award of exhibitions; Classics carried a maximum of 2000, Divinity 150, history 150, mathematics 350, French 150, German 150, and natural science 300. Perhaps the greatest change that came in the balance of the curriculum was the development of the Army Class, under the very able management of W. N. Wilson, from which a steady and increasing stream of boys won their entrance to Woolwich or to Sandhurst.

With the impending retirement from his House of John Collins, the new policy of School ownership of the Boarding Houses came into the sphere of practical politics, and in December 1906 the Governing Body made him an offer of £7000. They had to raise it by £500 before Collins would accept, but in 1907 the deal was completed, and G. F. Bradby was appointed Housemaster as tenant of the School at a rent of £450 a year. Purchase on this scale of the remaining six Houses in private ownership was clearly going to involve the Governing Body in extensive borrowing, but during James's time no further acquisitions were made, though negotiations for the purchase of Donkin's House had started at the time of his departure.

R.S.A.—II

For boys in the School the period of James seems to have been a fairly happy time. J. H. Simpson, for all his criticism,[1] clearly enjoyed himself and was proud of his School. So, too, was William Temple; 'I want you to know', he wrote to his wife in 1916, 'why some Rugbeians are so intolerably conceited about their School.' And the feeling seems to have been very generally the same throughout. The sense of repression which had been the corollary of Percival's reforming zeal had been lifted, and there was a tremendous amount going on. Work was hard, but a boy who was not unusually stupid could find spare time; Temple himself was exceptional; he could do his two hours' preparation in half an hour and used the remaining hour and a half for his own reading. To a new boy everything, of course, was exciting. J. W. Henderson wrote to his parents on 21 January 1899 a detailed account of his first day. He did not like the food at School Field. 'I went into what *they* called supper i.e. a hunc of stale bread, a piece of cold meat and a cup of miserable tea.' Breakfast consisted of 'vile porridge, bad tea and huncs of bread and butter with dried haddock'. But it did not depress him, for 'now I am not a bit homesick, in fact I am awfully happy here'. He had to have his voice tested in New Big School.

> The chap [presumably Basil Johnson] heard me sing and asked me if I had ever been in a choir before. He said I had a good enough voice and asked me if I wanted to be in it. I promptly said no. Then we all (New boys) had to go to School House dining room where Dr. James (I ought to say Jimmie or the Bodger) said he had three points he wished to speak about. 1stly that we ought all to begin and work from the very

[1] *Schoolmaster's Harvest.*

beginning and please our parents at mid-term when a report is sent in. 2ndly that we should be careful in choosing good companions and 3rdly that we should never forget our prayers etc. Dr. James is rather a short man with very seedy clothes and long, wiry hair and beard. After he went away we were taken by the School Marshal to our respective forms.

Mutatis mutandis, it might have been written today. Henderson must have watched with interest in his first summer the unveiling by Frederick Temple of the statue of Thomas Hughes and, during his first term, the fixing on the 'Doctor's Wall' of the tablet commemorating the exploit of William Webb Ellis in 1823 when 'with a fine disregard for the rules' he first took the ball in his arms and ran with it, thereby establishing the distinctive characteristic of Rugby football. The tablet was presented by the Old Rugbeian Society (founded in 1889); the O.R.s were becoming very active in their assistance to the School, and in James's time the foundation of the Bowen prize in 1895, in memory of C. S. C. Bowen, brilliant both academically and athletically, who had become a distinguished judge, and the Lees Knowles Exhibition in 1908 are only two among many examples of their generosity. It was they who were very largely responsible for the erection of the new buildings.

The School Marshal who showed Henderson to his form was A. C. Blake. The office of Marshal had been instituted by Goulburn in December 1850, when he brought in George Edward Patey as his personal man-of-all-work. Patey's duties developed gradually; he was the bearer of the Headmaster's messages, carrying round notes to be read out by form-masters, collecting lists of those stopping out of school, keeping his eyes open for malefactors among the boys or for masters who were

having difficulty in the classroom and reporting his observa-
tions to the Headmaster. He summoned those who were due
for headmagisterial punishment and formed part of the dread
procession to the birching-tower, where he was responsible for
the arrangements though not for the execution. He was the
Chapel Clerk, and, arrayed in his special gown, led the preacher
up the aisle to the pulpit. He was said to be the only man who
was allowed to enter a school during form hours without knock-
ing. Patey became a 'character' and developed a presence which
caused timid new boys to mistake him for the Headmaster—
and the same has been true of his successors; there have been two
only. His duties demanded tact of a high order, involving as
they did relations of a peculiar sort with Headmaster, assistants,
boys, and indeed with the townsfolk of Rugby. So successful
was Patey, so careful in distinguishing between offences due to
mere thoughtlessness and those which were wilful or vicious,
that he won the respect and even the affection of the School. He
relinquished some of his duties in 1887 and retired finally in
1890, though he remained Chapel Clerk until 1899; after his
death in 1902 a bronze tablet was put in Old Big School to
commemorate him. He had set a high standard, but it was
nobly followed by A. C. Blake (the belief was widespread
among the boys that he came from Scotland Yard), who held
the office until 1925, and by the present Marshal, J. F. Johnson,
who succeeded him.[1] And so useful did the Marshal prove that
Benson carried the office to Wellington and Percival to Clifton,
and there are other schools today, such as Repton, where it exists.

---

[1] Since this was written, J. F. Johnson has retired and has been succeeded by
R.S.M. F. Bates, B.E.M., who had previously, for a number of years, served the
Rugby School Combined Cadet Force.

The intellectual standard of the VIth form in James's time has possibly never been surpassed. It contained, in his early days, Arthur Steel (who later changed his name to Steel-Maitland), who, after winning a Balliol Scholarship, took a triple First in Classics and Law, won the Eldon Scholarship and a Fellow-ship of All Souls and still found time to become President of the Union and get his rowing blue. But Frank Fletcher, who taught them all, considered R. H. Tawney, later Fellow of Balliol and Professor of Economic History at London, and Lionel Smith, later a Fellow of All Souls, a hockey interna-tional and Rector of The Edinburgh Academy, to have been even better scholars, and William Temple, later Archbishop of York and of Canterbury, though he was never Head of the School or of his House nor so distinguished a scholar, and who was no athlete, to have been the greatest all-rounder of them all. A little later there was Rupert Brooke, athletically gifted—he was in the XV and the cricket XI—as well as a scholar and later Fellow of King's College, and a poet who captured the imagination of his generation. All these were members of a select Upper Bench society called Eranos, presided over for a number of years by Frank Fletcher, which met several times a term to hear papers on literary subjects. Brooke, too, was the prime mover in the publication of the *Phoenix,* which was first brought out in June 1904; indeed, he was the principal con-tributor to it, and himself wrote a very large part of its third and last number in March 1905, when it was closed down by authority. Probably Brooke's young questioning philosophy offended the religious conservatism of the Headmaster.

> Men cried to God. I heard the sound of it
> Go moaning heavenward as a smoke, and there

Fall blindly before the pitiless Infinite
And cold unheeding faces of the stars.

James would not have liked that. But the *Phoenix* was almost immediately (October 1905) succeeded by the *Venture*, which, avoiding matter liable to be objectionable to authority, lasted until 1907. Both of them were too learned for the bulk of the School population, and a rival, the *Vulture*, was started in July 1904. The editors hoped that 'the intense interest at the present moment taken in literature might even extend to those who have attempted to keep their sanity undefiled by the tainting claws of the *Phoenix*, their judgment undazzled by the false glitter of its wings', and declared roundly that it was their purpose 'to trample on the efforts of the Bird at which we have aimed as at our lawful game'. But contributions to the *Vulture* were not of a very high order. Another publication produced a single number, all copies but one of which were confiscated imme-diately after publication. This was *Lulu*, undated but during the South African War and probably belonging to 1900. The sur-viving copy was in the hands of a small new boy in one of the waiting-Houses, who was overlooked, and it is now in the Temple Reading Room. The offending article, entitled 'My Social Diary' by 'Cynthia' contained very lightly veiled allu-sions to staff ladies. They mean nothing now, but must have meant much at the time. The whole production—it was only six pages long—was very outspoken ('In the winter the Masters' meeting calmly abolished the Sixth match, and the Censor of the *Meteor* stifled protest . . . they haven't a vestige of authority for so doing') and in parts very witty; one is glad that a copy has survived. Yet another magazine, the *Quadrangle*, to which Godfrey Elton was a considerable contributor, appeared in

January 1909. It mocked the *Meteor* and the 'New New Big School', and produced four issues before it died for lack of financial support. All in all the literary output leaves the impression that it was a time of vigorous intellectual activity and independence of thought.

Concern with the boys' health caused certain changes. Two deaths in the sanatorium in the spring of 1907, from pneumonia following influenza, caused the Governing Body to overhaul the medical supervision. Up to this time Dr. Clement Dukes had been physician to the School on rather a loose, parttime basis. It was now decided that he should become 'consulting physician' and Dr. A. I. Simey, who had been Head of the School in 1892, was appointed a fulltime medical officer, responsible for preserving health as well as for curing illness. One of the first results was the abolition of early Chapel and early school in the Easter term, as one of a number of precautionary measures. This was popular except, probably, with Robert Whitelaw, who spoke caustically about morning prayers in Houses as 'that dismal ritual among the teacups'; but when the doctor began interfering with games and limiting the number of Bigside runs and deciding who could take part in them, the Levée and the House Sixths thought that he was going much too far. 'There would have been a record field for the Crick this year,' writes the Donkin's House annalist in March 1909, 'but for the interference of the new School doctor and others, with the result that the numbers were reduced to four.'

The fifteen years of James's headmastership must be seen as the last great phase of an order that was passing. Outwardly little was changed. There seemed, to all but a few economists, to be a stability which was immutable. Britain had risen on the wealth of the industrial revolution to a position of dominance; her navy ruled the seas and, with apparent comfort, she controlled a world-wide empire such as had never before been seen, and she was proud of it. Her citizens, brought up at schools like Rugby, went to all parts of the earth to develop and to control the destinies of peoples who were not British. They went with a sense of mission and with a supreme self-confidence, never doubting the essential rightness of the order that called them to their duty. For just a few, for the thinkers, for those like Rupert Brooke and William Temple and Godfrey Elton, there came doubts, but for the mass of that generation Kipling was the established prophet and it seemed a God-given dispensation which gave supremacy to Britain and power to her wealthy upper-middle classes.

> The rich man in his castle, the poor man at his gate,
> God made them high and lowly, and ordered their estate.

That verse was still sung in churches—and men still went to church.

Yet there were signs even within the School that change was in the air. The intellectual ferment that produced such a spate of school publications was slanted against the acceptance of any authority that claimed an eternal and unchanging value. Even the motions proposed in the Debating Society are significant of the approach of a new order. 'That regal splendour and national display are a waste of the country's money'; 'That this House laments the present condition of the daily Press' (the *Daily Mail* was first published in 1896); 'That this House deplores the growth of the Labour Party in the House of Commons' (Arthur Waley, Rupert Brooke and Philip Guedalla all spoke in this debate—the motion was lost); and 'That no danger exists from Imperial Germany', in which the House showed itself as blind as the rest of the country by passing the motion. But these were no more than uneasy stirrings, and for the most part it seemed that, in this golden evening of Victorian greatness, the School was riding the crest of a wave of prosperity and success, which could—and should—carry it forward indefinitely and unchecked.

In December 1909 James left Rugby to become President of St. John's College, Oxford. Within a decade of his departure, of something over 2200 boys whom he had accepted into the School, nearly 450 had been destroyed by war.

6

The New Age and the New Man

ALBERT AUGUSTUS DAVID, 1910–21

Rugby needed modernising. The School had experienced under James fifteen years of almost unexampled success, but it was success in the old tradition; the new trends and theories in education and the new national concern, which found expression in Balfour's Secondary Education Act of 1902, caused but few ripples on the placid surface of the School's life. The habits and methods, tested by long usage, which had done such splendid duty since, at least, the time of the first James, and the unforgotten work of Arnold, commended in the Report of the Public Schools Commission and proved by a formidable list of university successes and an even longer record of success in public life, had become ingrained in the life of the School. They worked; what need was there to change them? There was danger of a certain complacency settling on the place.

But the world was changing, and the change was soon to become almost frighteningly rapid. The signs were already there, and perhaps the members of the Governing Body were becoming aware that mere conservatism would no longer do and that a man was needed who would bring to Rugby fresh ideas and fresh life; one who would not be afraid to experiment.

And so they appointed Albert Augustus David. And with his coming a new, vigorous breeze seemed to blow through the School. Certainly to those who, like P. H. B. Lyon, were just reaching a place of seniority there was a remarkable sense of release and of uplift. The contrast was very marked between the rather crusty elderly bachelor, remote and somewhat awe-inspir-ing, and the new young man with his lovely young wife. ('Rugby Chapel', wrote a new boy to his parents, 'is very beau-tiful. So is Mrs. David.')

David was no stranger to Rugby. He had already served, from 1892 to 1898, as an assistant master and tutor at School House. He had been educated at Exeter Grammar School and at Queen's College, Oxford, where he was a Scholar and took a double First in Classics. Thereafter his career was distinguished. After two years teaching at Bradfield (1890–2) and the six years at Rugby, he returned to Queen's as Fellow and Tutor, and then, in 1905, he was elected to the headmastership of Clifton College—the fourth man and the third ex-Rugby master to hold that office. Later he was to be distinguished in another field as Bishop first of St. Edmundsbury and Ipswich (1921–3) and then of Liverpool.[1] He could have gone on from Rugby much earlier than he did; in 1911 he refused the Bishopric of Lichfield; in December 1913 he was offered the Bishopric of Bristol or of Sheffield and was pressed in May 1914 to reconsider his refusal of Bristol; in June 1916 he refused to consider the request of M. R. James, Provost of King's, that he should be a candidate for the headmastership of Eton; and in June 1918 he could have

---

[1] Of the eight clerical Headmasters in the period covered by this book, two became archbishops, two bishops, two deans and one head of a college. Hayman alone did not go on to high preferment.

had the Deanery of Manchester. The earlier offers he considered to be too soon after his appointment to Rugby, where he felt he had a valuable work to do, and one which deeply interested him; later he thought it his duty to see the School through the difficult period of the war.

David's headmastership divides itself into three fairly distinct phases; there were the first four or five years, when there was much to be done and when he was engaged in rapid and vigorous reform; then the years of the war with all its attendant difficulties; and finally the last three years or so, when he was deeply immersed in social work of all kinds and, under the influence of Homer Lane, much interested in the new develop/ ments in psychology and psycho/analysis, and when perhaps his control of the School became a good deal less firm.

When he arrived at Rugby in January 1910 there seemed to David to be a good many changes needed. There was first the problem of the Housemasters. Percival's rule of a fifteen/year tenancy had not applied to those already in office, such as White/ law or Michell, and younger men had to wait many years before there was any chance of Housemastership. B. B. Dickinson, for instance, waited twenty/three before he took over from Donkin in 1910. It was important, in David's view, that there should be a fairly quick turnover in his early years. One House, School Field, was made available at once by the sudden tragic death of W. P. Brooke in January 1910, and here H. C. Bradby was installed after an interim term of Rupert Brooke, who was not a member of the staff. The young Brooke professed to have enjoyed the experience, but he was an unusual schoolmaster and his Sixth found it rather difficult to support him. With other Houses the policy of purchase by the Governing Body helped

David. Older Housemasters were offered a price considerably
above the market value of their Houses; thus St. Hill purchased
Michell's for £10,100, though its estimated value was £9480,
and was prepared to spend £700 on alterations; the House was
bought from him by the Governing Body in 1913 for £10,300,
and in that year Steel accepted £9000 and Stallard £11,000,
though Whitelaw refused to part with his for £8800—'You
may take away my boys,' he is reputed to have said, 'but the
house is my own.' This last difficulty—and as Whitelaw was
resigning his mastership that year, it was a real one—was overcome when J. M. Hardwich bought the House for £10,000 on
the understanding that the Governing Body would take it over
for £8800, would be responsible for necessary alterations, would
guarantee him a lump sum of £600 if he left the House within
six years and would allow him a sixteen- instead of a fifteen-
year tenancy. The whole affair must have savoured to Whitelaw
of sharp practice; but, as will be seen, he had no opinion of the
Headmaster anyway—and it was quite essential for the School
to have his House. Thus six of the eight Boarding Houses
changed hands in David's first two and a half years, and the
imperium in imperio of the Housemasters, which had been a
matter of some comment by junior members of the staff, was
broken. The cost to the Governing Body was met by bank loans
totalling £34,100.

The next problem was the establishment of a pension scheme.
When John Percival was asked, shortly after he had been
appointed, what he intended to do at Rugby, he had replied
that the one thing he was determined on was to provide pensions for masters; he had, however, found so much to do in
other directions that he had never tackled the problem, and

James made no move to touch it. David attacked it at once. In his first year he produced a scheme, which was approved in principle by the Governing Body in August 1910, and which came into force as a contributory scheme in 1911, to provide a pension of £300 a year maximum. Of the £58 10s. premium the master was to pay two-thirds. Eight years later the scheme was altered to one on a non-contributory basis providing £250 a year after thirty years' service. It does not seem particularly generous, but it was at least a recognition of the fact that, with the reduced value of masters' emoluments (a new salary scheme ranging from £350 to £750, with an extra £50 for senior masters without Houses was introduced in 1919), only House-masters could be expected to provide adequately for their old age.

Finance generally received David's vigorous attention. The report for the year before his appointment showed that the total income of the Governing Body, including endowment and entrance fees, was £8825. The income of the bursars—at this time two masters—from fees was £69,600. Thus the School's total income was about £78,400 and the expenses for 1909 had been £77,200. The margin was much too small, particularly with the extra anticipated expenditure on bank loans and pensions. The raising of the School fees by a further £3 a year in 1911 did something to relieve the immediate difficulty, but David wanted a more radical solution; he felt that the management of finances should be taken out of amateur hands and that a professional bursar should be appointed. It was some time before the Governing Body could be brought to share his opinion, but with the very great expansion of School property and of the consequent School debt in the next few years, the

force of his argument became unanswerable; in 1916 the proposed appointment of an assistant bursar was on the agenda of a
committee appointed to examine the School's business affairs,
the following year enquiries were being made for a suitable
candidate, and in May 1920 Lt.-Col. G. E. Sharp, an Old
Rugbeian of Michell's House, who had served with great distinction in the South African War, became the first paid
Bursar of Rugby School. Three months later Donkin resigned
his office of Bursar with his mastership.

Within the School, too, there was rapid change and reform.
David's appointments to the staff seemed to be of a new type,
young, go-ahead men who brought a leaven of fresh life to the
place. Some of the best, such as Hubert Podmore and H. S.
Wilson, were killed in the war; others, such as E. F. Bonhote,
J. H. Bruce Lockhart, H. H. Symonds, J. H. Simpson and
E. E. A. Whitworth, were later to become headmasters; yet
others, like R. A. Raven and F. W. Odgers, both from Os-
borne, stayed to give many years of service and to become
Rugby characters. Fourteen were appointed before the outbreak
of war. Numbers in the School rose somewhat—in the summer
of 1912 there were over 580—but even so the Governing Body
considered that numbers on the staff were excessive—in 1912
there were thirty-eight regular masters and eight others—and
laid down as a general principle a staffing ratio of one regular
master to every twenty boys; but to this David never adhered.

With the new men came a new organisation. The timetable
was remodelled; all set-subjects were brigaded into blocks from
the top to the bottom of the School; a new science side, separated
for the first time from the modern side was formed, and with
the completion of the new physics schools early in 1915 (at a

cost of £10,234) the scientists began an almost autonomous existence. The School was, however, still predominantly classi/ cal in character, and David, at his first Speech Day, declared publicly his hope that it would continue always to be so. David was interested not only in the scholars and the VIth; his concern was principally with the average boy—perhaps he was the first Headmaster since Goulburn of whom this was really true—and many of his changes aimed at benefiting the lower part of the School. Thus he put one man, R. A. Raven, in charge of the organisation and curriculum of the Lower Middle forms; he aimed at really good teaching of English from the bottom upwards; he introduced the direct method for the teaching of modern languages. And the results for the mass of the boys were undoubtedly good; their work improved as it was made more interesting.

For the School as a whole the first few years of the new Head/ master were a hectic time, and by no means all of the masters approved of the changes; indeed some of the older ones were bitterly opposed to them, and although their opposition was, for the most part, confined to complaining among themselves, one man was prepared to voice his dissatisfaction with what he regarded as arbitrary and dictatorial action by his chief. 'You are so accustomed', Robert Whitelaw wrote to him on 7 July 1913, 'to settling what is called a discussion with an *ipse dixi*, that you don't know how it strikes others.'

This complaint forms part of a correspondence between Whitelaw and David on the subject of the latter's remarks at Speech Day, 1913. The dispute is worth recording as it sheds some light on the difficulty that Headmasters from Hayman onwards had had in dealing with that very great teacher and schoolmaster. Whitelaw had asked—had, indeed, demanded—that David should say nothing about him on Speech Day; David, naturally enough, had thought it impossible to accede to this request; Whitelaw was to retire in July and he was, after all, the most distinguished of the assistant masters. So David made in his speech what reads as a graceful tribute, giving the history of 'the Twenty', a form introduced by Arnold and which had always been ruled over by men of real distinction, of whom Whitelaw was the seventh in succession—Prince Lee, Bishop of Manchester; Bonamy Price, Professor of Political Economy at Oxford; Cotton, Bishop of Calcutta; Charles Evans, Professor of Greek at Durham; Jex-Blake, Dean of Wells; and A. W. Potts, Headmaster of Fettes. To these, said David, Robert Whitelaw was more than a worthy successor. Whitelaw was furious. 'I am bound to say', he wrote on 4 July, 'that you avoided with unerring precision the qualities (such as they are) by which I have attained such success as I have.' 'Can't you understand', he continued on the 5th, 'that . . . half a dozen words of encouragement and sympathy, said from the heart, and with appreciation of the things near my heart, would have been worth cartloads of formal laudation of my work, even if that had not missed the mark. I knew too well that I could not expect this, and therefore I asked (as a favour) that you would forbear.' And three days later: 'Of course it comes to this, that I do not recognise your right—your moral right—to return thanks for me in the presence of the School.'

What was David to do? He passed the letters to G. F. Bradby for advice and received in reply no advice worth having, but a good deal of amusing comment. '*This*', wrote Bradby on the 5th, 'is entirely amusing—quite Gilbertian. . . . The only satisfactory solution would be for the little man to write his own laudation, or half a dozen words of inconsequent sympathy, and deliver them himself—the picture of R.W. confining himself to half a dozen words starts me cackling afresh.' And a little later:

> I can just smile, but no more. When he has gone, R.W.'s out-bursts will probably seem wholly comic and one will get them in proper perspective with his other activities. Meanwhile I often feel regretfully that he *might* have served much nobler uses than providing the rough material on which the rest of us make ourselves fit for Heaven by the exercise of patience and genero-sity. If he had not been so small and petty he might have been, well, such a *great* man and not merely such a *quaint* man. I can never analyse him to my own satisfaction, but I feel certain that somewhere in his early childhood there was a sad neglect of the rod. Let us hope the Angels will do their duty thoroughly on the Mount of Purgatory or there will be quarrelling in Paradise when he gets there. Anyhow he has been a splendid discipline for successive Headmasters of Rugby—and I don't see who is to take his place.[1]

But to write off Robert Whitelaw as a comic and irritating little man would be not only ungenerous; it would be entirely wrong. He was without any question a very great schoolmaster. For forty-three of his forty-seven years on the staff he had been form-master of the XX. Daily he had lost himself in the beauty of the Classics, and his own sheer delight in them had infected the majority of his pupils.[2] He had driven his form to a pitch of

---

[1] David papers.

[2] The present writer has been able to find only one man who, in retrospect, did not find Whitelaw's teaching very stimulating and valuable—though they did not all enjoy themselves in his form.

industry that made the Rugby XX famous in the academic world, and had forged, sometimes from the most unlikely ore, the rough material of scholarship to be finished and polished in the VIth.[1] Those who were in his House regarded him as a great Housemaster, too, and had a deep respect and often an affection for him. He may sometimes, particularly in his later years, have had favourites, but for him Whitelaw's was the only House that really mattered and he was prepared to defend his own boys to the last ditch. He would criticise them himself; but no one else, not even the Headmaster, was allowed to do so. And there was a softer side to him. In 1914 he moved into a house in Moultrie Road, and he wrote thus to his ancient friend E. M. Oakeley, who had first helped him to the Rugby post: 'It is meet that you should come and sample the little house to which your kind ordering of my life has conducted me at the close.' There, on 6 February 1917, he died. The portrait of him leaning characteristically on the reading-desk from which he always taught—and which, so it is said, he had installed in his house of retirement because he could not read the Classics in any other position—hangs today in Speech Room.

If David's vigorous reforming activity differed strikingly from the comparative lethargy of James, his attitude to boys, both individually and in the mass, differed even more. He was 'modern' in the sense that his policy was to 'trust the boy' until his trust was proved to be misplaced, and he was prepared always to give the benefit of the doubt where any doubt existed. In this he was doing little more than follow the example of

[1] The XX under Robert Whitelaw was known as 'Paradise Lost', while the Lower Bench, under F. J. Kittermaster, was 'Paradise Regained'.

Frederick Temple, but the principle did not commend itself to some of the older masters, who sometimes felt that boys had a more sympathetic hearing from the Headmaster than they did themselves, and that important changes were made at the suggestion of the VIth Levée without sufficient consideration or consultation with the staff. The outstanding example of this was the substitution of a voluntary for a compulsory Sunday evensong, a measure disapproved of certainly by a majority of the masters and one which did not survive the coming of a new Headmaster by more than a few weeks. Moreover, where previous Headmasters had dealt with moral offences with severity, David tended to treat them with an attempt at understanding and with sympathy. This was indeed 'modern' and progressive, and roused even so enlightened a man as G. F. Bradby to protest.

> You know [he wrote to David towards the end of 1913] you *are* destroying the safeguards which gave parents their particular confidence in the School, and which, more than anything else, I believe, made life here for masters such a hopeful thing. The safeguards I mean were, that in dealing with all forms of immorality,
> 1. We should recognise the significance of symptoms, the deadly peril of the disease to the community, our own inadequacy to deal with it and consequently the immense danger of being sanguine.
> 2. We should always 'give the chance' to the society and not to the individual; and if there *has* to be a sacrifice, sacrifice the one to the many and not the many to the one.
> 3. We should absolutely renounce the dangerous but tempting experiment of curing boys under the conditions of school

life and never attempt to combine a health resort with a hospital for infectious diseases.

4. *Never* trust our private judgment against facts.[1]

It was the same argument that Arnold had applied eighty years
earlier when he said that evil existed, but that a School was not
a jail to keep it in, but a place of education where they must cast
it out. It was the old argument of those who saw so clearly the
clean division between good and evil and who had no knowledge of half-tones in morality or of the discoveries that were just
beginning to be made in the curious workings of the human
mind. It was the argument between the 'reactionary' and the
'enlightened', which even today, half a century later, has not
been fully resolved. Today David may seem to have been on
the side of the angels; but to men who had known Percival he
must have seemed a dangerous firebrand, flinging away principles that had proved their worth and taking risks with the
good name of the School that were beyond all reason. But
David was nothing if not firm in his convictions, and the
warnings of Bradby and others went unheeded.

David's years before the war were, on the whole, a happy
time for the School. His first summer saw a remarkable victory
in the Marlborough match, when Rugby defeated by an
innings a side which had been described by the *Morning Post* as
'the best amateur team in the country'. (In this David was more
fortunate than one of his successors,[2] who, on the touch-line at
a football match in his early days, was heard to remark: 'I hope
these boys will win something soon; people will begin saying
it's me.') Apart from an alarming outbreak of diphtheria in 1912

---

[1] David papers.   [2] Sir Arthur fforde.

and again in 1913, which caused the Governing Body to spend £60 on an expert enquiry by Dr. E. W. Goodall into its cause, the health of the School was remarkably good and seemed to justify the improved arrangements for supervising hygiene and for medical attention. Just before David's arrival, Dr. G. A. Auden (father of W. H. Auden, the poet) had been appointed, provisionally, sanitary inspector to the School; in December 1910 his post was made permanent with the rather happier title of 'sanitary adviser'. With Dr. Simey now installed as full-time School doctor, Dr. Dukes was made consultant physician to the School for life (and five years later his daughter Alice joined the music staff and was to teach piano at Rugby for the next forty years). The smell of 'Dowson Gas' no longer defiled the air of the Close after 1911, when the School Electricity Com-pany was wound up and rewiring was carried out to draw from a mains supply—at a cost of £1200 and £300 compensation to masters who had shares in the School Company. Only Jex-Blake's swimming-bath remained of the old unhygienic instal-lations; it was the constant butt of humorists contributing to the *Comet*, which could scarcely produce a summer issue without some slighting reference to the 'Tosh'. Many boys, indeed, still preferred the river, though, for non-swimmers, immersion in the rather thick water of the bath was compulsory.

The *Comet*—surely the longest lived of private-enterprise journals in the School—continued to appear and to make a profit. The two original editors, H. Le Mesurier and M. L. R. Romer, both left in March 1913—they were to be killed within a month of one another in 1916—but the journal continued unchanged, and, though a House annalist could complain that it subsisted chiefly on 'abuse of the *Meteor* and the School

Marshal', it was read and appreciated by large numbers in the School and formed a useful organ for the expression of unofficial public opinion. It steered clear, if only just clear, of matters liable to incur official retribution, and in this proved wiser, or perhaps more fortunate, than *Rugby Opinion* a few years later, which produced one (heavily censored) issue and had its second confiscated on publication 'to the general dismay of the School'[1] in 1916.

The changes in School routine were on the whole popular. The long midday gap from 12.15 to 3.0 p.m. on whole school days gave a new opportunity for games practices or runs, and the abolition of whole-school callover in the middle of half-holiday afternoons, so that boys had until 5.30 to pursue their own activities, was part of the liberalising tendency of the times, and was as much distrusted by disciples of Percival, who thought it gave to the young too long a stretch to get into mischief, as it was appreciated by the boys. Much less popular was the new prominence given to physical training under the energetic Captain E. C. Brierly, who came from Eastern Command in 1911 to remodel the School's activity in this department.

The VIth still ran the School in all minor matters—and in some not so minor. David was not altogether happy about their organisation and powers. It was possible for quite young boys to achieve authority simply by rising to the Lower Bench, where they might have technical power over, but no respect from, older, perhaps more worthy boys who were not quite so clever. An article in the *Comet* entitled 'Rugby Characters: The Worm' emphasised the danger in exaggerated terms. So in 1915

[1] *Annals of Dickinson's.* But a No. 2a was produced rapidly and was allowed to circulate.

the Headmaster proceeded to limit the numbers with School Sixth power by confining it to a VIth form Levée composed of the Upper Bench, Heads of Houses and not more than two co-opted from the Lower Bench. It made a less unwieldy body, but was still too big—and too independent. In 1918 the Levée resigned as a body in protest against the Headmaster's demotion of the Head of the Upper Bench (Martin Bateson) from his position as Chairman, and his replacement by his own choice of Head of the School (E. A. Montague). The result in the end was a further limitation to provide a Levée of Heads of Houses and five others co-opted from the VIth, known as 'the Sixth'. On this the irreverent *Comet* published a delightful satire entitled 'Parliamentary Experiments (being a fragment from the umpteenth book of Harty-as)', which ends: 'But it came to pass that *afterward* he took thought and fashioned another assembly, and it was *much* as the other had been, and it worked exceeding great great folly in the land. . . .'

One other change in the direction of 'modernity' was the disappearance of top hats for Sunday wear. They were worn for the last time in the winter term of 1912. A few boys accepted the remarkable story that they would be useful for Morris dancers and should therefore be left in the ante-Chapel after the last Sunday evensong. Others took part in an impromptu dribbling race across the Close with the hats taking the place of footballs. Thereafter straw hats became Sunday wear, and it was not long before the war was to play havoc with the old clothing regula-tions.

The Speech Day of 1913 was the last of such celebrations before the war, since in 1914 it had to be cancelled owing to a severe epidemic of mumps. It was also the last at which Basil

Johnson performed at the Speech Room organ, newly embel-
lished with the decorated organ-screen, presented by W. B.
Gair, which was causing a certain amount of amused comment
in the School. On this occasion, J. A. G. Haslam recalls,
Johnson excelled himself. The distinguished visitors were very
late in coming to the platform and the School was becoming
bored and restless, when suddenly Johnson drew their attention
by a blast on the organ and proceeded to lead them in community singing, beginning with 'There is a Tavern in the Town'.
'The School was so amazed and delighted with the noise it
made', says Haslam, 'that it would have gone on until exhausted,
I think.' In those days, he adds, only the choir sang in Chapel.
Johnson left in 1914 to be Director of Music at Eton and was
replaced by George Dyson, who, in his short stay, won golden
opinions from the School. The story may be apocryphal, but
is worth repeating, that Dyson owed his appointment, against
such distinguished candidates as Martin Shaw, to having
arrived for interview on a motor-cycle, which the selection
committee thought would 'appeal to the boys'. He was succeeded
in January 1915 by A. H. Peppin, who controlled School
music with distinction until 1924 and was followed by his ward,
Kenneth Stubbs, who was in charge until his early death in
1949.

When war broke out in August 1914 it seemed at first to
make very little difference to the life of the School. Indeed,
compared to the more violent disturbance in 1939–45 (and even
then Rugby was infinitely more fortunate than many other
schools), there was throughout but little material change. There
was a drop in numbers, but not a serious one, in the first year,
but they had recovered by 1916, and by the time war ended they

were higher than ever before in the School's history. The most obvious immediate result of the outburst of patriotism that fol' lowed the declaration was that virtually the whole School joined the Corps, which doubled its activity—there were two weekly parades instead of one—and ran a special class for those about to take commissions. The Corps was naturally taken much more seriously, as the long terminal records in House annals bear witness, though as time wore on there were some, like Robert Collis, who wondered just how valuable the type of training would be in conditions of modern warfare. And one doubts that C. J. P. Ionides was taking entirely seriously the instructions for dealing with a captured enemy, that one should secure him and render him harmless, when, during an exercise at Fawsley Park, he used a captive's puttees to tie him to a tree and threw his rifle into the lake.

The war seemed to come much closer when lists of Rugby casualties began to come in and to be read out in Chapel. For senior boys who knew that they would soon be taking an active part, as well as for those who taught them, there must have been a feeling of unreality in the day'to'day business of academic work. And yet, as Robert Collis has recorded, the very know' ledge that they would soon be fighting caused them to 'care more fiercely about our little affairs than any other generation before or since'.[1] Rapidly the list of Rugbeians lost became hor' rifyingly long—in the end there were 686 of them—and it included many of the best; older ones such as F. C. Selous, who had entered the School as far back as 1866, but who joined up at the beginning of the war and was killed in East Africa at the age of sixty'five; younger ones such as Ronald Poulton, one of

[1] Robert Collis, *The Silver Fleece*.

the greatest of Rugby athletes—and much more—who had once, as the Rev. C. S. Donald, Manager of the Rugby Clubs, tells us,[1] spent the evening before playing in an international Rugby football match by the bedside of a dying Notting Dale child.

Many of the younger masters left early in the war to join the services. Three of them were killed, O. M. Samson, Hubert Podmore and H. S. Wilson; three returned only fleetingly in 1919—H. H. Hardy and J. H. Simpson, who went that year to headmasterships, and E. W. E. Kempson, who became an Inspector of Schools; and E. C. Brierly resigned his mastership in 1915. David was faced with the difficulty of war-time appointments, and there were a number of temporary masters, some of them good, such as G. F. Spaulding, who came for a year from America, some not so good, and the standard of teaching undoubtedly suffered to some extent. But there were some, such as E. F. Waddy, an Australian cricketer (and a great practical joker), and A. R. Tatham, who came to stay. And, in spite of the difficulties, of those boys whose main schooling at Rugby was during the war years, over seventy won awards at Oxford and Cambridge, though a tragically large number of them did not live to take them up.

For boys in the School there were, apart from the activity of the Corps, many minor indications that times were not normal. Weekly subscriptions were raised to the fund for relief of

---

[1] 'He had come to London to play for England against the unbeaten All Blacks at Twickenham next day. Forty thousand rose as one man with the shout 'Poulton's through!' as he made the ever memorable run from the England line the length of the ground. Only I knew how he had spent the evening before.' C. S. Donald, *Memoirs*. (Privately circulated.)

prisoners of war; economies were made in eating bread and sugar, and the money saved was used to provide 'comforts' for the troops (Dickinson's, in this way, produced £15 for mittens one term). Beer disappeared from the menu of School House. There was agricultural activity, and squads went out during term time to help farmers, particularly with potato picking—a cheque for £100 was sent in 1917 to M. Paul Cambon as part of the profits from the School potato field. Farming camps were organised by F. W. Odgers in the summer holidays, though these were not always entirely successful. There was no real scarcity of food, but the annual House suppers had to be abandoned, and House concerts were organised instead. To help relations between town and gown, David put food-shops out of bounds and forbade the receipt of parcels of food from home; there was indeed a feeling in the town that the School had advantages in the matter of food that were denied to the ordinary population, and rationing was not so skilfully arranged as to avoid the difficulties of periodic demand from a com-munity of six hundred which was not permanently in resi-dence. Games continued much as usual, though the Corps occupied some of what had been games hours. There were, naturally, fewer foreign matches; games with other schools were, in any case, much fewer than they are today, and they continued, though the Marlborough match was played in alternate years at Rugby and Marlborough instead of at Lords; matches against clubs disappeared from the calendar and were replaced, where possible, by games against teams from troops billeted in the district. As the war dragged on and ordinary activities became progressively limited, new enterprises were undertaken to stimulate interest. In the autumn of 1915 a chemistry exhibition was organised by the scientists, which was so successful that it was followed the next term by a physics exhibition. And just occasionally war-time shortages produced unexpected results; in 1918 Robert Collis, who as captain of the XV was *ex officio* starter at the athletic sports, was unable to secure blanks for the starting-pistol; instead, if we can believe his story, he took live ammunition from the armoury. He nearly shot a master, E. L. D. Cole, and was surprised to see a com-plete line of spectators fall flat until he realised that he was point-ing the gun in their direction while attempting to free the mechanism, which had jammed.[1]

When the Armistice was signed on 11 November 1918 the School joined in the general, hysterical rejoicing of the country; all rules were in abeyance—both the official School rules and those, much more strictly kept, imposed by the boys themselves. 'Ragging', said a House annalist, 'was allowed.' It was very vigorous, and, on the roof of what is now Bradley House, R. G. C. Levens, using one of the turrets as a stand, conducted an orchestra of eleven instruments in a concert listened to delightedly by an audience of several hundred in the Barby Road.

Meanwhile the Governing Body had not been having an easy time. Not only was there a general increase in prices, but they were faced with the necessity of paying salaries to those on war service (which they did, less £30) as well as to the tem-porary masters who replaced them; and there were a number of cases where they felt a moral obligation to reduce fees for boys whose parents were suffering hardship as a result of the war. In 1915 the School overdraft had increased and the Reserve Fund

[1] *The Silver Fleece.*

had to be drawn on for the payment of interest due. They were loath to increase fees, but by 1916 it was essential, and the boarding fee went up by £2 a term. A great deal of thought was given to methods of effecting economies, and in December 1916 they approved a proposal of David's for the formation of a committee to examine the possibility of central buying of supplies, and of establishing a School dairy and poultry farm, a laundry and a tuck-shop. The following year sites were being chosen for the laundry and the shop and for a bakery, and the Headmaster was examining the possibility of setting up a School book-shop. As things turned out, the war came to an end before most of these enterprises were started, and only the School shop, 'the Stodge', which was to put Hobley's and 'Gussie's' at last out of business, came out of all the planning.

In their desire to help those suffering hardship, the Governing Body gained a good deal of assistance from the foundation of scholarships, exhibitions and prizes as memorials to old Rugbeians who had been killed. From the period of the war and just after it there came the G. H. Gair Scholarships, the Ralph Evers Fund, the Arthur Percival Scholarships, the Humphrey King Hoyle, the Joseph Spencer Mitchell, the George and Ronald Wheatcroft, the William Spencer Judge, the Charles Wake and the Parry Memorial Exhibitions, as well as the Selous Memorial Fund and the F. C. O. Twist Prize. They did not cover the School's expenses in this matter, but were an indication of the confidence and affection in which Rugby was held.

On 11 December 1919 the Governing Body recorded a minute of appreciation of

the way in which the Headmaster and the Masters have carried
on the work of the School during the unprecedented difficulties
and anxieties of the last five years [and of] the courage, self-
sacrifice and resourcefulness which alone could have conducted
the School successfully through such a period of trial. To Dr.
David . . . they wish to express their gratitude for the wisdom,
tact and unfailing energy which he has uniformly displayed
and which make his name a conspicuous one in the illustrious
list of Rugby Headmasters. . . . If the School is now, as it
certainly appears to be, in a condition of unusual prosperity,
that fact is largely owing to the qualities displayed by the
existing Staff; and the Governing Body have very great
pleasure in recording their consciousness of what the School
owes to those who have piloted it through this time of trouble.

The Rugby Governors were not in the habit of issuing, often,
commendations of this kind; one can hardly doubt that on this
occasion it was deserved. But the prosperity to which they
referred was not financial, and School fees had twice to be
raised in the two years after the war, till they stood at £201 a
year as the consolidated fee for boarders and £75 for day boys;
and there was in addition a School entrance fee of ten guineas
and a House entrance fee of three. The increase made possible a
further modification of the masters' salary scale, to run from
£400 to £1000 in twenty-two years. At this it remained until
after the Second World War.

Two other developments of this period bore in them the seeds
of great changes in the future. One, occurring just before the
war, was the first inspection of the School by the Board of
Education, in February 1914. The report on the inspection
came in after war had started, and made less of an impact than

it might have done in peace-time; but it was a highly laudatory
document, reading more like a prospectus than a serious attempt
at criticism. A second inspection took place in the Lent term
of 1921 and again reported the School to be in 'a remarkably
healthy and vigorous condition', though this time some
detailed suggestions for practical improvements were made,
such as the provision of more drying-room accommodation in
Dickinson's House. It is difficult to imagine James inviting or
accepting interference of this sort from a government department,
but David was on the side of progress in the matter, and twice
lent School buildings for a Board of Education course of
instruction for science teachers. The other development, full of
portent for the future, was the entering of a few boys for the first
time, in the summer of 1918, for the School Certificate examination. From that time, the number entered increased annually
until the examination became a normal hurdle in the course of
every boy, and Certificate results assumed an importance that
some regarded (and regard today) as out of all relation to the
value of the examination. And today, when they are the essential preliminary to entry to the universities, and indeed to many
professions, the shape of education is dictated by public
examinations.

One very great service David performed for Rugby School.
Towards the end of 1918 some land south of the School on both
sides of the Barby Road came up for sale. David urged the
Governing Body to buy it, but, with the difficulty which they
were finding in reducing their existing debt, they felt unable to
do so. So important, however, did David regard the acquisition
of the land, which would quite certainly be used for building if
it were sold to anybody but the School, that he borrowed the

A. A. David

David's staff, 1921

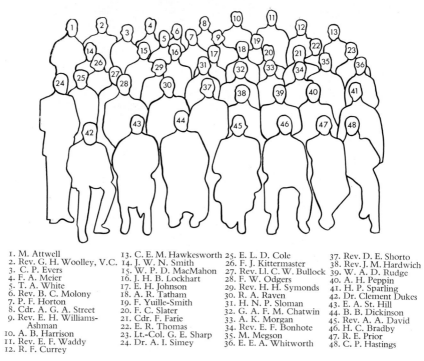

1. M. Attwell	13. C. E. M. Hawkesworth	25. E. L. D. Cole
2. Rev. G. H. Woolley, V.C.	14. J. W. N. Smith	26. F. J. Kittermaster
3. C. P. Evers	15. W. P. D. MacMahon	27. Rev. Ll. C. W. Bullock
4. F. A. Meier	16. J. H. B. Lockhart	28. F. W. Odgers
5. T. A. White	17. E. H. Johnson	29. Rev. H. H. Symonds
6. Rev. B. C. Molony	18. A. R. Tatham	30. R. A. Raven
7. P. F. Horton	19. F. Yuille-Smith	31. H. N. P. Sloman
8. Cdr. A. G. A. Street	20. F. C. Slater	32. G. A. F. M. Chatwin
9. Rev. E. H. Williams-	21. Cdr. F. Farie	33. A. K. Morgan
Ashman	22. E. R. Thomas	34. Rev. E. F. Bonhote
10. A. B. Harrison	23. Lt.-Col. G. E. Sharp	35. M. Megson
11. Rev. E. F. Waddy	24. Dr. A. I. Simey	36. E. E. A. Whitworth
12. R. F. Currey		

37. Rev. D. E. Shorto
38. Rev. J. M. Hardwich
39. W. A. D. Rudge
40. A. H. Peppin
41. H. P. Sparling
42. Dr. Clement Dukes
43. E. A. St. Hill
44. B. B. Dickinson
45. Rev. A. A. David
46. H. C. Bradby
47. R. E. Prior
48. C. P. Hastings

necessary money, largely from Housemasters, and bought it for the School on his own responsibility. And in 1919 the Governing Body was persuaded to take it over. To finance the purchase it was decided to sell the Benn property on the Hillmorton Road—the *Comet* published a sad lament at its passing.[1] And so David saved the last green lung of countryside for the School and for the town. In doing so it is hardly too much to say that he saved the School. Had he not acted so swiftly, the Close and Caldecott's might well have become a small island of green surrounded by a built-up area, and Rugby School might have been forced, as were the Charterhouse and Merchant Taylors', to move elsewhere. David's purchases were Hillbrow and the Water Tower Farm; when, shortly afterwards, the Spring Hill estate of 136 acres came on the market, the Governing Body had learnt its lesson and that, too, was acquired. Hillbrow and Spring Hill were to be levelled for playing fields, and Water Tower Farm was let to C. P. Hastings, who farmed it, if gossip was correctly informed, none too efficiently.

The Hillbrow house, which had previously been a preparatory school, went to the Director of Music, A. H. Peppin. As well as his private rooms it contained two masters' flats, four rooms for music, and a workshop for science. It proved a useful addition to the School's buildings, and twenty years later its site was used for the new Kilbracken. David's initiative in purchasing land south of the School led to the Governing Body's adopting it as policy, and when later on more land in the area became available they were prepared to incur heavy debt until, in the time of David's successor, all the fields and houses on both sides of the Barby Road as far as the crossroads became

[1] Printed as an appendix to this chapter.

School property. One other purchase made just after the war was the house and garden known as 'The Firs', which some years later was to provide a site for the Music School and the new sanatorium.

The question of a suitable war memorial was being considered very shortly after the Armistice. As early as December 1918 the Governing Body voted £200 towards the production of war-memorial books 'provided the Headmaster and Bursars provide a similar sum'. Next year Sir Charles Nicholson's designs for a war-memorial chapel and for a cross were accepted, and a great summer gathering to celebrate the conclusion of peace, attended by over five hundred Old Rugbeians, helped to swell the subscription lists. But David did not stay to see the completion of the new 'Little Chapel'; he departed in July 1921 to his new work as Bishop of St. Edmundsbury and Ipswich. Nicholson wrote to him on 6 June of that year:

> You know I warned you, when we started this memorial job, that there was an impending fate which would prevent our finishing it together.... Well, there is only one comfort—if you get tired of burying St. Edmund you can always reckon on getting a fresh sphere of occupation by sending for me to mend your cathedral tower.... May I venture to suggest that you should engage a couple of strenuous archdeacons who do not object to the Church's one foundation and who enjoy functions and mustard and cress sandwiches on the vicarage lawn.[1]

Nicholson knew well enough that David was a man whose energy always went beyond the formal and the traditional.

By the time war ended David must have been a tired man.

[1] David papers.

The strain of those years would have been telling anyway, but, at the end, the health of the School, which had been remarkable until then, proved unable to resist the wave of influenza that swept the country, and indeed the world, in 1918 and 1919, and the anxiety of widespread and often grave illness in the School was added to the cumulative anxieties of four previous years. Whether or not this strain was the cause, as the charitable among his opponents in the matter suggested, it is a fact that in the last few years of his headmastership David developed an almost obsessional interest in the new 'science' of psycho-analysis, and fell completely under the influence of Homer Lane.

Homer Lane was either a saint or a charlatan, according to one's view of him, but in either case he was a man of outstand-ing charm and persuasiveness. He was a self-taught American of humble origin who had developed a philosophy of education akin to that of Pestalozzi, but in application entirely his own. In the course of a varied career he had been a grocer's clerk, a rail-way clerk, the superintendent of public playgrounds in Detroit and in control of a self-governing 'republic' of children in America, before coming to England in 1913 where he took over responsibility for a reformatory school under the Home Office, which he called the 'Little Commonwealth'. From this post he was dismissed after an enquiry into allegations of unsavoury conduct—which were never proved—in 1918. He was an amateur psychologist, much influenced at first by Freud, but developing theories all his own (his biographer[1] suggests that he was not far, at the end, from equating himself with Jesus Christ), and his next move was to set up as a psycho-

[1] W. David Wills, *Homer Lane*.

therapist in London, where he 'gave lessons' to 'pupils', since his entire lack of medical qualification prevented him from claiming a doctor–patient relationship. And there is no doubt that in his psycho-analytical practice he had many cases of remarkable success, and that he convinced a number of influential people, among them Lord Lytton, Governor-General of India, of the value of what he was doing. His career ended with another court case, which became a *cause célèbre*, in 1925, when again allegations against him were not proved, and at which Dr. David, among a number of distinguished people, was prepared to give evidence on his behalf.

This was the man who converted David to a belief in the value of psycho-analysis for treating moral difficulties in the young, and to whom he even offered a post on the Rugby staff. David, as has been seen, was always 'advanced' in his views on discipline. Now his 'progressiveness' took another leap forward, and he became convinced that moral problems could best be treated by the methods of Homer Lane. In this he was backed by a few of his staff, H. H. Symonds and J. H. Simpson in particular, but the bulk of his masters, and the older ones almost to a man, viewed the new development with the gravest concern. It caused a final breach between the Headmaster and G. F. Bradby, whose lampoon on Rugby, *The Chronicles of Dawnhope*,[1] dates from this period. The book, amusing as it is, provides a gross misrepresentation of conditions, and was the subject of a severely critical review by E. W. Ashcroft in the *Rugbeian*,[2] yet another literary venture started just at the end of the war. Exaggerated, too, were the stories circulated about the results of David's new interest. There cannot have been very

---

[1] Heinemann, 1921.   [2] Vol. II, no. 5; 16 November 1921.

many boys, though there were certainly some, who managed to convince the Headmaster that they were suffering from 'a complex' and thereby secured a trip to London to consult the specialist—and a night and perhaps a theatre in town. Stories were multiplied and lost nothing in the telling, but the very rumours were enough to alarm the Governing Body. It was even said, though Dickinson declared this to be 'a malicious lie', that David was threatened with dismissal if he did not accept a bishopric when it was offered him.

Probably, then, it was wise for him to move on when he did, before his reputation as Headmaster became tarnished; for there is little doubt that, with his new views and the division they caused on the staff, his grip on the School became less firm and discipline was beginning to suffer. If he was appointed to Rugby to 'modernise', to break the ties of tradition that were becoming outdated, he had been successful; though one might argue that the war would have done this for the School whoever had been at its head. His administration and the reforms of his earlier years were both enlightened and highly successful; but to take new and unproved psychological theories and apply them in a School such as Rugby according to the teachings of a man who had neither training nor qualification was surely, at its mildest, a mistake. As a bishop, David was great; and he never lost his interest in educational method, philosophy and experiment. His later published conclusions[1] contain much of wisdom. And two of his pupils, P. H. B. Lyon (1907–12) and A. F. B. fforde (1914–19), were to be successively Headmasters of Rugby School.

---

[1] E.g. *Life and the Public Schools* (Alexander MacLehose, 1932).

Lament for Benn's

In the *Comet* of 20 June 1919 there appeared the following lament for Benn's. Its prophetic nature makes it worth preserving.

EHEU FUGACES

'It is rumoured that Benn's are to be sold for building and replaced by fields near the Water-Tower.'

> Shades of the most unprofitable Boshes,
> Neither a wonder nor a wild desire,
> Shades of the subsequent assault of Toshes,
> (Providing one had lit the boiler fire)
> And shades of Mr. Hastings' speckled hens!
> Are you aware that they are selling Benn's?
>
> Where you and I would loiter in the background,
> Evading carefully the frenzied scrum,
> Rejoicing that we'd struck upon a slack ground,
> Builders and bricks and carpenters will come.
> There shall the proletariat live and thrive,
> And hang their washing on our Twenty-five.
>
> There shall we see those architectural wonders,
> Streets of 'Rupertias' and 'Mon Repos',
> Inhabited by Nature's grossest blunders,
> Profaning sanctuaries we used to know.
> What! Lose those priceless pitches once for all
> On which we took our first, and final, ball?

How art thou fallen, Benn's! It can't be thought on
   That thou, abettor to our infant stride,
A most conveniently Short Hillmorton,
   Should thus be—vulgarly—allowed to slide.
Surely the sheep will find it passing strange
To find your miniature a kitchen range.[1]

'Well, well! Time flies,' you'll hear us come and mutter,
   When your new streets have spoiled your ancient trees,
Poking our alpenstocks beneath a gutter,
   You'll hear us doddering of our memories.
'How well I knew the place! In days gone by
That's where I scored our fifty-second try!'

The rising generations never knew you,
   Your gaudy bricks shall fill them with disdain;
They'll leave the Central railway-station to you;
   Their conscript 'leisure' 's on another plane.
Spare me the degradation of that hour,
Boshes and Rems, beneath the Water-Tower.

POSTUMIUS, O.R.

[1] There was a miniature rifle-range on Benn's.

7

The Layman

WILLIAM WYAMAR VAUGHAN, 1921–31

From medieval times, when all education had been the province of the Church, until the second half of the nineteenth century, headmasterships of schools in Britain had been, almost without exception, in the hands of men in holy orders. The fundamental purpose of education in the early days was to produce clerks, men who could read and write and who could deal in Latin, the universal language of Church and Law. With the sixteenth century, under the influence of men such as Erasmus, Colet, More and Lily, there was a broadening; Greek was added to the Latin curriculum in a few schools; in the seventeenth century mathematics crept in, and these three remained the basis of education until the scientific and industrial revolutions compelled a further broadening. Thomas Arnold's original contribution to educational theory had been, as has been seen, to make the training of Christian gentlemen his first priority, and from his time headmasters of Public Schools had regarded preaching as the most important part of their teaching, and training in religion as, in a sense, the most important subject; and since the Classics provided the language of theology, philosophy and ethics, they remained the basis of all educational practice.

One result of the increasing importance attached to studies other than Classics in the second half of the nineteenth century and their gradual adoption as serious subjects in the schools was the appointment of a steadily increasing proportion of laymen as assistant masters. Goulburn's four appointments were all in orders, as were half of Temple's and Hayman's; of Jex-Blake's nineteen appointments and of Percival's seventeen, only three in each case were in orders; James appointed six clergymen among his nineteen, David only four among thirty-eight, one of whom later renounced his orders, though three others subsequently took them. It was inevitable that this process of secularisation should spread in the end to headmasterships; as the same phenomenon was occurring in the universities, the clerical proportion of the academic world was becoming too small to provide suitable candidates for all the posts available.

The first layman on the Rugby staff to move to a headmastership was A. W. Potts, who in 1870 was appointed to the new school of Fettes. This, as a Scottish appointment, might have been regarded as exceptional, but others rapidly followed, such as those of J. S. Phillpots to Bedford Grammar School and F. E. Kitchener to the new High School at Newcastle under Lyme, both in 1874. But for the rest of the century it was to the smaller or less important schools that the laymen went. It is true that J. M. Wilson was a layman when he was appointed to Clifton in 1879, but he took orders before entering on his office, and the first major Public School to accept a layman as headmaster was Marlborough when Frank Fletcher went there in 1903. Others were slow to follow Marlborough's example, and before the war only W. W. Vaughan and Cyril Norwood were lay headmasters of other leading schools; perhaps it is significant of the reluctance of their governing bodies to abandon the principle of clerical direction that Bertram Pollock, the outgoing Master of Wellington, with the approval of Lord Derby, his chairman, tried—and failed—to persuade Vaughan to take orders after his appointment to that School in 1910.[1]

William Wyamar Vaughan was only the fourth Rugbeian to be appointed Headmaster of his old school,[2] and he was the first of three in succession. Unlike all his predecessors except Henry Hayman, whom he resembled only in having secured a double Second at Oxford, he could lay claim to no very great scholarship; but he was a man of immensely wide interests, most of them educational, and of dynamic energy. His reputation, and by 1921 it was a very great one, had been made as a practising schoolmaster; he had never been a don or held a Fellowship, as had all his predecessors since Arnold. Thus not only was he the first layman, he was also the first complete schoolmaster to be Headmaster of Rugby School. After leaving New College he had taught at Clifton College from 1890 to 1904, and had then gone as Headmaster to Giggleswick School, where he was so outstandingly successful in raising the reputation of what had been regarded as a rather second-rate institution that, when a new Master was required for Wellington College in 1910, Vaughan was invited to accept the post. Only two other men were seriously considered, Dr. St. J. B. Wynne Wilson, an old Rugby master, at the time Headmaster of Haileybury, and Lionel Ford, Headmaster of Repton, who was later to move to Harrow. Both were in orders and both had

---

[1] David Newsome, *A History of Wellington College, 1859–1959.*

[2] The three others were Knightley Harrison, 1670–5; John Plomer, 1731–42; and T. W. Jex-Blake, 1874–87.

paper qualifications and experience that might have seemed superior to those of Vaughan, the strength of whose candidature lay entirely in his achievement and character. And his per formance at Wellington during the great difficulties of the war period so far justified the judgment of the Governors that by 1921 he was regarded as one of the outstanding headmasters, possibly the greatest in the country. Like David, he had been invited to be a candidate for the Eton headmastership, but the Eton selectors had chosen C. A. Alington instead.

In 1921 Vaughan was fifty-seven years old; in only three years he would be of age to retire from Wellington, and it was natural that he should hesitate for some time before accepting the invitation of Lord Kilbracken to undertake the headmastership of Rugby. He had gone through a period of strain and overwork at Wellington, which had affected his health in 1918, and although he had entirely recovered he could not but regard with some misgiving an undertaking that would again test his powers to their limit, and which, if the stories he had been told of the condition of Rugby were true—they were in fact exag gerated—would involve a good deal of anxiety. But all the friends to whom he turned for advice urged him to accept the post; and he would have been less than human if he had not been attracted by the prospect of crowning his career by occupying one of the highest posts in the schoolmastering world,[1] and pres iding over the destinies of his own old School. And so Vaughan came to Rugby, like Percival at an age when some considered him too old; and, like Percival, he proved how wrong they were.

That a new Headmaster should provide a marked contrast with

---

[1] David, in his farewell speech to the Old Rugbeians, 6 July 1921, said: 'Let no man speak of my promotion; they cannot promote the Headmaster of Rugby.'

the old is common enough. Most men of any quality have the faults of their virtues, and often governing bodies feel it wise to appoint a man who is likely to correct the results of an excess of zeal or of too much mildness in his predecessor. The contrast between Temple and Goulburn has already been noted; Percival's reforming energy was followed, suitably, by the milder rule of James; and now the ultra-modern theorising and experiment of David seemed to require some modification. Quite certainly Vaughan, both in appearance and opinions, provided a very marked contrast to the outgoing Headmaster. Rugby boys, looking curiously, and perhaps with some apprehension, at the 'new Bodger', saw a big, rather clumsy, figure, dressed in untidy secular garments, his hair a little longer than was usual and wearing a full moustache. Someone described him as resembling a huge shaggy dog with a disconcertingly loud bark. Very rapidly they found that he was a man who would stand no nonsense; more slowly they came to realise that behind the gruff, alarming exterior there was a fund of sympathy and real human kindness. To the malefactor, the idle or the dishonest he could be a terror; but anyone with a genuine problem could approach him with confidence that he would have a sympathetic hearing and sound advice. They soon found, too, with the shrewdness of their kind, that there were suitable and unsuitable methods of approach. A request beginning 'Please, sir, may I . . .?' was apt to draw the rejoinder 'Why should you?', whereas one that started diffidently 'I suppose it wouldn't be possible for me to . . .' as often as not drew the reply 'Why not?' Vaughan liked, even in small matters, to be the initiator of events.[1]

[1] George Smith, in conversation with a colleague, once described Vaughan as 'contra-suggestive'.

Before he arrived at Rugby Vaughan had heard some rather alarming accounts of the School and may even have believed that he was faced with the work of cleaning up an Augean stable. This was by no means the case, but he did find discipline slack in a number of respects, and he lost no time in tightening it up. Action of this sort by a new man is never popular, and it was with some distress that the boys learnt that in future stiff collars would be worn by all, and that Sunday evensong was no longer to be a voluntary service. They grumbled—but not to the Headmaster. From the very start they realised that that would get them nowhere. But their criticism very rapidly turned to respect, for it became evident that the new Headmaster was taking a real and detailed interest in them. In a very short time he knew the name of every boy in the School; he was always about the place; in the New Quadrangle before lessons, keeping an eye on his watch to make sure that they started on time (and his rebuke to a tardy master: 'Ah—I wanted to see you, but I see you're late; it will do another time' was enough to keep the staff as well as the boys up to the mark); on the Close at games times, with an eye on behaviour; even in the swimming-bath, for he liked to be able to recognise his pupils in all conditions, clothed or unclothed. And no boy ever passed a day in the sanatorium without receiving a visit from the Headmaster. New boys did not always find him so alarming as did C. R. Evers;[1] there was an occasion, one January evening after lock-up, when after dismissing the term's new boys, to whom he had been giving his regular talk, down the steps to the gravel, he was surprised ten minutes later to receive another visit from one of them. 'Sir,' he said cheerfully, 'you said that, if we were ever in

[1] *Rugby*, pp. 100-6.

any difficulty, we were to come to you.' 'Well, what is it?' 'Sir, how do we get out of the Close?'

It is doubtful if Vaughan would have echoed David's pious hope that the Classics would always remain the chief characteristic of education at Rugby. Though his own degree was a classical one, his interests were predominantly modern. After leaving Oxford he had spent some time in Paris, and he became one of the great supporters of the direct method of teaching modern languages; he even became President of the Modern Language Association, though he was not himself a distinguished linguist, and his pronunciation of French caused amusement even to his pupils. His interest in and the help he gave to the Science Commission, the British Association, the Workers' Educational Association and the Schools Broadcasting Service of the B.B.C. marked him as one of the leading 'moderns' in education.

Like his predecessor, Vaughan was interested not only, perhaps not principally, in the VIth form. The work of the whole School was kept under his constant and detailed supervision. In December 1922, after only four terms at Rugby, he was able to report to the Governing Body:

> I have taken every form in the School in one subject or another and have heard very many masters teach. . . . The difficulty at Rugby, as at other schools, is to teach the boys who will never rise to the top forms. In dealing with these boys, on whose education a great deal of the professional work of the country depends, we are torn between the alternatives of keeping their interest or of exacting thorough work. I have the impression that in forms where the former aim has been most successfully

attained, the thoroughness of the work has suffered, and vice versa.

His classroom visits extended to the Science Schools, a department in which he took a particular interest. 'Is this the cream or the scum?' he once asked, on entering a room where a small group of three or four boys were being taught. Among a mass of pencilled notes—many of them difficult to decipher—in the possession of H. J. Vaughan, there is the declaration that 'Science must be offered to *young* boys' and a complaint that 'Prep. Schools have turned a deaf ear to recommendations on Science.'

Masters were acutely aware that their work was under constant scrutiny. Junior men whose appointments were still probationary were made to feel conscious that they were very much on trial, and in more than one case the period of probation was extended beyond the customary two years. Even if they had received no classroom visit during a term, there was always the end-of-term examination, on which the report to the Headmaster was, in those days, no mere formality. 'It is always difficult', Vaughan wrote to the Governing Body in 1923, 'to combine the two purposes of an examination, that of testing the teacher and of testing the taught.' It is perhaps significant that he put the teacher first. There were some, particularly among the younger masters, such as J. A. G. Bruce—one of the most brilliant and stimulating teachers that Rugby has known, who was to die tragically young in November 1944—who found the strain almost beyond bearing. But for most of them it proved a stimulant, and standards of industry, and indeed of achievement, during the decade of Vaughan's headmastership have seldom been equalled. In 1929 he was able to report that

Rugbeians, in that year alone, had taken twenty-six Firsts at the universities and that three had been elected to Fellowships, one of them at All Souls.

There is plenty of evidence that, among the boys too, there was a keen awareness that a new and more vigorous control was at work. A House annalist might state in the autumn of 1921 that there had been 'no startling innovations', but the Levée were clearly a little uneasy about their powers. At a meeting on 9 October 1921 the Head of the School, J. B. Miller, stressed the importance of 'vigorous action on the part of all School Committees and of individual members of the Sixth . . . in view of the fact that the self-governing activities of the School were inevitably under close scrutiny at such a time', and the tone in which the Levée's decisions were couched underwent a gradual but a marked alteration. Where in February 1922 they were demanding rather peremptorily 'that Mr. Johnson's jurisdiction over the School playing fields be better defined', by June 1924 they were minuting that 'the Headmaster should be asked if some alteration could be made' in the time of summer evening callover.

To some it undoubtedly seemed that the more personal and direct control exerted by Vaughan had the grave disadvantage of discouraging initiative in his staff. 'He seems', wrote B. B. Dickinson after his retirement, 'not to be able to trust anyone to decide the smallest detail without reference to himself . . . to have kept everything in his own hands and to have decided everything without any discussion.' And a senior master, with perhaps unpardonable exaggeration, said, 'The fact is that Vaughan is breeding a set of rabbits.' And yet the autocracy of the Headmaster was not the rigid thing it had been under Percival, and

W. W. Vaughan

Sir Arthur fforde and P. H. B. Lyon

in theory at least he believed in a measure of liberty. 'It is far better', he wrote, 'that a cricket match should be lost or a concert have a hitch in it, than that the overzealous watchfulness of the teacher should leave nothing to the initiative of the taught. It is far easier for the teacher to interfere too much than to stand aside and watch.' And there were times when the visionary in him broke through and seemed to contradict the intensely practical activity of his daytoday work. 'The object of education, through all its stages', he wrote, 'is to release the imprisoned splendour.' Those who sat through his Scripture lessons in the VIth might have found this a little difficult to believe. Nor was he entirely unbending in his adherence to a fixed routine. In the hard weather early in 1929—a term in which the School was hit by scarlet fever, mumps and influenza—he more than once, to the delight of his pupils, remitted the first lesson on a Monday afternoon to give time for skating. He had, of course, no Robert Whitelaw to restrain him. In matters of religion he was certainly a liberal. He spoke of 'the manifest reluctance of the leaders of the Church even to allow others to make the new bottles which alone could hold the new wine'. And although he restored a compulsory evensong on Sundays, he insisted that Communion 'should be voluntary, not only in name but in fact. It is better that a boy who neglects this duty should go on neglecting it than that those who come should feel that their presence is noted with approval, or the reverse.'

The first problem facing Vaughan in 1921 concerned the numbers in the School. In David's last year the Governing Body had expressed their concern that the number (619) 'was considerably above what it ought to be', and had ordered that it should be reduced to a maximum of 600 as opportunity occurred. They did not, they declared 'intend to allow the present extension of the small House system to become per‑ manent', and they fixed a limit of three years beyond which small Houses might not be continued. David had done some‑ thing to obey the injunction, and handed over only 589 boys to his successor in September 1921. But there were still five small waiting‑Houses,[1] and pressure of entries was such that numbers almost at once began to rise again; by May 1923 they had reached 620 and during his last four years Vaughan never suc‑ ceeded in keeping them below that figure. There were only three ways of dealing with the situation—to raise the standard of entry to a point that would exclude a good many whom the School would normally have wished to accept and thereby to reduce numbers; to enlarge the existing Boarding Houses, which would have been a very costly, piecemeal operation; and to build a completely new House. It was this last alternative that was supported by the Headmaster, and by December 1922 it was being seriously considered by the Governing Body. A committee, composed of W. G. Michell, A. F. Buxton, W. B. Gair and the Headmaster, was set up to advise on the subject, and their first report, in July 1923, recommended the conver‑ sion of Hillbrow into a Boarding House and the building of new music‑rooms and classrooms adjoining the Speech Room to accommodate the musicians displaced from Hillbrow and to ease the existing pressure on teaching schools. The recommen‑

---

[1] A great objection to the small Houses was that, to run them, it was necessary to charge an extra fee of £12 a term for each boy in them. The Governing Body was anxious to get rid of this charge. They had considered abolishing it and increasing the entrance fee for all new boys by £6.

dation was accepted, as was a further recommendation that was to have its influence on the new House, that the only property above the hospital on the Barby Road still not in the School's possession—Miss Pennington's house and fields between Dickinson's (Bradley) House and Hillbrow—should be purchased. And so Southfield House and garden, and the two fields adjoining it, were acquired for something under £5000, and the danger of any of the land between the Barby Road and Caldecott's 'falling into unknown hands' was at an end.

The School was now entering another great period of building. Sir Charles Nicholson's war-memorial Chapel was complete and in use by 1922. It provides a marked, and to many people a pleasant, contrast to the main Chapel, though Dr. Nikolaus Pevsner regards it as 'very anaemic after Butterfield'. It is built entirely of stone, a cruciform building with arms of equal height, and 'the main feature of the design', in the words of its architect, 'is its extreme simplicity, it having been felt that a monumental character would be best attained by severity of treatment'. Nicholson was anxious that, as the primary object was to produce 'a monument rather than a utilitarian building', his treatment should be quite distinct from that of the main Chapel so that it should not be thought of as a mere addition to that building; though 'to preserve a certain amount of consistency, the architecture is of a Gothic character'. The length and breadth of the Chapel are both forty-six feet and the roof, rib-vaulted in the centre, tunnel-vaulted in the arms, rises to forty feet. The impression of dignified loftiness is increased by the fact that the four great windows, equal in size but varied in their tracery, spring from high up on the walls, above the reredos in the east, the tablets bearing the names of the fallen on the north and south, the ante-Chapel on the west, and reach to the vaulted ceiling. These windows are the work of Harry Grylls, and their main subjects are the Passion, Crucifixion, Resurrection and Ascension of Christ; and worked into some of the smaller panels are parts of the School buildings and a scene of a war-time field-communion in France. They provide the only positive colour in the Chapel, and when the evening sun shines through the rich glass of the West window, it touches the grey walls to a warmth which gives to the whole Chapel a haunting loveliness. The panels bearing the names of those who lost their lives in the First War are today on the northern wall and the eastern wall on either side of the sanctuary; the southern wall carries the names of those who fell in the Second War and a tablet on the west wall commemorates those who fell in Korea, Cyprus and Egypt in later years. An octagonal lectern, surmounted by a bronze figure of a soldier, by Esmond Burton, carries seven volumes of memorial books with biographies and portraits, and a war register of all Rugbeians who served in the First War. A smaller lectern, surmounted by a wooden figure of St. Michael, carved by E. F. G. Barraclough, carries a memorial book for those who fell in the Second War. These and all the equipment of the Chapel were gifts of relations of the fallen and friends of the School, and the Chapel itself was generously endowed for its upkeep by W. B. Gair, an Old Rugbeian and member of the Governing Body.

The first building of Vaughan's initiation was the new Music School. On 5 December 1923 Sir Charles Nicholson attended a meeting of the Governing Body to submit his plans for a building estimated to cost £10,500[1] and work rapidly got

---

[1] The estimate of the contractors, Wooldridge & Simpson, was £17,300.

under way. The site chosen, east of the Speech Room, involved the demolition of the 'Tin tabernacle', the old home of science and geography and by that time used as the Natural History Society's museum; the N.H.S. was moved 'temporarily' to Lawrence Sheriff House, north of New Big School, where it remains to this day. The new building, which came into use in 1926, besides the 'New Music Room', admirably suited for chamber music and VIth-form lectures, and the practice cubicles, contains the geography school and three ordinary teaching schools. But although the opening of this new accom-modation released the Hillbrow House, the purchase of the Southfield property had provided an even better site for the new Boarding House for which Vaughan continued to press, and in July 1926 the decision was made to erect an entirely new building on the smaller of the two fields recently acquired. But it was to be another two years before the work was put in hand.

Meanwhile other projects were under consideration. The first to be proceeded with was the new swimming-bath. By 1925 it had become clear that the old Jex-Blake bath could no longer do duty; apart from the fact that it was constantly in need of repair, it was very much too small for a School of over 600 boys. In February 1926 the Governing Body discussed the possibility of converting the existing bath to a larger open-air one and appealing to Old Rugbeians for subscriptions to this work. The technical difficulties of such a conversion were for-tunately recognised as too great and in July the decision was made to build an entirely new bath, twice the size of the old, on a new site; and John Coleridge was appointed architect. Early the following year the Governing Body agreed to provide the site—on the east of the Southfield garden—and £1000 towards the estimated cost of £9000, and an appeal to Old Rugbeians was launched. Fortunately they responded generously, for the actual contract price proved (as usual) a good deal more than the architect's estimate, and before the work was finished it had cost little short of £10,500. The result was certainly worth the cost and today's 'Tosh' must be one of the finest and most decorative swimming-pools possessed by any school. It was used for the first time on 28 May 1928. Approval had already, in February, been given to the conversion of the old bath for use as a miniature rifle-range to replace the one at Benn's.

Other projected developments were listed in order of priority by the Headmaster in a memorandum to the Governing Body in July 1927. They were: (i) the new Boarding House; (ii) a new sanatorium; (iii) a new Natural History Society's museum; (iv) a new art school; (v) a house for the medical officer; (vi) the conversion of Southfield House to make accommodation for two masters. This was an ambitious programme of capital expenditure, but the School was flourishing and no one could then foresee that only two years later an economic blizzard was to break over the world; and when a committee, which included W. B. Gair and Sir Maurice (later Lord) Hankey as well as the Headmaster, was set up to examine building needs, it supported Vaughan's proposals, and in February 1928 the programme was accepted in principle by the Governing Body.

Southfield House, the least important and costly, was in fact the first to be tackled, and by July 1928 it was in course of conversion at a cost of something over £2000. There Dr. Simey took up his abode for the last two years of his service as medical officer. For the new Boarding House Messrs. Forsyth & Maule were appointed as architects, and in February 1929 their plans were accepted for what is now Sheriff House, estimated to cost £45,000. Again it was an underestimate, partly owing to the fact that extras, such as steel window-casements, were added to the plans, and the lowest tender—which also carried the earliest completion date—was that of Foster & Dicksee for £48,103.[1] This was accepted, the work got under way and E. H. Johnson was appointed Housemaster in February 1930. He opened the new House in September 1930 with twenty boys, eight of whom he brought with him from his small House, and none of whom had been more than two terms in the School. The first Head of the House, R. D. G. Meek, was a fatherly figure of fourteen years old. For some time it was obviously impossible for the new House to take part in inter-House competitions, and on half-holidays they lived a life of their own. But both Vaughan and Johnson were convinced that to fill it up gra-dually was better than to give it a ready-made normal age-range by importation from other Houses, and events seemed to prove their wisdom; certainly they avoided some difficulties that were met when the other policy was adopted in restarting Houses after the Second World War.

The adoption of the name 'Sheriff' for the new House brought to the fore the question of permanent names for the other Board-ing Houses, which, up to this time, had been known by the names of their masters for the time being. There was a good deal of resistance among Old Rugbeians to any change in the system, but the advantages of a permanent nomenclature were clear, and with Governing Body support the permanent names were gradually adopted, beginning in 1931 when 'Cotton' was accepted for Evers's House and 'Tudor' for Megson's; but the

[1] It cost in the end £52,972 11s. 2d.

process was not complete until 1945 when J. R. A. Smith took over Harris's (H.J.H.) and it was renamed 'Bradley'.

By the time Sheriff House was opened, Vaughan was pressing vigorously for a start to be made on a new sanatorium. He had medical opinion powerfully behind him. There had been serious epidemics of influenza and measles, with severe complications, in 1922, which had shown up the disadvantages of the existing building. Apart from an old-fashioned design, it contained no suitable provision for extra nurses in times of pressure. Although the following year was one of remarkably good health, further epidemics in 1924 led Dr. Simey to submit to the Governing Body a very strong memorandum on the inadequacy of the existing arrangements. Vaughan's plan of letting 'The Firs' as a small House at a low rent, on the understanding that it could be commandeered on demand as a sanatorium overflow, was no more than a palliative. A very heavy epidemic of influenza came in the spring of 1925, when no fewer than 202 simultaneous cases were being treated; and an outbreak of scarlet fever in March 1929, which caused the School to break up twelve days early, after a year that had been a bad one for health, underlined the necessity for action. But it was some time before the Governing Body could decide between the alternatives of enlarging the existing building and creating a new one, and by 1930, when they had at last decided to build anew, the great depression was making capital expenditure progressively difficult.

Moverover, there had been unforeseen expenditure on a smaller but significant scale in other directions; the memorial chapel gave trouble; in 1924 there was a breakdown and near explosion of its new heating apparatus, and in 1929 serious

cracks appeared, owing, apparently, to flues let into the thick-
ness of the walls. In the Easter term of 1929 the organ of the
main Chapel broke down completely, and its repair was a major
operation. And the Speech Room organ had to be tuned down
a semitone—which cost £350 and necessitated a further expenditure of £100 on retuning the orchestral instruments to match it.
There was also the necessity of providing a filtration plant for
the new swimming-bath, which would cost about £1000, and
of adapting fields on the Barby Road for hockey and tennis—
about £750—on the move from Benn's farm, the last portion
of which was sold in 1929 for upwards of £11,000.

This last sale was to provide part of the funds for the purchase
of more land. Early in 1930 the Rokeby Estate and Higher
Rokeby, on the west of the Barby Road, were on the market
and it was virtually certain that some fields near Springhill
House and the Thornfield property east of the hospital would
soon be for sale. As it was quite certain that all this land would
be used for building if no action was taken by the School, the
Governing Body decided that it must at all costs be acquired.
The first three of the properties were bought for an aggregate
of £24,000, the operation being financed by a bank loan of
£28,000 to allow for the purchase of Thornfield when that
should become available. Some of the Governors were very
doubtful of the wisdom of such expenditure at such a time, but
today's open land to the south of Rugby surely justifies it, and
the Old Rugbeian Society was delighted; on their behalf
G. A. F. M. Chatwin addressed to Lord Kilbracken a letter
of congratulation on the purchase.

In the circumstances it is perhaps not surprising that the
Governing Body were hesitant to commit themselves to another

major operation in a new sanatorium, though they were being
strongly urged by Vaughan and Simey to do so. In July 1930
they went so far as to consider a specification, and in February
of the following year they debated the matter seriously. Sir Will
Spens argued that, even at that time of financial stringency, not
to build the sanatorium might affect entries—and numerous
entries were important to give a wide freedom of choice—and
might even affect numbers. He was supported by A. W.
Pickard-Cambridge, who thought that the financial position
of the School was strong; but there were others who favoured a
building on a smaller scale than the one projected, and some,
such as Sir Maurice Hankey, thought that the financial situation demanded delay. It is certainly true that there had been a
good deal of criticism from parents of the School's medical
arrangements. But it is a remarkable fact that, though there were
some withdrawals and the pressure of entries slackened a little,
the slump, which hit other schools, such as Clifton, so severely,
had no significant effect on the numbers at Rugby. In the
depression years 1929–32 the average numbers in any year were
never below 620, the lowest in any one term being 614 (summer
1930) and by the autumn of 1932 they topped 630. None the
less the Governing Body agreed to accept their Finance Committee's advice to proceed cautiously, and in July 1931 they
decided to get plans and estimates, but to incur no other expense
on a new sanatorium until the final liability on the swimming-
bath and Sheriff House had been discharged. After that, they
were prepared to borrow up to £40,000; and, at the Headmaster's suggestion, they decided to cut down the original plan
of a building with eighty beds to one with sixty. And so it was
left to Vaughan's successor to see the plan through.

Evidence that the Old Rugbeians were aware of how much was owed to the Headmaster for the material development of the School came in one of the *Vive-las*, written by 'Evoe' (E. G. V. Knox, S.H. 1895–1900) and sung at the O.R. dinner in 1930:

> Underneath his austere and benevolent rule,
> New rods and new acres are found for the School,
> New houses spring up in his prosperous path,
> And I think they should make him a Knight of the Bath.

There was a considerable turnover of masters in Vaughan's ten years. Twenty-six left, more than half of them during his first three years. There was a fairly widespread belief among the boys that this, in the words of one of their annalists, 'could be attributed to Mr. Vaughan's influence'; but though this may have been true in one or two cases, it was certainly not generally so. Of those who left, six were men of over thirty years' service— H. C. Bradby had been a master for thirty-seven years and B. B. Dickinson for thirty-six—and four more were men of many years' standing; some, for example A. H. Peppin, who had not been at Rugby so long, had spent long periods in other schools; five, for example E. E. A. Whitworth and H. N. P. Sloman, went to headmasterships, and four, including J. T. Christie and J. W. N. Smith, to university posts. There may have been some, with whose views he did not agree, whom Vaughan encouraged to apply for other posts, but he had, in fact, inherited a very fine staff. That many of them were senior men who would soon be due to retire and that others were of quality to move to posts of greater responsibility gave him the opportunity of creating a staff entirely to his own liking, and among his forty appointments there were a number of remarkable men. Twelve of them subsequently went on to headmasterships, at schools as widely divided as The Edinburgh Academy (R. C. Watt) and Lima (O. R. C. Prior) and as different in character as Westminster (J. T. Christie), Uppingham (Martin Lloyd), Nottingham High School (C. L. Reynolds) and Cargilfield (H. J. Kittermaster). This was the beginning of a process that later caused a Headmaster who did not come from Rugby[1] to refer to the Headmasters' Conference, rather caustically, as the 'Old Rugbeian Club'.

Of those who stayed and made Rugby their life, though it may be invidious to single out names, one must mention a few. There was Richard Broxton, a great teacher of mathematics, Housemaster in turn of Cotton and Tudor, who seemed to have found the secret of perpetual youth and who remained completely unchanged in appearance and energy until within a year of his death; and W. N. Hughes, who served for forty-one years, fifteen of them as Housemaster of Whitelaw, whose brilliant shafts of wit prompted his pupils to make two collections of his sayings, the second of which (the first, alas! is lost) is preserved in the Public Library of Rugby. There must have been something rather stimulating in sitting at the feet of a man who would greet a late-comer courteously with 'Doubtless you have missed your train', who would check a discourse, when two hands went up simultaneously, with 'One moment—there are two prophets sitting on Pisgah', or who might cry in exasperation: 'Get on, creature! Do not rest on your laurels; you haven't any!' And there was the occasion, one November, when he flung open a window to rebuke some urchins who

---

[1] A. M. Gamble, at the time Headmaster of Denstone.

were too loudly demanding 'a penny for the Guy' with: 'Go away! We're all papists here.' Then there was E. H. L. Jennings, who had won a First in both the Classical and the Modern Language Tripos and who had a more minutely detailed knowledge of certain periods of history than any of the 'professional' historians. No man was ever a more delightfully biased supporter and defender of his own House (Kilbracken), and his hobby of historical portraiture—his collection runs to over a quarter of a million reproductions—made him nationally famous in his own field. These—and there were many others— were 'characters' in the old style who could challenge comparison with the great ones of the past, and they give the lie to the suggestion that Vaughan was 'breeding a set of rabbits'. The staff, in so far as he created it, was one of most vigorous and diverse individuals.

The 1920s were unsettled years; the war had broken down some of the standards that had been accepted without question in earlier times, and there was a certain intellectual and moral unrest in the country, which inevitably found a reflection in all Public Schools. That Rugby suffered very little from this phenomenon must in large part have been due to the personality of the Headmaster. His directness of mind—which led him to accept what he regarded as good in the new ideas and approaches to life and to education and to shear mercilessly through the false, the sham and the shallow—made him exactly the right man at the right time for a school such as Rugby, which prided itself on a certain rugged individualism and independence of character. And his humour saved him from being pompous. 'The most wasted of days', he said, 'is that on which one has not laughed.' The boys he found not very different from their predecessors. One of his pencilled notes reads, 'Worst boy as bad as worst boy 60 years ago; best boy no better; average boy better and happier.' Certainly such written records as the Rugbeians of his years have left suggest that they were not so very different. They seem to have appreciated the same kind of humour. 'Mr. Hardwich', they recorded, in writing of a concert in the winter of 1923, 'sang two entirely unsuitable songs, and was encored.' The *Comet*, which had gone into eclipse for most of the war years and had been restarted in 1918, welcomed the new Headmaster carefully. 'Since our last issue another Pharaoh has sprung up. We can only hope it will not be a case of "He knew not Joseph" for we would always wish to be—His humble servant, the Comet.' Its contributors used the same targets for their humour and their satire—the Corps, the School clock, the (old) swimming-bath, the Natural History Society—to which were added any innovations of the post-war period that seemed suitable, such as the new tuck-shop or the intelligence tests which were given an experimental trial. In a poem entitled 'Sameness', written in 1930 by G. C. Allen for the *Comet*'s fiftieth number, we read:

> The generations still succeed
> Each other; and we all deflate
> Into O.R.s: and still the breed
> Remains unalterably great.

In case this may be thought to represent an intolerably Kiplingesque pride of breeding, let it be understood that it is taken clean out of its context, and that the 'Sameness' refers to seasons and routine, and not at all to individual uniformity. Those generations could hardly have been stereotyped which could throw up such diverse products as a Patrick Dean to be Ambassador to the United States, an Anthony Quayle to manage and act at Stratford's Royal Shakespeare Theatre, a Philip Toynbee to make his name as a literary critic, a J. M. Wood to promote ballet at Covent Garden, and a P. G. Rendall to be Headmaster of Achimota College. In every field of activity Rugbeians of Vaughan's period were and are to be found. There were artists, such as J. R. Beddington; politicians, such as A. E. U. Maude; journalists, such as A. G. Jeans (Deputy Chairman of the Press Association); playwrights, such as D. A. Parry; musicians, such as R. B. Ferry; paediatricians, such as J. P. M. Tizard; headmasters, such as T. E. B. Howarth (now High Master of St. Paul's), a Secretary to the Prime Minister, J. M. Addis; a professor of Classics at Chicago, J. G. Hawthorne; and a professor of Theology, J. P. Hickinbotham; and sport was well represented with J. M. Hodgson playing Rugby football for England for six years, Peter Kershaw as world rackets champion, A. A. Duncan as Army golf champion, and D. N. Stewart as a member of the team that won the horse jumping in the 1952 Olympics. There was, perhaps, a change in the type of career aimed at; fewer went into the Church or the Services, more made for openings of a newer type, such as the B.B.C., the British Council, or aircraft research (where the mathematician D. M. A. Leggett became Secretary of the Royal Aeronautical Society). Here was no stereotyping or dull uniformity, and if there was a 'sameness', perhaps it was in a habit of honest application to the job in hand that was insisted on and drilled into them by a very great Headmaster.

'There are just two kinds of Headmaster,' someone once said,

'Vaughan and all the others.' When he retired in July 1931 there was a deep awareness among all Rugbeians who had been under him that something great was passing; it was like the end of an epoch. And when a tragic accident at the Taj Mahal, while his powers were still undimmed, led to his death in November 1938, it was not only Rugby, but Britain and the world that were the poorer.

8

The Latest Age

PERCY HUGH BEVERLEY LYON, 1931–48

ARTHUR FREDERIC BROWNLOW FFORDE, 1948–57

WALTER HAMILTON, 1957–66

With the coming of Hugh Lyon we enter the region of contemporary history. Lord Acton once said that 'the living do not yield up their secrets with the candour of the dead', and if *de mortuis nil nisi bonum* is a sound maxim, perhaps, for the historian of a living institution such as a school, *de viventibus nil* would be an even sounder. At the time of writing, the latest three Headmasters are all, fortunately, vigorously alive, as are the majority of their staff and of their pupils, and what follows can be little more than a record of events.

P. H. B. Lyon had been a scholar of Rugby from 1907 to 1912, under James and David. He went as Exhibitioner to Oriel College, Oxford, but had got no farther than taking Classical Moderations when the war interrupted his studies. His service with the Durham Light Infantry was distinguished, and he returned to Oxford in 1919 with the Military Cross, after a time as prisoner of war, to win the Newdigate Prize and a First in Greats. Thereafter he taught at Cheltenham for five years and in 1926 was appointed Rector of The Edinburgh Academy. Thus, like his predecessor, he was not only an Old Rugbeian but also a layman and completely a schoolmaster. But these, and a single-minded concern for those for whom he was responsible, were perhaps the only ways in which he did resemble Vaughan, and the School entered a period of less authoritarian and, some would say, more humane direction.

Lyon came at a time of considerable difficulty, when the economic depression that had hit the world in 1929 was reaching its most severe point, and when the declining birth-rate at the end of the war might have been expected to have a damaging effect on entries. Although numbers at Rugby do not appear to have been seriously affected by these two factors, there was a good deal of concern felt by the Governing Body, who considered themselves bound to regard sympathetically requests for assistance from parents who had been hit by the slump and by the increased taxation that went with it. So serious did the situation become that a proposal was put forward early in 1932 for a 10 per cent. reduction[1] in salaries of the teaching staff; it did not, in fact, have to be put into effect, as from this time onward the economy of the country gradually improved, and with the improvement there came a slow upswing of numbers in the School, which reached 650 in the summer of 1935. But from 1938 the impending world catastrophe began to have its effect and in September 1939 the roll of the School was down to 603,

---

[1] A committee of masters had put forward a scheme for a graduated reduction, ranging from 5 per cent. to 10 per cent., but the Governing Body preferred a flat 10 per cent.

and of these eleven were absent for the term. The tide was not to turn again until the flood of victory began to flow at Stalingrad and El Alamein in the autumn of 1942.

The first major building operation with which Lyon was concerned was the new sanatorium. This, as has been seen, had already been decided on in principle, but such was the financial stringency that the decision had been made in August 1931 to go no farther for the time being than to secure plans and estimates and to wait until the final settlement for Sheriff House had been completed, in a year or eighteen months, before making a start on building. The addition, at such a time, of large and expensive items to the School's amenities was regarded with disfavour by some. 'The open air Bath', wrote B. B. Dickinson to Lyon in June 1931, was 'a good advertisement no doubt, but was it a good investment? The new palatial House ... If it be true that it cost £30,000, well!!! I rather fancy that you may find these a difficulty, and the proposed rebuilding of the Sanatorium on the site of the Firs will need your anxious care.' (One wonders what Dickinson's 'well!!!' would have become if he had been told that the figure he quoted for Sheriff House fell short of the fact by £22,000). But, though criticism was heard on all sides and even the Governing Body was not united in the policy, it was decided that the potential advantages of a new sanatorium were worth the risk, and in July 1932 H. W. Fairweather was retained as architect and six months later the tender of Foster & Dicksee for the work was accepted. This was for a gross figure of nearly £42,000, but, by charging certain items to special accounts (such as the Simey bequest), the cost to the Governing Body's funds was reduced by £5000. The new sanatorium was ready for use in 1934, and although the Prince of

Wales (later Duke of Windsor) refused an invitation to open it formally in June, he did pay an informal and much-appreciated visit to the School on 3 July. (The *Comet*, ever irreverent, printed the following note in its number of June 1934: 'The rumour that Herr Hitler refused an invitation to open the New San., but will be delighted to pay the School an unofficial visit in the near future, is discredited by our Berlin Correspondent.')

The building of the sanatorium aggravated the financial difficulties of the Governing Body, but they found themselves compelled to undertake two other pieces of capital expenditure. These were the purchase of Thornfield house and fields at the south-east corner of Caldecott's, for £8000, in February 1933, and the acquisition for £2400 (it had been decided to offer up to £100 an acre if necessary) of thirty-one acres bordering the Ashlawn Road, which completed the Governing Body's policy of acquiring land on both sides of the Barby Road as far as the crossroads. The use of the Thornfield property was complicated by the existence of a right-of-way across the field to the Barby Road, but the offer of a part of the fields to the Rugby Corporation for an extension to their recreation ground persuaded that body to extinguish the right, which in any case was very seldom used, and by the autumn of 1933 the ground had been levelled and Caldecott's, Hillbrow and Thornfield had become one L-shaped field.

The negotiations for the purchase of land, from the inception of the policy in David's time to its completion in Lyon's, had been the responsibility of C. F. Harris, Clerk to the Governing Body, who recorded their appreciation of his work in a minute of July 1934. He also saw the beginning, after the Rugby Statutes had been modified to allow the investment of Trust funds in real-estate, of the policy of house-purchase for the accommodation of masters. By the time he retired in 1949, he had been Clerk for fifty years; and he was the fifth in an unbroken father-to-son succession of Clerks to the Trustees and the Governing Body since 1740. There was a strong movement among Old Rugbeians to try to secure the appointment of a Rugbeian Clerk to succeed him, but the Governing Body considered that two centuries of unbroken service gave an overriding claim to Harris's firm, and it is a partner of that firm, Seabroke, Harris & Co., Mr. P. D. Bennett, who is the Clerk today.

The cost of the new sanatorium, of the conversion of 5 Barby Road (Bradley House), which exceeded £10,000, and of the property purchases left the School's financial affairs in such a delicate condition that it was decided in July 1934 to incur no further capital expenditure for the next five years. No minute of the Governing Body, however, could prevent the Headmaster from planning, and, but for the outbreak of war, Lyon's head-mastership would probably have proved the greatest period of School building since the days of Temple. As it was, quite a lot was done, as will be seen, and much more was projected. Meanwhile there were certain items of expenditure that could not be avoided. There was first the question of what was to be done with the old sanatorium, and it proved the answer to some of the criticisms made by F. B. Stead and F. R. G. Duckworth when they attended a meeting of the Governing Body on 8 November 1933 to report on the recent Ministry of Education inspection of the School. Their report was generally a very favourable one, but they felt that there should be much better accommodation for art in the School, and that, in view of the high fees paid by parents, forms should be smaller. As a result the Headmaster proposed, in February 1934, that the old building, 'though most unsightly', should not be demolished, but should be retained and converted for temporary schools until a new block could be built; and that the two large wards should be used as an art museum, leaving the first floor of the Temple Reading Room as an art school. This work was com/ pleted the following year at a cost of about £2500. At the same time alterations were made to the art master's house and to the medical officer's house, at a cost of over £1000 each. Other unexpected items of expense kept cropping up; in 1937 the Thornfield house was discovered to be so riddled with fungus and dry/rot that it had to be demolished; the Chapel organ again required extensive repair; new floors were needed at Stanley House and in the gymnasium; also it was becoming clear that Kilbracken House at 1 Hillmorton Road was really in need of rebuilding, and the question arose whether the existing building could be satisfactorily repaired or whether it would be better to build a completely new House somewhere else. By February 1938 the five/year pause in capital expenditure was nearing its end and a very extensive plan and time/table of new building was considered and largely approved by the Governing Body.

The plan included a classroom block of at least nine schools to be erected on the vacant ground between the old sana/ torium and the Barby Road; this would cost not less than £1000 per classroom, but was regarded as urgent and was to start in 1939. Next there was the building of the new Kil/ bracken—the decision was to build anew—on Hillbrow, at a cost of £30,000, which it was reckoned would take a year from

January 1939. In the same year there were to be extensions to the Music School (£4750) and to the Science Schools (£3750), the rebuilding of the study and library blocks of Whitelaw House (£3500), the provision of a new changing-room at 5 Barby Road (£3500), and extension of the dormitories and provision of better sickroom accommodation at School Field (no estimate made). For the future, to begin in 1940 or 1941, School House was to be provided with a new hall by the absorption of two schools on the south of the Old Quadrangle, there were to be wood- and metal-workshops built on the west of the Close near the gymnasium, extensions to the Temple Reading Room and the private side of School House, a modelling shed, and a groundsman's cottage on Thornfield. In view of the world situation it looks today an over-optimistic programme, but in November 1938, after the Munich agreement had seemed to presage greater security, it became even more ambitious, the estimate for the renovation of School Field being given at £9000 and those for the extensions to the Music School and the Science Schools increased to £6500 and £9500 respectively. And in February 1939 the Governing Body minuted that 'the present is without doubt a favourable time for building operations' and decided to continue with all the proposed schemes. But one piece of stark realism crept into the planning, when it was decided to include an 'A.R.P. basement shelter' with the Music School operation and a gas-proof shelter in the new Kilbracken.

This is very largely a list of things that never happened; of all the planning, only the new Kilbracken and the Bradley changing-room were completed before war put a stop to all building operations. But the very programme is significant of a positive and progressive policy of development and expansion, interrupted by the war and modified by the conditions that followed it, but never abandoned. The great developments that came in the post-war years, though differing in detail from the earlier planning, were in fact its logical consequence.

Although most of the planned operations had to be postponed, one most useful new building had cost the Governing Body nothing, since it was financed entirely by subscription; this was the James Pavilion, the site for which was approved in July 1935 and which was built to the design of A. L. N. Russell (O.R.) in 1936. It was first used in the cricketing season of 1937.

In spite of all the optimism there was clearly an uneasy feeling that grave danger was just round the corner. In February 1938 the question of the defence of the School against air attack was raised for the first time at a Governing Body meeting; in May of that year the Governors were sanctioning arrangements for shelters in houses and the protection of windows; and it was decided that the changing-rooms of the gymnasium and the James Pavilion might be used as decontamination centres. And, although the editors of the *Meteor* regretted, after the Munich agreement, that 'we shall not after all see the staff riding down to first lesson in their respirators', £116 had by that time been spent on sand-bags; in February 1939 the Governors instructed all Housemasters to make 'blast- and splinter-proof shelters' and to lay in supplies of non-perishable food; and by the summer 'A.R.P. trenches' were being dug and an extra charge of £1 a term was added to each boy's bill to cover the cost of these preparations.

One cannot leave the proceedings of the Governing Body in

these years before the Second World War without recording the grievous loss that was suffered in 1932 in the death of Lord Kilbracken, who must rank as one of the most faithful Rugbeians of all time. As J. A. Godley he had been in the School under Temple from 1862 to 1866, had been elected to the Governing Body in 1890 and had been its Chairman since 1903. During over forty years of service, he had never missed a meeting, except when he was ill, and more than any other man he had guided the policy of the School. To the very end he kept his detailed interest in its affairs—and his sense of humour. A letter from him was printed in the *Meteor* as late as 1 June 1932, in which he gave an appreciation of two Rugbeians who had recently died, J. A. Babington and J. M. Wilson, the last survivor of the masters who had taught him at School. 'I am now', he said, 'a "masterless man", a condition which, in the reign of Queen Elizabeth, would have qualified me for arrest and imprisonment.' With his passing it must have seemed to the Governing Body that an era had come to an end.

Rugby has, indeed, been fortunate in its twentiethcentury chairmen. Lord Kilbracken was succeeded by Sir Austen Chamberlain, who served until 1937, to be followed by William Temple, whose broad wisdom helped the School through the difficult years of the war until his death in 1944. Sir Will Spens, who succeeded him, exerted a direct and detailed control over School policy for fourteen years. On his retirement in June 1958 Lord Cilcennin was elected, and had already established himself as one of the very greatest chairmen at the time of his sudden and tragically early death in July 1960. Today the office is held by Lord Parker of Waddington, the first Old Rugbeian to become Lord Chief Justice.

If the planning for material development during Lyon's eight years before the war was in the direction of expansion and modernisation, developments in the internal running of the School were no less so. In 1933 there was a radical alteration in the curriculum, the main object of which was to give fewer periods of class work in the lower part of the School and more time to drawing, workshop and physical training; at the School Certificate level boys were to choose between French, German and science, and were to take five instead of six subjects in the Certificate examination. Forms of the Upper School below the VIth were to have two periods a week of physical training, all non-scientists were to take two lessons of general science, there was to be an option course in economics and geography and a special business course for those intending to enter commerce or industry. And in 1936, to the delight of all except the very earnest, the Headmaster abolished early school before breakfast, and a humorist celebrated the change with a jingle that is worthy of record:

> Let us hymn the Headmaster in suitable rhyme,
> Whose pupils are having a halcyon time.
> For 'We rise up too early', they cried in New Zion—
> So what could he say to them other than 'LYON'.[1]

A further indication of the liberalising tendency of the times came in the same year with the alteration of School dress from the old black coat uniform to a grey tweed worn with grey flannel trousers. This encouraged the Levée to renew a request that had been put forward from time to time in the past for the

---

[1] I am indebted to Mr. E. J. Harris, whose memory has preserved this rhyme. No written version of it appears to exist.

abolition of House caps; the request came up, always unani-
mously, again and again, but always it was vetoed by Housemasters, though the Headmaster told the Levée that their
efforts might have effect 'in time, like water dropping on a stone'.

The Levée at this time showed themselves a liberal body;
they were concerned to reduce the frequency of corporal punishment by the Sixth; they abolished 'fag calls'; they set up a committee on Sixth privileges, which recommended the abolition of
'all restrictions whose sole object is to stress the inequality which
is supposed to exist between older and younger boys', and
declared that in such matters as carrying books in any particular
fashion, carrying rolled umbrellas or doing up a specific number
of buttons 'any member of the School is free, within the limits
of good taste, to act as he pleases'. They even urged the Headmaster to limit the numbers of Sixths in Houses, since they
found the whole Sixth too numerous to be effective as a disciplinary body, and were so insistent in their demands that
Lyon noted curtly in their minute-book, 'The Headmaster will
not be bullied.' But they would brook no interference with the
self-governing traditions of the School in matters they considered their own concern. 'The assistance of masters' in out of
school activities, they minuted in January 1937, 'should be
given only when invited, and should be in a purely advisory
capacity. Within these limits assistance is welcomed.' In their
duty, for instance, of controlling such things as smoking and
drinking on expeditions, they thought that School rules in the
matter applied only in Rugby, and though they 'condemned
smoking altogether', they 'saw no harm in a little alcoholic
refreshment on such occasions'. This was in 1936; later on,
early in the war, discipline in the matter seems to have become

loose, and the Levée organised a 'round up of public houses'. In some matters they remained traditionalists, and were insistent that the custom should be preserved of the lesson-reader in Chapel wearing a white tie, even after the alteration in the clothing regulations. It lasted until the autumn of 1941, when white ties went into abeyance 'for the duration of the war'. The custom has never been revived.

One very sad casualty of these years was the *Comet,* which produced its last number in November 1934. In Lyon's first term it had paid him a tribute by reprinting a comic poem entitled 'A Ballad of Fleet Street', which he had himself con-tributed to the magazine in December 1913. Two years later, in November 1933, in producing the sixtieth number, the editors, R. C. C. Hunt and R. C. Symonds, had 'begged to remind the public that *The Comet* has survived fifty-nine numbers. This is remarkable because it is in no way official and does not owe its longevity to the fact that "it goes on the bill".' But, in spite of excellent cartoons and other drawings by P. F. Stewart and O. J. W. Hunkin, the later numbers became over-burdened with references to the peculiarities of the staff. Most of the references were innocuous, but cumulatively they created mild irritation, and when the editors, in an illustrated article entitled 'The Rugby–Melbourne Air Race', allowed their shafts to be directed against staff ladies, it was felt that the mark of propriety had been overstepped. The aeroplanes were all easily recognisable ladies and the pilots members of the staff. And so there passed the last of the regular private-enterprise magazines, and the *New Rugbeian,* under official control and with a guaranteed sale, was launched in 1935 and became the only literary magazine in the School. Occasional attempts have

been made to establish competitors to it, but modern printing
costs have always proved prohibitive; and although the con-
trollers of the *New Rugbeian* have tried to allow the maximum of
latitude in accepting material, comment in an official organ
has never felt quite the same as what was produced in the old,
independent journals. There remained for completely honest
expression of opinion on paper only the House annals, jealously
guarded from publication and even from prying eyes; not even
the *Comet* could have recorded of a lecture in February 1934, on
'Landscape Painters', that 'most of it was inaudible and the
whole thing rancid'. But comments were not always derogatory; the same volume of annals spoke two years later of a concert, at which K. A. Stubbs conducted the B.B.C. Midland
Orchestra in a broadcast of Brahms's Requiem Mass, as
'altogether admirable'.

The Second World War hit Rugby, as it hit most other
schools, much more severely than the First. By comparison with
many others—Clifton and Malvern, for example—which were
uprooted from their homes and had to make do with temporary accommodation and what, in peace-time, would have
been considered impossible conditions, or which stayed where
they were and suffered bombing from the air, Rugby was fortunate indeed. But the impact of war none the less created many
difficulties that had not before been encountered, and a good
deal of ingenuity was necessary on the part of the Governing
Body, the Headmaster, the staff and the boys themselves to
overcome them.

The first and immediate result of war was the drop in numbers
already referred to. From a terminal average strength of 627 in

1938, they shrank to 614 in 1939, 588 in 1940, 533 in 1941 and 499 in 1942—the lowest point touched since 1893. Thereafter, with the tide of war turning and increasing confidence in the country, they began rapidly to recover, and by the end of the war they had again passed the 600 mark. The reduction in numbers created immediate financial problems for the Govern⁄ing Body. With declining income there came also a rapid rise in expenses; the banks, which had advanced money for new building, demanded a higher rate of interest on their loans; masters on war service—there were already six by November 1939—had to have their service pay made up to the figure of their salaries; substitute masters had to be paid; boys were withdrawn without the statutory term's notice and it was difficult for prac⁄tical or moral reasons to demand a term's fee. And there was continuing expense on air⁄raid precautions—by May 1940 it had risen to well over £5000. Prices were already beginning to rise. By 1941 it was estimated that the fee income was down by £20,000 from the 1938 figure, and total income by £10,000, and expenditure had been reduced by only just over £6500. A year later the annual deficiency was stated as £6400.

To meet the situation the first and obvious course—and one in any case forced on the School by the increasing difficulty in obtaining labour and materials—was to put a stop to any build⁄ing operations not actually begun. Of the great pre⁄war schemes, only the Bradley changing⁄rooms and the unfinished Kil⁄bracken were continued; almost immediately after the com⁄pletion of the latter in April 1941 it was requisitioned by the Government, but its release was secured before the summer term opened. In 1940 it was arranged to lease the old Kil⁄bracken to the Copper Development Corporation, but the house was taken over by troops before the lease was signed. With little likelihood of a rapid improvement in numbers, in February 1941 the Governing Body sanctioned the policy of closing Houses; a few months later Cotton became a Ministry of Labour hostel, and at the end of that year Stanley became a reception hostel for women. Part of the old sanatorium had already been let to the Ministry of Supply.

A second measure of economy was a reduction of the salary bill, and in November 1940 an overall 10 per cent. reduction was held to be necessary. By this time thirteen masters were on war service, and it was hoped that, with the smaller numbers in the School, it might be unnecessary to replace all of them; some economy was achieved in this way, but early in 1942 a scheme had to be adopted for reduction of salaries on a scale ranging from $12\frac{1}{2}$ per cent. for those of over £900 to 5 per cent for those of under £700. At the same time an allowance of £20 was made for each dependent relative. Further economies were made in the cost of music, of the sanatorium and of science and suggestions were also put forward for central feeding, group heating of buildings and a school printing press, but these were deferred as being impracticable for the time being.

With very careful management and the exercise of stringent economy in all possible ways, the Governing Body got through the difficult period; but it was at a cost of leaving undone much work that should normally have been carried out, and when in the summer of 1944, with numbers up to 579, the accounts showed a surplus of nearly £5000, it was regarded as fictitious since it represented 'the enforced neglect of the buildings during war-time'. There were indeed, in the years which followed, very serious arrears to be made up.

These difficulties were naturally not apparent to boys in the School, for whom the first term of war seemed, apart from the difficulties of the black⁄out, to make very little difference. The early air⁄raid practices were a matter for joking rather than an inconvenience, and House suppers that December took place, though they were modified, with very few Old Rugbeians attending. The black⁄out did indeed cause difficulties as the days grew shorter, and the Levée had to make and enforce strictly rules for one⁄way pedestrian traffic on Barby Road and the Close to avoid collisions and confusion, particularly when boys were changing schools in the dark between afternoon lessons. After Christmas 'war conditions' began to multiply; snow came to complicate the situation, and persisted for the first half of the Easter term, and the only really serious epidemic during the war (influenza and German measles) kept the sana⁄ torium full and necessitated nursing in Houses. Rationing began that term. In June a company of the Local Defence Volunteers (L.D.V.), soon to be rechristened the 'Home Guard', was enrolled—it was to become a rival to the Corps. That summer of 1940, during the holidays, parties came back to Rugby to help farmers and to guard the Armoury. For the more senior boys there was less and less leisure; the Levée commented on the fact that they had too little and that juniors had too much, and needed direction. 'Between agriculture and A.R.P.,' wrote a House annalist in his comments on the sum⁄ mer term of 1940, 'between fire⁄squad practice, L.D.V. and armament work, this term can only be described as a muddle. . . . The Corps faded more and more into the background as L.D.V. advanced in numbers and importance, and time grew shorter and shorter for any other activities.' The situation arising from the collapse of the Western Front led to the abandonment of Speech Day, and—a much more cheerful development— owing to paper shortage, all examinations except the Certificates were cancelled. And then the sirens began to blow— though Rugby was never a target. 'Two hundred or so airraid warnings without a raid', recorded one who experienced them, 'made all organised activity a labour.' And, as 1940 dragged on towards a bitter winter, 'A concrete shelter floor is not the place to sleep a cold winter's night.' Though the nearest real attack was at Coventry and only a few stray bombs fell closer than miles away from the School, the Second War was coming closer to Rugbeians than ever the First had come.

But, in spite of all the disturbances, the academic standards of the School do not appear to have declined. During the six years of war 98 open awards were won at the Universities; and, even more remarkable, in the following four years, when, if ever, the results of inadequate teaching might have been expected to make themselves felt, there were 78 more, a record that compares honourably with those in peacetime. These satisfactory results must, in part at least, have been due to the fact that some of those who came temporarily on to the staff were men of high teaching distinction, such as F. C. Geary, Fellow of Corpus Christi College, Oxford, who took the Upper Bench, and Dr. B. L. Garrad, from the University of London, who for a few years was in charge of the English department. But, for the success to have the unbroken character that is evident, the teaching in the lower part of the School must also have been generally good, and a debt is owed not only to the hard core of regular masters, too old for military service, who carried on through the years of difficulty, but also to such shortterm tem poraries as the Jewish refugees Schulhof and Rosenberg, who were immediately and universally known in the School as Rosencrantz and Guildenstern.

One of the ways in which the Second World War differed, for Public School men, from the First was in the method of choosing officers. Where, between 1914 and 1918, any man from a Public School with an O.T.C. training would almost automatically be granted a commission, in the Second War he had, like anyone else, to pass through the sieve of a War Office Selection Board and prove his quality at an O.C.T.U. This was a natural and reasonable result of the development of democratic sentiment between the wars, one manifestation of which was a discussion that developed in the 1930s of the place which Public Schools should have in the national system of education.

The independent schools themselves were increasingly anxious for some change that would bring them closer to the grant⁄aided schools, and a few, like Clifton, which before the war began accepting six bursars from primary schools each year, made individual moves in that direction. Early in 1941, to facilitate inter⁄school consultation and co⁄operation, there was formed the Governing Bodies' Association, on which Rugby was represented by A. W. Pickard⁄Cambridge; and it was to some extent as a result of pressure from the Schools that the Fleming Committee was set up, which, in 1944, reported in favour of the acceptance by the Public Schools of a 25 per cent. entry from grant⁄aided schools.

This at once brought the whole question into the region of urgent and practical debate. The Headmaster of Rugby urged

the acceptance of the report in principle, since it was 'a coura-
geous and reasonable attempt to solve a problem that cries out
for solution', but the Governing Body was divided in opinion.
William Temple, now Archbishop of Canterbury and Chairman of the Governing Body, considering that many schools
would, in the future, need public support, was anxious that
Rugby should not dissociate itself from its weaker brethren, and
held that it should be prepared to sacrifice some preferences 'in
order to lend support to this whole type of school', provided
that a real independence could be maintained. Sir Will Spens,
in a memorandum circulated before the Governing Body met
to discuss the matter on 2 October, argued powerfully against
accepting the proposals, stating that Public Schools would 'be
failing in their duty to posterity and to the nation' if they accepted
the scheme. 'If we accept the Report', he said, 'the Public
Schools are doomed.' Lord Hankey came out as strongly
against acceptance on the grounds that Public Schools were the
only schools of leadership. 'Neither the nation, nor national
education, nor the Public Schools, nor Rugby, nor the majority
of the intended beneficiaries are likely to derive advantage from
the scheme. . . . On merits it ought to be rejected. . . . Acceptance is a policy of appeasement to an outcry of political origin.
Let us be under no illusions; this is the thin end of the wedge.'
But Pickard-Cambridge, himself a member of the Fleming
Committee, was able to answer some of the objections, and in
the end the Governing Body minuted that they 'would welcome
a scheme which secured the admission to Rugby School of a
substantial number of boys from grant-aided Primary Schools,
who intellectually or otherwise would be likely to benefit', but
wanted a great deal of clarification of the details of the proposals.

Later, in 1945, after a conference with the Eton authorities and discussions with the Ministry, they declared themselves to be in 'strong and growing sympathy with the objects of the Fleming Report', though they were still worried about the possible political attack on the fees that would be necessary to support state bursars at some schools. But nothing substantial was done; a few schools took a few boys from grant-aided schools; one of them was Rugby, which in 1953 began providing places for two boys annually from the Hertfordshire County Council; but the report as a whole was shelved and, although the Headmasters' Conference continued to put forward proposals that might lead to a closer integration of the Public Schools with the state system, it was not until the coming to power of the Labour Government in 1964 that the problem again assumed a character of immediacy, this time with the probability of more radical proposals.

Lyon's last few years were a time of slow recovery. It was not possible, owing to continuing shortages, to repair swiftly the results of war-time neglect of essential work on the buildings, but a beginning was made, and in 1946 the Headmaster submitted a comprehensive memorandum on the development of buildings when building operations should again become possible. Numbers continued to rise until, by the summer of 1947, they were again up to those of the peak period of the 1930s. In July 1946 there was a great reunion at the School of Old Rugbeians; there were many missing who might have been present, for losses in the war had been grievous, though numerically only a half of those suffered during the 1914–18 struggle. The meeting, like that after the First War, in a sense recognised the fact that the war was really over, and gradually the school settled down to peace-time conditions. The peculiar and sometimes colourful variety of costume, which the difficulties imposed by clothes-rationing had made it difficult to forbid, gave place to more regulated garments, though never again to uniform. The kilt, adopted during the war by some Scottish boys for Sunday wear, was allowed to continue.

But there is no doubt that the war and the disturbed condi-tions that followed it had a psychological effect on the School. There had probably never been at Rugby, certainly not during the twentieth century, any general tendency to accept authority just because it was authority—in a community of any intellectual quality, this is perhaps inevitable. But now, with the uncer-tainties of the world and the future, doubts were magnified. Shortly before the war, in November 1938, the *Meteor* had con-sidered the changes that had come about in the previous three-quarters of a century, and had declared that 'there yet remains in the sleek, civilised Rugbeian of today something of the solid worth and conscientious energy of his forefathers'. It is doubtful if the editors would have written that (even if they had not regarded it as rather smug) ten years later. Whatever doubts existed in 1938, Rugbeians of that day, for the most part, cer-tainly looked on their School as a sound institution and one to be proud of. Ten years later there was not the same certainty. The vast majority, certainly, still regarded Rugby with affection and recognised the high quality of its academic achievement; but the Fleming Report had given official voice to a growing feeling that Public Schools, in their existing form, had to some extent outlived the age to which they were relevant, and that, in the modern democratic world, they stood too much apart, little enclaves whose inhabitants were protected from the developing forces of the world around. Of their value as places of purely academic education not even their bitterest enemies had any doubts; of their suitability in the social conditions that were developing even some of their members were uncertain. Much of the uneasiness among the School population was not the result of conscious reasoning, and found its expression in an increasing irritation with the petty restrictions of School rules, the more irksome as the post-war generation matured more rapidly than their predecessors. There was a mounting desire, though not a formulated demand, for more freedom. And certainly less reverence was paid to institutions and traditions whose value seemed to rest on no claim but that of their antiquity. Change was in the air.

On Speech Day in June 1948 P. H. B. Lyon publicly wished his successor 'good f-fortune', and in September the School found itself once more under new management.

Sir Arthur fforde was something quite new in the history of Rugby School. He had been a boy in the School under David for the whole period of the First War (1914–19) and a Scholar of Trinity College, Oxford. Thereafter his only official connection with education had been as a member of the governing bodies of the Froebel Institute and of St. Mary's School, Calne. His experience had been legal and administrative, as a partner in the solicitors' firm of Linklaters & Paines, as a member of the Council of the Law Society, and, during the war, as Deputy Director-General in the Ministry of Supply and an Under-Secretary in the Treasury. The announcement by Sir Will Spens of his appointment to Rugby School was couched in terms that invited argument, suggesting that there was not to be found, in the academic profession, anyone with the type of experience needed to deal with the peculiar problems of the time. It caused a considerable stir, largely in the academic world, where it was felt as something of a slight on the teaching profession, and for a while there was a brisk newspaper corres/ pondence. A member of the Clifton College staff wrote to a friend at Rugby a verse beginning

> Oh, brother, let us now be ffranke

(the 'ff' was a gift to humorists), which, while accepting

> Dons from Pot/House, men from King's[1]

ended with the complaint

> But now we come to business men
> To teach us all our teaching gen.

But there was something to be said for the appointment of a man with the kind of business experience fforde had had by 1948, at a time when, against a background of material short/ ages and developing financial inflation, the School had to set about making good the inevitable aftermath of the war years, the repair and modernisation of buildings, the provision of housing for masters and other staff, the revision of salary scales and pensions and such/like problems, partly material, partly financial, and seldom wholly impersonal in an institution such as a school. The teaching staff was quite strong enough to keep up academic standards, even with a Headmaster who had no academic experience.

---

[1] B. L. Hallward, Headmaster of Clifton, was a Kingsman and a Fellow of Peterhouse.

In any case, fforde was not a 'business man'. As an under-graduate he had felt a vocation for teaching, which failure to secure a First in Greats had prevented him from fulfilling; for three years he had done evening work with London East End boys; he had a keener mind than most of his colleagues, was no mean literary scholar and linguist, and was a poet of some dis-tinction. Moreover he was humble enough to realise the dif-ficulties. 'I wake up at 5.0 a.m.', he wrote shortly after his appointment, 'contemplating vast abysses of ignorance'; and not long before his retirement he said that the most terrifying experience of his life, so far, had been that of teaching, as Head-master, the first lesson he had ever taught—Greek Testament to the classical Upper Bench, whose formidable scholarship he still found truly alarming, though the situation had been saved for him by their courtesy and helpfulness. And, if some of his methods and some of the things he did were unusual in a Head-master, and caused irritation sometimes to his older-fashioned colleagues and jerked them out of their comfortable ruts, this was, perhaps, in the long run, no bad thing.

fforde came to Rugby at a time of rapidly increasing expenses. Prices were rising and with them wages; before long it was going to be essential to increase staff salaries if men of the right calibre were to continue to be attracted to Rugby. The outlook in finance was not happy; by 1949 the deficiency was over £10,000, and the following year it had risen to £14,000 and radical action was going to be necessary to bring about a healthy situa-tion. This could be done in three ways, increase of fees, major measures of economy and a significant increase in the numbers in the School. And for capital expenditure it might be possible to launch an appeal. In the matter of numbers fforde was certainly successful; by 1952 the School passed the maximum figure of 675, which he had stipulated, and for his last two years the average was 703. The increased fee income made possible an improvement in the salary scale, which came into operation in 1949. Fees were raised by £15 a term to £105 in 1951, and again in 1954 and in 1956 until they stood at £411 a year.

One of the major items of increasing expenses was in fuel and the heating of school buildings, and in November 1949 it was decided to investigate the possibility of a 'district heating system'; early the following year a committee of the Governing Body was set up to consider the whole matter, and in June 1950 the decision was made to go ahead with a scheme estimated to cost £42,500. But inflation rapidly overtook the planners—by June 1951 the estimated cost had risen to £85,000—and although the scheme was persisted in for some time and some of the equipment was actually ordered, in 1953 it had to be finally abandoned. Prophets of doom had always said that it would never have worked, and there were many who were relieved that there was not, after all, to be the power-house on Caldecott's which had been planned. The appointment of a part-time engineer to advise on modernising the existing heating plant may, at the time, have seemed by comparison a very minor event, but it led to the gradual installation in all School buildings of the modern system of oil-fired central heating by which they are warmed today.

This was illustrative of a policy of expansion and modernisation, which, although the pre-war building programme could not, in the new circumstances, be carried out as originally planned, remained a cardinal point of the Governing Body's policy. The increase in numbers made it essential that more spacious accommodation should be provided in Boarding Houses; the policy of providing School accommodation for the staff demanded the purchase, conversion and even building of new properties; the increasing proportion of boys specialising in science and the rapid advances being made in that department necessitated enlargement, new equipment and modernisation in the Science Schools; the Chapel had received no radical atten﹣ tion during the century and its restoration was going to be a major operation. The expense of such a programme could clearly not be met from the School's existing resources, and in the autumn of 1952 a capital appeal was launched for £250,000, with J. C. Dunkin, who had been Bursar since 1927, in charge of the arrangements under an appeal committee. In the stated objects of the appeal the District Heating Scheme took a pro﹣ minent place, which proved, in the Headmaster's opinion, 'a positive deterrent to subscriptions', and when, after a year, a 'first progress report' was issued, a figure of only £82,000 had been reached in gifts and covenants. The priorities were there﹣ fore changed and the partial reconstruction of Boarding Houses took first place, followed by the renovation of Speech Room, the reroofing of the squash courts and repairs to the Temple Reading Room. Subscriptions still came in slowly until, towards the end of 1954, an anonymous gift of £50,000, the first charge on which was to be the redecoration of the Chapel, brought the total up to nearly £207,000, and two years later, with another very generous anonymous gift from an Old Rug﹣ beian, the target was reached. The results are to be seen in the new building at Stanley House, where K. G. Kellett's design won a Civic Trust Warwickshire award, at School Field, Cotton, Whitelaw and, most recently, Michell Houses, in the renovated big Chapel, in which S. E. Dykes Bower, surveyor of the fabric of Westminster Abbey, decided to out-do even Butterfield in colour, and in the improved and redecorated Speech Room. But these improvements were not completed until some time into the period of fforde's successor. A beginning was made too, during fforde's headmastership, to the great developments of more recent years in the Science Schools, with the provision—helped by a grant from the Industrial Fund—of two new teaching rooms, one of them with laboratory apparatus.

If the attention of the Governing Body was anxiously directed to the development of the School buildings, it was not to the neglect of the School estate. Here it was not merely a matter of getting back the grounds into reasonable condition, and reseeding those fields that had been given over to agriculture during the war. There was also the Town and Country Planning Act of 1947, with its provisions for the compulsory purchase of land for development, to cause anxiety. In November 1948 application was made for the classification of the Barby Road estate as 'essential ground for the operational purposes of the School'. This was accepted by the planning authorities the following year, and when, in 1951, the county development map was published, it left all School property 'uncoloured or marked as used for educational purposes', which the Governing Body regarded as 'a very satisfactory position'. David's green lung was, for the time being at any rate, to be preserved. One other rather alarming possibility existed—the driving of an East–West road across School property from the Barby Road to the Dunchurch Road. This, from the point of view of the general public, though not of the School, had a good deal to be said for it and would be much more difficult to resist than 'development' of

the School property. The scheme got as far as the planning
stage, but after official protests by the School to the planning
authorities and the Minister, it was, for the time, abandoned in
1952. It is, however, by no means a dead issue.

In all these difficult matters of administration and negotiation
Sir Arthur fforde had played a leading part. There had been
heaped on him a volume of business such as few previous
Headmasters had had to undertake; and it was to relieve him of
some of the internal work of the School, the mundane administration—time-table, allocation of work, the hundred petty
details on the efficient management of which the smooth
running of the School so largely depends—that the Governing
Body, at their June meeting in 1954, decided to appoint a
'Second Master'. There was precedent for this, but it lay as far
back as the headmastership of Thomas James (1778–94). A
dozen years of experience of A. J. Hunt in the post makes it
fairly certain that, this time, it has come to stay.

Within the School, where many of these matters of high
policy went unnoticed by the boys, academic standards
remained high. Another full-scale inspection by the Ministry
of Education took place in the autumn of 1951, and found the
School in a healthy condition, while making suggestions that
led to improvements in curriculum and organisation. The
physical health of the School, during these early years after the
war, seems to have been indifferent; there was a fairly widespread
incidence of minor complaints, though the increasing use of
antibiotics led to a progressive decrease in short stays in the
sanatorium, and, as time went on, there were increasingly
frequent periods when that building was occupied by only a few
accident and operation cases. In fact, only during the periodic

epidemics was it ever really full. One curious feature of the time was a remarkable increase in the number of injuries at Rugby football—420 in 1951 as against 183 in 1940. J. P. Sparks, who succeeded R. E. Smith as medical officer in 1950, suggested, in his 1951 report to the Governing Body, that conditions during and after the war had reduced boys' resistance to both infection and injury.

But it was not matters concerning their own health—except for disturbances caused by occasional widespread epidemics—or the high policy of the Governing Body that caught the attention and aroused the interest of boys in the School. Like their predecessors in every generation, they were struck principally by things, in almost infinite variety, that touched them personally— many of them small events and fundamentally unimportant— and which varied the day-to-day routine of School life. Town boys in particular had found excitement in their migration from their small abode on the Close to the more spacious accommodation in the old Kilbracken, a move which, in 1952, gave a new home, in the old Town House, to the Bursary, and released a room for use as an extra school in the Old Quadrangle. The School as a whole was amused and entertained when, in 1950, the Renown Pictures Corporation did much of their filming of *Tom Brown* at Rugby, and about a hundred boys were presented with top hats to give nineteenth-century verisimilitude to the scenes; many of them took part in an old-fashioned football match for the benefit of the cameramen. Later the Corporation completely redecorated Old Big School and provided it with new lighting; and the old Exhibition boards, which had covered its south wall, disappeared for ever. A similar excitement occurred six years later when B.B.C. television engineers descended on the School, and a half-hour's programme of Rugby School life, much of it 'live', was shown to the public. And there were occasional unforeseen excite-ments, as when, in 1955, careless and entirely illegal use of an electric soldering-iron caused a fire in School House which gutted two studies.

But these were no more than passing items of interest and excitement for the boys, as the war and its limitations and shortages slipped gradually out of their experience. The reign of Arthur fforde was a period of recovery, when the School was making good the losses and the neglect inevitable in the years of war and was gathering itself together for another great step for-ward. When he resigned the headmastership to become Chair-man of the B.B.C. in July 1957, its financial difficulties had been to some extent resolved, it was at a high level of academic success and its numbers were greater than ever before in its history.

With the coming of Walter Hamilton in September 1957 this survey of the history of Rugby School must come to an end. Unlike his predecessor, he had spent his whole life in education, as a Fellow of Trinity College, Cambridge,[1] assistant master and Master in College at Eton and Headmaster of Westminster. Not long after his arrival a doctorate was conferred on him by Durham University and, for the first time since the departure of Vaughan the 'Doctor's Wall' acquired a literal and not merely a traditional meaning.

[1] Hamilton is the first Cambridge man to be Headmaster of Rugby since the appointment of Henry Ingles in 1794. Of the 34 Headmasters, 25 have come from Oxford, 6 from Cambridge; of 3 there is no record.

During his time in office, the great building operations made possible by the appeal have been completed, and a progressive policy of expansion and modernisation has been pursued. Numbers in the School, in spite of some fluctuation, have risen and in September 1962 reached an unexpected peak of 771. This was too many—in the Headmaster's words, the figure 'pleased no one but the Bursar'—but that they could be accommodated is a proof of the success of the policy of material expansion, particularly as a disastrous fire at Tudor House demolished its dormitory accommodation a week before the boys returned for that crowded term.

But mere increase in size would be a poor criterion by which to judge the School; there has been much more. Under the direction of Walter Hamilton, Rugby has kept abreast of—in some respects led—the advances demanded by modern trends in education. If there has been no abandonment of old principles of discipline which over the years have been characteristic of the School, if there has been no falling away from the quality of classical scholarship so dear to the heart of David, if the humanities still hold their place, there has yet been, in the department of science, a truly remarkable development. Every boy, at some period of his school career, today studies science, and many who do not intend to pursue it later sit the 'ordinary level' Certificate examinations in the subject; the number specialising in scientific subjects has doubled since the war; and developments in the Science Schools have made possible courses that only a short time since would have been unimaginable, as in electronics and, most recently, in radio-activity—courses, moreover, that are practical as well as theoretical. Surely the spirits of Berdmore Compton and J. M. Wilson and those other pioneers who struggled, with pitifully inadequate resources, to overcome a great deadweight of prejudice and to establish despised studies, which they had the vision to see as a great subject of the future, must today be resting happily.

In a more general way, too, there has been a development of attitude and of outlook. Games are still played with vigour and enjoyment, and indeed are taken seriously, but they do not carry the overriding importance that they held half a century ago; this is perhaps merely the accentuation of a trend which has been evident since the 1920s, but certainly the 'games buck' cannot today expect to command respect merely because of his athletic competence. The disappearance of the compulsory character of the Corps, the development, instead, of a choice of 'Alternative Activities'—among which social service in the town of Rugby has its place—the organisation of arduous training, the interest in the Duke of Edinburgh's Award and in voluntary service overseas, all these indicate an outward-looking attitude that is in line with modern thought. But below and making possible all the changes of these later days there yet remains the rock-foundation of a tradition laid by former generations of boys and masters, by Arnold and Temple and Percival and those who followed them—a tradition difficult to lay hold of or define, but fundamentally demanding a habit of industry and of service, showing itself in varying ways at different times, but with a basic character which is unchanging.

Today, standing on the threshold of what must be an era of great developments, and looking back over the 120 years covered by this book, one can see that there have been very great changes at Rugby—changes of objective, changes of practice, changes of intention. Arnold's ideal, inherited by Tait and Goulburn,

Walter Hamilton

Bigside, 1861

was to produce 'Christian gentlemen'; by the time of Percival and James the aim was good citizens who would take the lead in the Church, the Services and the civil administration at home and in the Empire. Two world wars destroyed some of the old certainties and created a world of a new kind, and perhaps today's objective is to produce a habit of straight thinking and honest work in the service of the community, a habit which can be achieved as well by scientific and other modern studies as by the Classics, which provided the only pabulum of former generations. As Robert Birley wrote in 1958:

> The Public Schools are part of England's history. Anyone looking back on the changes in the life, the social structure and the education of the Public Schools during their long history is not likely to be afraid of the future. Institutions with a strong tradition know how to change—or they would not have survived—and yet to preserve that tradition intact.[1]

Rugby, more perhaps than any other school, developed in the nineteenth century a tradition of work and service which became a moulding force in British education. So long as that tradition stands in its integrity, the changes of the new era that is being ushered in need hold no terrors for the School.

[1] Preface to *The Public Schools . . . as published by Ackermann in 1816* (Traylen, Guildford; 1958).

A Century of Games*

At the head of the picture entitled 'Lawrence Sheriffe: Hys Dreame', drawn by A. Fellowes in 1862, there is a still-life design which includes a football, a cricket bat, a racket and a fives bat. For more than the first half of the period covered by this book the games symbolised by these objects, together with running and leaping, formed the principal athletic pursuits of the boys of Rugby School. Football and cricket reigned supreme, with running an honourable third.

When Tait became Headmaster in 1842, it was less than twenty years since William Webb Ellis had performed the feat that—if the tradition is true—initiated the game to which the School gave its name. The game played in those earlier days bore little resemblance to the Rugby football of today, but through all its phases and changes it retained its popularity. The very first issue of the *Meteor*, in 1867, reported that 'the old God of Football is not yet tottering on his throne, and will probably bear sway in all his pristine glory and vigour over the heads of all true Rugbeians at least as long as the three trees and the goal posts last'. The last of the 'three trees' fell in 1893, and new posts

* This section is based on research done and articles written (and largely incorporated) by D. J. Skipper (Rugby football), J. C. Marshall (cricket), M. F. Robins (running and athletics), J. Inglis (fives), Rev. J. A. M. MacDonogh (hockey), P. H. Gray (rackets), I. G. Miller (lawn tennis), T. C. Swinfen (swimming) and G. M. Helliwell (sailing).

(since replaced by an even grander set from Twickenham) were presented to signalise the Webb Ellis centenary match in 1923, but football holds its popularity still.

A century ago almost all Rugby football was played at Rugby School, since few outsiders were familiar with the game. Apart from the three great matches each football half, in which the VIth, the two Cock Houses and the Old Rugbeians played the School, there were regular Bigsides played each week, presided over by the Head of the School and the VIth. In these games only 'caps' were allowed to play; 'caps' were awarded by the Head of the School to those who had already been awarded their 'flannels'. By 1867 any member of the VIth was allowed to 'take his cap', but this right was a recent innovation, and, although there was no limit to the number of 'caps', rapid promotion was rare and was frowned upon; one Old Rugbeian spoke scornfully of 'a fellow who got his cap his second football half, and in his first match on Bigside completely lost his head and made the most awful mistake in the very heat of the crisis'.[1]

The rules were those drawn up by a Levée of Bigside in 1846, and fair play was judged by two umpires who 'it was hoped would be as tiger-eyed as they conveniently can'. Infringements were many, and, even when a fine of half a crown for each offence was levied, the offside rule was rarely obeyed.

There were not a few hazards. There were, in those days, no touch-lines and 'the chance of severely injuring the physiognomy in a long tight scrum against one of the three trees was considerable', and 'the gravel path by the white gate on the Barby Road was a very awkward place to fall upon'. Hacking, though

---

[1] This and other quotations in the section on Rugby football are from the *Meteor*.

officially forbidden by Dr. Temple, was still, in 1867, considered by many to be a virtue because 'it promoted running
scrummages which were the beauty of the game', and 'developed
the passive virtues by teaching those who play to keep their
temper sometimes under trying circumstances'.

The VIth match, early in the term, was the first great occasion;
on the last day of term the two Cock Houses—chosen first by a
Levée of Bigside, later by the Football Committee, on the
evidence of House matches—played the School. Old Rugbeians came down to play in both these games as well as in
their own match against the School. There was no limit to
numbers, and if the sides were equal it was purely by chance.
In 1896 seventy of the VIth defeated nineteen of the School by
39 points to nil. Later in the same term fifteen from the VIth
also defeated a XV chosen from the School. There were always
three backs and two half-backs on each side and the remainder
played as forwards. For the Old Rugbeian match of 1871
'fifty-seven caps followed up for the School while the old boys
played about ten more'. It struck a spectator on this occasion
that 'the School did not play on the ball with their usual energy
and determination, perhaps owing to the enormous scrummages
which 120 forwards necessarily entailed'.

These matches continued until, in 1900, a Masters' Meeting
decided to discontinue the VIth match. At this time, when the
Levée managed all games arrangements (including financial
ones), the decision was much criticised because it was felt that
such matters were not in the jurisdiction of the common-room.
In 1901 the Levée changed the Old Rugbeian fixture to a fifteen-
a-side match, but the Two Cock House match continued until
1940.

On four days in the term the School had to 'keep goal'. Three hundred boys were penned in an area ten yards by fifty, where they indulged in either a 'Littleside', gastronomy or tormenting the VIth. Until Dr. Temple's arrival this practice was compulsory at all Bigsides, but he limited it, and in 1871 it was abolished altogether. This produced a need for touch-lines, to confine the spectators rather than the players, for although the VIth, with their canes, were supposed to control the School, they still encroached upon the pitch, often preventing backs from running with the ball at all. Touch was changed as trees fell down or flagstaffs and the like were moved, until in 1897 the captain of football 'courageously cut down the ground to its proper dimensions'.

In these matches all 'caps' were expected to play, but it was complained that for ordinary Bigsides they rarely all appeared and the *Meteor* noted the danger that Bigside might suffer from 'an excess of devotion to House matches'. These were one of the three kinds of House games, the other two being 'Below caps' and 'Littlesides'. House matches were a knock-out competition between the best teams from each House, and have continued until the present day. 'Below caps' were later called 'Counting Belows', which was shortened to 'Countings'; normally they consisted of three competitions for three separate teams in each House, and all except Bigside players were eligible to take part in them. This competition, too, has continued annually. Little-sides were simply pick-up games organised by individual Houses. A fourth activity, known as 'puntabout', took place on Pontines, with balls supplied by the School. It was an event-ful pastime; in the early days the 'town louts' often comman-deered the balls until a groundsman appeared, when they made

off, sometimes taking a ball or two with them. The ground at
Pontines, in those days, is described as 'unpleasant to stand on,
a suppressed marshy odour lurked under one's nostrils and the
puntabout left a marshy deposit on one's hands'. Nevertheless
the ground was frequently used, and the discontinuance of
puntabout in the Easter term, because of expense, was bemoaned.

The first foreign match took place in 1867, when Temple
allowed twenty 'caps' to be chosen to oppose twenty men brought
down by A. C. Harrison. They were almost all Old Rugbeians, and gradually, as more clubs were founded by past
members of the School—including those of Richmond, Liverpool and Oxford and Cambridge universities—the number of
foreign matches increased. The *Meteor* of 1869 records that
'good Rugbeians, when they leave, go to Oxford. When they
get to Oxford they find no Rugby football. They hear of football of other schools, or, worse, they go and play an amalgamation game. All the intricacies and difficulties of real football are
swamped in a huge round ball.' (Yet even the *Meteor* saw some
merit in this amalgamation game, for in 1895 'an eczema plague
was stopped by playing it for one week'.) A meeting at Wad-
ham put the matter right at Oxford, and at Cambridge a
similar meeting in Trinity founded the C.U.R.F.C. Since this
time 158 Rugbeians have been awarded Blues.

Apart from one occasion at Cambridge when 'only nine men
appeared, so that single-wicket cricket was played' instead of
football, both the university clubs flourished, and were soon
proving too strong for the School. 'A' teams and college XVs,
however, provided excellent opposition; in fact, in 1876 Jex-
Blake (who was something of a snob) banned all foreign
matches except against sides from Oxford and Cambridge,

since he considered that other club sides were too old and that they contained non-Public School men. Later the ban was relaxed and a number of clubs were played until 1963, when all except the Rugby town fixture were replaced by grammar school matches. The town match has been played since 1895. Perhaps its most notable occasion was on the Close in 1932 when '3,000 people watched and the Mayor would have kicked off had he arrived in time'.

It was not until 1896 that the first foreign school match was played. Opponents of the idea, who 'thought such matches would never be practicable, or, if practicable, certainly not expedient', may well have detected the hand of God when, after the fixture had been arranged, scarlet fever struck the School and caused the postponement of the match for a term. The opponents were Cheltenham, and they defeated the School on the Close—a victory they repeated for the next three years. A second match, against Uppingham, was arranged in 1899, and until 1915 these were the only two foreign school fixtures. Even as late as 1945 there were only five such games. This contrasts with the fifteen played twenty years later.

As the game spread and foreign matches multiplied, indig-nant Old Rugbeians suggested many reasons to explain the comparative failure of their successors. Cheltenham were superior because they practised gymnastics, Clifton played four times a week, while at Wellington there was coaching arranged on a School instead of a House basis. In 1896 an Old Rugbeian wrote: 'There is no nursery for Bigside. If men are not coached until they reach Bigside, a good XV must be the result of mere chance.' Seventy years later a coaching pattern to meet all these points has at last been evolved. Gymnasium training, frequent

Bigside practices, and basic training for boys from the time
when they enter the School are now common practice. And
Young Guard teams at various ages began playing matches of
their own in 1932.

The increased attention to coaching has of necessity involved
masters. As early as 1900 two men were coaching the XV;
sixty years later fourteen are regularly involved and many more
referee the Countings, with a few boys, where in the earlier days
there were no umpires at all and later boys had sole charge. An
Old Guard team of masters can still be raised, though they do
not always defeat the XV as convincingly as their predecessors
in 1896. Yet, despite the interest taken by masters, the tradition
whereby the boys control the game is, as far as possible, jealously guarded. The Head of the School no longer takes the last
lesson off on Saturday morning to pay the groundsmen, as he
used to; but it is the captain of football who invites 'caps' to
'follow up' for the School and awards XVs, 'caps' and 'bags'
(which 'flannels' became in 1925). He organises Bigside training
and, with his secretaries, administers all games arrangements.
But certainly much has changed from the customs described
by a former member of the XV, who, visiting Rugby to meet
the newly appointed master in charge of football, remarked, on
crossing the Close with him, 'Are you allowed to walk here?
In my day it was the privilege of the XV.'

Few things remain as they were a century ago. All teams still
play in white or stripes, but the stripes are now always dark
blue, where once each House had its own colour (worn only
by 'caps'); from 1870 the XX, later the XV, played in blue,
white and red, colours chosen by the captain, deplored by
many, and changed to white in 1887. Velvet caps, the prototypes

of all caps worn by football clubs, are still in use—but no longer on the field of play. The shorts of today may not compare with the blue serge knickerbockers of 1879 that merited the descrip' tion 'a considerable decoration', nor are they decently fastened below the knee as in Percival's time, but they are still long enough to invite amused comment from touring sides training on the Close. Balls are still supplied by W. Gilbert, of the family who sup' plied them in 1867, but the annual bill now exceeds the £12 10s. of that day.[1] The ball, then, took the shape of the chosen pig's bladder, but standardisation became possible in 1870 with the invention of the rubber bladder and the hand pump.

Bigsides have always been played on the Close. In earlier days two other pitches existed on Reynolds' Field, behind Holy Trinity Church. They appear to have been unattractive to play on after cattle'fairs, but were good enough for the North *versus* South England trial game in 1874. Later the acquisition of Caldecott's and Benn's provided many more pitches, and today, with the land on the Barby Road, twenty'two are available— though this is said to be eleven fewer than in 1923.

Of the many great names of footballers few need be selected for mention. Poulton remains a legend. Of him W. J. A. Davies writes: 'For four years preceding the war no personality more completely dominated the Rugger world than Ronald Poulton. He was my ideal captain. His extraordinary, deceptive run and swerve made him a most difficult player to tackle. He pos' sessed abnormal football sense and was always there to carry on a movement.'[2] At Rugby he began his career by playing in his

[1] The service was shared by Mr. Jiggle of School Street, who supplied the balls, a new one for each half, for the centenary match of 1923.

[2] *Rugby Football* (Webster's, 1923).

first term for Town House, and ended in the School XVs of 1905, 1906 and 1907. He played for England from 1909 to 1914 and was killed in the First World War. Adrian Stoop was in the XV of 1900, the year when the Webb Ellis tablet was placed on the Doctor's Wall and when Cheltenham were defeated 29–8 and Uppingham 59–0. V. H. Cartwright, the England skipper in 1905–6, who also refereed the centenary game in 1923, was his captain. *The History of the Rugby Football Union*[1] records that Stoop had a polished technique and ideas that made themselves felt. With the Harlequins he revolutionised modern football and changed the tactics of the game completely. Altogether seventy-six Old Rugbeians have won international caps on the football field.

The game Rugby gave to the world has changed in the course of a century almost beyond recognition. From a sort of tribal warfare it has developed into a sophisticated, tactical, fifteen-a-side game. Conservatives of each generation deplored the changes as they came; those who believed that 'football was meant for internal use within the limits of the School' distrusted the institution of foreign matches. These might do for cricket, but 'you could not compare the deep interest with which the community throbbed during some of the tragic struggles for Cock House with anything in the summer term'. They found the limiting of numbers first to a XX, then to a XV, and the divorcing of the Head of the School and the VIth from football duties, individual disasters. But others appreciated the changes. 'One hour, ten minutes of misery, with scrummages going on for fifteen or twenty minutes at a time—quite unsuited to the children of luxury recruited now.' So wrote a correspondent of

[1] By O. L. Owen (Playfair Books, 1955).

the *Meteor*. 'Weight', he went on, 'is no longer the greatest asset. Activity, pace and mind are now required. . . . No longer do the purely muscular and ponderous rise to the top of the tree as forwards.' There has been no lessening of the enthusiasm or the excitement of House matches, but Rugby football, as played today within the School, is played as a game to be enjoyed.

Cricket was a very much older game than Rugby football and must have been well established by the time Webb Ellis made his famous run. The season, for the School, was a longer one a century ago than it is today. 'On account of the weather', runs the first sentence of the first cricket report of the first issue of the *Meteor* in 1867, 'no cricket was played until Thursday, March 28th', and that same year the XXII played a match against Burton-on-Trent on 30 August. The XI had eleven foreign matches. Marlborough were played and beaten, at the Oval, in June. Three Oxford colleges, Corpus Christi, Trinity and University sent sides to Rugby, the last having a difficult return journey as the L.N.W.R. refused to stop the train at Bletchley. 'We cannot imagine what has come over the L. & N.W. as they are always so ready to oblige anyone,' writes the *Meteor*. Matches were also played against M.C.C. (at Lord's), Butterflies, Rugby C.C., and, on a tour after the end of term, Tooting, the Civil Service, and the Free Foresters. The 1867 XI won only three of these games, but contained five future Blues. B. Pauncefote, who played four years for Oxford; W. Yardley, the first Cambridge man to score a century in the Varsity match; A. A. Bourne, F. Tobin and C. K. Francis, who in 1869 achieved bowling figures at Lord's against Marl-borough that are never likely to be bettered—7 for 25 and 10 for 15! Arnold's (School Field) were Cock House in 1867, but it was Wilson's (Whitelaw) who were to dominate House cricket at this time and emerge as Cock House in each of the next six summers.

It was not until 1873 that the Marlborough match was played at the end of the term. Before this, to give the boys at the two schools a chance to watch the match, the 1868 match was played at Rugby and in 1870 at Marlborough. The 1868 and 1869 Rugby XIs were particularly strong; in 1868 the *Meteor* reporting the Tooting match wrote: 'Notwithstanding the Tooting team was a very formidable one, the School succeeded in beating them by no less than 214 runs'—Yardley scored 150 not out; while in 1869, after Marlborough had been destroyed by Francis, the editor of the *Meteor* said: 'It was not a disgrace to be beaten, when we could bring into the field an eleven which had done such great deeds throughout the year and had almost, if that were possible, eclipsed its predecessors.' One of these 'great deeds' was the defeat by one wicket of B.N.C., who included six members of the Oxford side in their team. But, of course, the wheel soon turned and Marlborough won in 1871 and 1872. After the first of these defeats all that a disgustingly condescending *Meteor* editor could bring himself to write was, 'Every dog has his day.'

Cricket, unlike football, was not a compulsory game in the 1870s—chiefly because of the shortage of grounds—but many demands were made for 'fagging' (fielding) by small boys for older ones at the ends. It was not until 1871 that 'leg nets' were introduced for the 'out ends', thus enabling a batsman in these ends to bat with more confidence and 'not live in perpetual dread of a hard leg-hit from his neighbour'. In 1872 Dr. Hayman gave £5 for bowling prizes 'to induce fellows to cultivate more that branch of cricket'. The editor of the *Meteor* gives this advice to budding bowlers: 'First obtain straightness and then go in for a little headwork,' and goes on to yearn for 'fellows to cultivate good slow under-hand bowling'. But complaints were made about boys who were 'too lazy even to handle a bat, least of all after dinner, watching with eagerness the play of the more active and weakening their growth in the art by premature flattery'.

In 1874 the XI beat both Marlborough and the M.C.C. at Lord's—a rare feat this—but in 1876 a hitherto-unbeaten side, captained by E. T. Hirst, who played three years for Oxford, were surprisingly beaten by Marlborough, a defeat that was repeated in the following year when A. G. Steel made 128 and took 12 wickets for Marlborough.

In 1878 when there was no resident professional at Rugby— Diver, who had been twenty years at Rugby, had died in 1876— loud demands were made for the appointment of one. 'Some O.R.' was urged 'to send a good one down'. Despite this and stern criticisms of the XI's bowling and fielding, Marlborough were beaten by an innings—C. F. H. Leslie, who was to tour Australia with M.C.C. in 1882–3 and play in four Test Matches, scoring 98. Leslie dominated the School cricket for the next two years, scoring 661 (av. 55·08) in 1880, when the XI was very strong.

Despite these good results, criticism of the organisation of cricket in the School was rife in the 1880s. The coaching was considered so bad and the opportunities for play so scarce that it was considered impossible for a boy to learn the game if he had not been well coached before coming to Rugby. In 1881 a correspondent to the *Meteor* believed that 'one or two masters would be found willing to play the part of cricket mentors to the School', a far cry from the 1960s, when masters run all School games in conjunction with the captain of the XI and as many as nine or ten masters may be seen coaching at the nets on the Close on a whole schoolday evening. The state of Reynolds' Field, the only other cricket field apart from the Close, was an almost annual cause for complaint; in 1881 it was suggested that the School seemed to be trying to make money from the hay crop in this field.

Lawn tennis, first introduced in 1877, 'particularly for the loafer', is blamed for the poor play of the 1881 XI, whose play was 'quite spoiled' because they did not practise, but spent their time playing tennis. In 1883 members of the XI and XXII were forbidden to play tennis. Many complaints about the standard of umpiring in House matches show that little has changed in at least one department of Rugby cricket in the last eighty years. In 1882 the Old Guard played the XI for the first time.

Between 1882 and 1893 Rugby beat Marlborough only once. In 1883 H. H. Castens, who later played for South Africa, is described as 'an admirable, energetic captain'. Rugby followed on at Lord's and set Marlborough 178 runs to win in less than two hours, a target that was regarded as 'impossible' and which was not reached. Brown was appointed as full-time professional in 1883 and hopes for the 1884 XI seemed brighter, but they were not lucky at Lord's. Marlborough batted and made 130. Soon after three o'clock Rugby batted, but by 4 p.m. 'there was a regular London fog'. The fog was so thick that 'the wickets could only be dimly descried from the pavilion'. Rugby were bowled out for 49 and, following-on (it was compulsorily enforced and 80 was the limit in those days), lost four wickets the same evening. It was in 1884 that H. W. Bolton put forward the idea of a permanent memorial to C. M. Caldecott, who for many years had shown great interest in all School activities, but particularly cricket. This led to the purchase of some land 'occupied by Mr. Cross as a Nursery garden' and the opening of 'Caldecott's piece' in 1885. In his original letter H. W. Bolton said: 'Cricket at Rugby is not flourishing as it was, partly because more time is devoted to work than used to be, but still more on account of the many other attractions that have sprung up, notably Lawn Tennis, but also Gymnasium, the Baths, Bicycle, Rifle Corps and N.H.S.'; words, with one or two amendments, that could so easily have been written eighty years later. The 1885 XI were not very successful, but the captain, E. H. F. Bradby, scored 764 runs in 11 innings, including a fine 170 against Marlborough. It was the much-criticised 1886 side that won at Lord's, H. Bowden Smith scoring 95, batting at no. 7, in a low-scoring match. The 1887 XI did well, except at Lord's. A second school match (it did not become a regular fixture until 1909) was played for the first time, against Clifton, to celebrate the Queen's Jubilee. Rugby won by 8 wickets and H. C. Bradby, who scored 122 not out, was carried in triumph to the pavilion. In 1889, when a 'useful all-round cricketer' called P. F. Warner first played for the XI, Rugby played Harrow Past and Present at Althorp Park. F. S. Jackson (their 1889 captain) and A. C. McLaren were in the Harrow side, so three future England captains played in the match. It was in 1889, too, that Tom Emmett came to Rugby as profes-sional, a master hand to mould the XI.

Sir Pelham Warner, captain of Middlesex and England, President of M.C.C., Rugby's greatest cricketer, did not have an outstanding record as a schoolboy player. He scored 177 against the Free Foresters at the age of sixteen in 1890, when he scored 530 runs. In 1891 he was never able to do himself justice as he suffered from a 'severe strain'. He was captain in 1892; the month of May was very dry—'pitches have reached a climax of bumpiness'—and the XI was not very successful. Tom Emmett was invited to write a few lines in the *Meteor* on cricket at Rugby School. He speaks of the fine fielding against Balliol, but 'the batting was too much of the milk and water style, with an abundant scarcity of the milk. Mr. Warner, of course, was the exception . . .' Marlborough scored 490 at Lord's and won by an innings, Warner making 1 and 0. This heavy defeat at Lord's led to much heart-searching—'The School in general do not show the same enthusiasm as other schools do' and 'the discouragement of other pursuits has produced wrong results' (perhaps not surprisingly!). 'Bulldog', writing to the *Meteor*, said that Rugby games were bad because the boys were made to work too hard!

In 1893 the Young Guard came into being and received its own professional, Wall, in the following year when Marlborough were at last beaten again. J. Stanning (152 not out) and C. P. Nickalls (109) put on 207 for the second wicket in an hour and three-quarters and Rugby's total of 398 was scored in under two and a half hours. Another fine match, between two good sides, was played at Lord's in 1895, Rugby winning after being bowled out for 41 and following-on. Nickalls made 97 and then W. F. Gowers, the Rugby captain, took 6 for 30, bowling Rugby to a remarkable 70-run win. Another very

'Football at Rugby', 1871

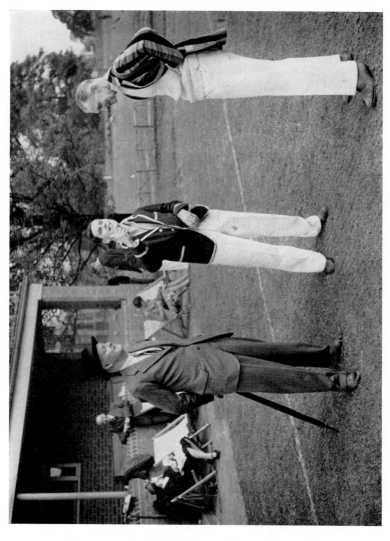

*Sir Pelham ('Plum') Warner, J. A. Boyes, and R. S. Rait-Kerr (Secretary of the M.C.C.)
tossing up at the M.C.C. Centenary Match, 1942. P. H. B. Lyon in the background*

good Rugbeian cricketer in the 1895 side was E. R. Wilson, described by Wisden as 'one of the best amateur slow bowlers of his time'. Cambridge, Yorkshire and England (in Australia in 1920, when he was over forty) all benefited from his skill, as did many generations of Wykehamists.

In 1896 time alone saved the XI from defeat at the hands of Haverford College, U.S.A., whose fielding is described as 'very flashy and showy but not sound', but Marlborough were beaten by an innings, Wilson taking 6 for 19 in their second innings. The 1897 XI looks, to a very distant observer, one of the best, even though it just lost at Lord's. Wilson opened with 206 not out against New College, and Uppingham (another Jubilee match), who had not lost a school match for ten years, were beaten despite the absence of Wilson from the Rugby side. H. V. Spencer, who took 95 wickets in 1896 and 1897, was unfit to bowl in the second innings at Lord's. The next two Lord's matches were dominated by the Marlburian R. H. Spooner, but in 1900 E. W. Dillon, who scored 620 runs and took 33 wickets and then played for Kent in the holidays, played a fine innings of 110 not out to gain victory for Rugby against the clock. After the 1900 match Rugby's lead over Marlborough after 41 matches was 10; before the 1966 match this lead is 11 after 106 matches.

V. H. Cartwright, the 1901 captain, scored 549 runs in a dry summer of bad wickets. 1902 was wet, but there were 'plenty of halves on Mondays' as 'peace came on exactly the right day'. The XI were not successful, but won at Lord's where A. O. Snowden, a slow left-hand bowler, took 6 for 56 in Marlborough's second innings. Snowden captained a good side in 1903, which won a moral victory in a one-day match in the Nursery at Lord's, the main ground still being unplayable after heavy rain. The *Meteor* describes 'the futility of the M.C.C. arrangements under these novel conditions' as 'amusing'. For example, the score was posted on the main scoreboard, which was practically invisible from the Nursery. 'It is hard to believe', the *Meteor* concludes, 'that the M.C.C. is not a government department.' D. Watson, a very good all-round cricketer, first appeared in 1905 and took 5 for 60 in another rain-ruined game at Lord's. In 1906 W. R. Cuttell became the senior professional and soon won the reputation of being a fine teacher of the game. Watson played a big part in Rugby's win by 227 runs as did C. L. Cole, a fast bowler, who took 7 for 27 in Marlborough's second innings. The bowling averages this year were headed by Rupert Brooke, who was described as being 'a slow bowler who at times kept a good length and puzzled the batsmen'. The 1907 side did little except win the fiftieth match against Marlborough. Watson averaged 71·4 in his six innings at Lord's and in this side, too, was R. W. Poulton, who was to win such great fame on the football field; he is described as a fine fielder and 'a vigorous batsman with a partiality for the leg side'.

In 1909, on the day that Edward VII opened Speech Room, P. S. Fraser, who had already scored 143 not out against Trinity, Oxford, made 134 against M.C.C. A second school match, against Clifton, was introduced; a high-scoring draw was played in 1909. This was a successful Rugby side, but it lost at Lord's, where R. S. Rait-Kerr, who was to be Secretary of M.C.C. from 1936 to 1952, scored 51. In 1910 nine of the XI averaged more than 20 with the bat. The Clifton match ended in a tie, Rugby losing its last five second innings wickets for 22 runs. Marlborough, 'the best school side of the year', were overwhelmed at Lord's—'the triumph of the Improbability', as the editor of the *Meteor* put it. P. W. le Gros took 9 for 49 in the Marlborough second innings and caught the tenth batsman.

Writing about Rugby cricket at this time, R. A. Boddington, who played for the XI in 1910–11 and later for Lancashire and is now (1966) President of the Rugby Meteors C.C., recollects that 'the Bigside pitches were very good and true, though not very fast'—as they are in the 1960s—and that in those days all the XI wore a white blazer with light-blue edging at Lord's, although boys in their second year in the side had worn the dark-blue blazer with light-blue edging before Lord's.

In 1911 Rugby, not for the first time nor by any means the last, collapsed on the first morning at Lord's (17 for 4), but recovered to win by five wickets. The 1912 XI lost both its school matches, but beat Liverpool C.C., who used to make a tour of schools during Whit week, by one run by means of a throw that hit the wicket. The 1913 side was a good one, although its captain, A. de Selincourt, was fit enough to play only one innings. C. P. Johnstone led the side to an innings victory over Clifton and a win by ten wickets at Lord's where the Rugby fielding was excellent; J. L. Bryan, who was outstanding at cover, scored 118 and, like Johnstone, later played for Cambridge and Kent. Bryan also went to Australia with the M.C.C. in 1924–5, but did not play in a Test Match. Although Marlborough were beaten again in 1914, Speech Day had to be cancelled because of 'pestilence' (mumps) and the XI lost at Clifton on a wicket described as 'very lumpy'.

In the four summers of the First World War Rugby won ten out of eleven school matches, and two of these, against Clifton in 1915 and Marlborough in 1916, must rank amongst the finest played with these schools. Rugby, following on 245 behind Clifton in 1915, scored 418, of which C. G. Boddington made 249 (the highest score ever made by a Rugbeian in a match) and then bowled out Clifton for 121. At Marlborough in 1916 Rugby won by 8 runs after 1238 runs had been scored in the two days. M. D. Lyon, a wicket-keeper and hard-hitting batsman, who later played for Cambridge and Somerset, was captain in 1916 and was responsible for making 'games throughout the school more efficient and interesting'. Again there was no Speech Day in 1916—for fear of Zeppelin raids—and Malvern were played and beaten by four wickets. Two good all-rounders, C. D. McCarthy, whose leg-breaks had proved decisive at Marlborough the year before, and G. A. Rotherham, yet another Cambridge Blue, dominated the 1917 season. Malvern, Uppingham and Marlborough were beaten, but no game was played against Clifton. Malvern and Uppingham were again beaten in 1918, but Rugby's fine run of success in school matches ended when Marlborough won at Lord's by an innings. In a game against the Machine Gun Corps from Grantham, Major the Hon. L. H. Tennyson scored 159 and hit one ball 'over the top of the tallest elm'.

In the 1917 and 1918 XIs was B. H. Lyon. He headed the batting averages in 1918, but as he left school at the age of sixteen and a half to go into business for two years before going to Oxford, he did not make a great mark in school cricket. Later he captained Gloucestershire with great distinction. One imagines that he is the last Rugbeian to appear amongst Wisden's 'Five Cricketers of the Year', an honour he achieved in 1931 in company with a young Australian, D. G. Bradman.

1917 marks the half-way point between 1867 and 1967, and it is tempting to select a 'best' XI from the cricketers for these fifty years; tempting but also dangerous, for if there can be little argument about the inclusion of perhaps six of the following names, the last five may well have been the lucky ones out of about twenty or thirty. In chronological order (the captain apart) one might select:

P. F. Warner (W. 1892) captain, B. Pauncefote (S.F. 1867), W. Yardley (B. 1868), C. K. Francis (W. 1869), E. T. Hirst (C. 1876), C. F. H. Leslie (K. 1880), E. R. Wilson (M. 1897), E. W. Dillon (W. 1900), J. L. Bryan (Tu. 1914), M. D. Lyon (S.H. 1916), G. A. Rotherham (S.H. 1917).[1]

The 1919 XI beat Clifton but lost a match at Lord's, which caused a correspondent to the *Meteor*, who signed himself 'XI 1888', to be severely critical of both the 'dirty' Rugby shirts and the 'disgraceful' Rugby fielding. Liverpool scored 529 for 7 dec. this year, the School bowling 'not being all that could be desired or expected'. Liverpool won by an innings. 1920 was an unlucky year: it was wet, there was an influenza epidemic at Rugby, which caused the cancellation of the Clifton match, while at Lord's, after much rain, Rugby, set only 23 to win, finished 9 short as there was time for only one over to be bowled. 1921 was J. G. Pugh's year. He scored 1034 runs, an aggregate that was to remain a record for thirty-nine years. Strangely, Pugh scored less than 400 runs in the following year and totalled barely 1500 in his three years in the XI. At Lord's in 1921 Rugby were set 236 to win in just over two hours and were castigated by the newspapers for not making a better effort to get them. Two poor years followed, Marlborough twice

[1] The date in each case is that of the player's last summer term in the school.

winning by ten wickets. H. C. Pattisson, in his second year of captaincy, led an unbeaten side in 1924. E. F. Longrigg won a close and low-scoring match at Lord's with an innings of 77 not out, and D. S. Milford took 57 wickets in the season. Longrigg scored 840 runs in 1925, including 90 and 89 at Lord's, where the last Marlborough pair survived for half an hour. 1926 was Cuttell's last year as professional, a season of close and mainly adverse finishes, and a big win at Lord's, where H. L. Leedham-Green, a leg spinner, took 15 wickets for 135 runs in the match. Wisden describes the 1927 XI as 'a vigorous side' with a good opening pair of batsmen in J. M. Monkhouse and J. E. G. Pearson; Pearson was also the leading bowler. In 1928 G. V. F. Dawson, in the opinion of H. T. H. Snowden 'probably the fastest bowler produced by Rugby' between 1900 and 1950, took 53 wickets at 11·9 each. Tragically Dawson died very shortly after leaving school.

Three rather moderate years followed, but an improvement came in 1932 in K. L. T. Jackson's second year of captaincy. Eight Marlburians had been dismissed for 36 when rain prevented any further play at Lord's. Jackson took 91 wickets in his four years in the XI and played for Oxford in 1934. J. A. Gemmill, the 1933 captain, took 33 wickets in the season, and led a strongish batting side—seven members of it averaged 20 or more—to victory at Lord's.

Repton were played for the first time in 1934 and won by 3 wickets (it was not until 1944 that Rugby was to beat Repton). M. M. Walford, later to have a distinguished career for Oxford and Somerset, was the captain of this side but did not have a very successful season, although his all-round play did much to defeat Marlborough by 9 wickets. D. E. C. Steel, a very good wicket-keeper, and P. Kershaw were the leading run-scorers. There was a high-scoring draw at Lord's in 1935; Rugby, facing a score of 351 for 9 dec., replied with 480. The 1937 XI was a good one. D. P. G. Elliot scored 102 against Uppingham and 660 runs in the season. Both D. G. Clark, later to captain Kent, and A. Kershaw made centuries in another high-scoring draw at Lord's. Writing about the early days of Rugby cricket in the *Cricketer*, E. R. Wilson concludes his article by saying that he had 'never seen a Rugby side as strong in batting as the side captained by Elliot' in 1937. To celebrate the fiftieth anniversary of the Jubilee match against Clifton, the James Pavilion was first used for Clifton's visit in 1937. After Sir Kenneth Swan had mentioned Percival and James, Sir Pelham Warner replied in these words: 'Swan has spoken of *his* two headmasters. I had only *one*, Tom Emmett.' J. R. Bridger, a good all-rounder, captained the 1938 side and played during the war for Cambridge. A. Fielder, who played for England six times, was the coach between 1929 and 1937.

H. C. Munro scored 614 runs in 1939, when only one match was won, but the 1940 side was a splendid one and it was very disappointing that it could not be seen at Lord's. L. G. H. Hingley scored 741 runs (av. 74·10) and shared in many fine opening stands with M. R. Holman. Hingley in three years in the side scored 1745 runs and in 1940 hit three centuries, 175 not out against Malvern being his highest score. Oundle (played in place of Clifton, and regular opponents since 1940), Malvern and Uppingham were beaten, while at Repton the scores were level with four Rugby wickets still standing when the game ended. It is sad that the 1941 XI was a weak one, for a match was played at Rugby to celebrate the centenary of the first visit of the M.C.C. to Rugby—the great match described in *Tom Brown's Schooldays*. J. A. Boyes captained this side and the 1942 XI, which bowled well, only one opposing team scoring more than 150. E. R. Wilson has suggested that 1943 was the centenary year of the wearing of blue shirts by the XI, although there is no definite proof of this. There is no doubt, however, that the 1943 XI was a good one. It won eight matches, but lost at Lord's after playing much attractive cricket on the first day. M. A. Boddington (50 wickets) and M. M. Morton (29) were a very good pair of opening bowlers and were well backed up by a slow left-hander, A. C. Guthrie, who took 35. In 1944, the flying-bomb summer, Marlborough were played and beaten on their own ground, as were Repton (at last) in a two-day match to celebrate the arrival at Repton, as Headmaster, of Mr. T. L. Thomas, ex-Housemaster of School Field. Morton took 41 wickets and the captain, J. H. H. Anton, was a fine all-rounder who was later 12th man for Cambridge. Eight matches were won again in 1945. Marlborough and Repton were amongst the victims, but there was a disaster at Uppingham. This 1945 side contained, as did others of this period, a number of good all-round athletes—a world rackets champion, two (and it must have been three but for a sad illness) international Rugby footballers, an Oxford golf-captain, an Oxford cricket Blue, the best swimmer in the school and, above all, W. S. Wardill, the captain, a very good off-spinner and possibly the finest schoolboy cover-point ever seen on the Close. W. M. McColl, the 1946 captain, was another good all-rounder. Practically the same Uppingham side as had won the year before by ten wickets was beaten by two runs in a thrilling game. Repton and Oundle were beaten too, but at Lord's, after a very good Rugby recovery, a declaration was made, which lost the match and displeased some eminent Old Rugbeian cricketers. In 1947 an outbreak of poliomyelitis at Rugby prevented the XI, a good one captained by J. C. Marshall, who won a Blue at Oxford, from playing at Lord's, but Repton were beaten by 10 wickets, T. M. B. Guy and W. R. Mason (one of the best of recent Rugbeian wicket-keepers) scoring 169 for 0 to win the match. The next three XIs were not particularly good sides, but J. E. Robinson, a good out-swing bowler, took 77 wickets in his two years in the side and D. R. Wright, an all-rounder, made 118 against Clifton in 1949. It was after the 1947 season that W. H. Ashdown retired from the post of head groundsman and professional. He was a wonderfully kind and good coach, who in his ten years at Rugby made a host of friends and worked miracles on the grounds in the difficult war years.

The next four Rugby sides contained many good players, and during this time Rugby gained two exciting victories at Lord's and two favourable draws. In 1951, after one of the draws, R. S. Rait-Kerr, then Secretary of the M.C.C., wrote to the *Meteor* praising the 'enterprise and zest displayed by the Rugby team' and going on to say: 'I can remember no post-war side from any school whose approach to a school match, from its start, has been more virile.' The 1952 XI was probably the best of these four teams and perhaps the best Rugby XI since the end of the war. In this year, when nine games were won, R. A. Hunt, a fast bowler, took 50 wickets and M. J. S. Preece, an off-spinner, 55. Preece made 99 at Lord's in 1953, while M. A. Eagar, who played four years for Oxford and then for Gloucestershire, scored almost 1300 runs in the two seasons 1951 and 1952. R. M. H. Boddington, J. A. Dyde and D. A. C. Marshall were very good all-rounders, and E. M. Rose, twice 12th man for Cambridge, a very steady left-handed bat. G. A. A. Currie, wicket-keeper for three years, kept for the Public Schools in 1953. Between 1951 and 1954 the XI won 25 matches and lost 9; all in all vintage years, although it is sad to record that Repton were not beaten during this period. But, perhaps the most astonishing innings of these years was played by A. J. Pickard, an O.R. who had been a member of the 1939 and 1940 XIs, for the Butterflies against the School in 1952. Facing a score of 228 for 8 dec., the Butterflies had replied with 54 for 7 when H. L. Leedham-Green joined Pickard, who launched such an assault on the XI bowling that he scored 160 not out in exactly two hours, winning the match with five minutes to spare.

The 1955 side was less good and narrowly lost the low-scoring match at Lord's, which celebrated the centenary of Rugby's first match against Marlborough—although the hundredth match between the two schools was not played until 1960. In the mid 1950s the wickets at Rugby had deteriorated noticeably, so it was not surprising that bowlers held sway in these years. T. B. L. Coghlan, captain in 1956 and 1957, bowled fast and furiously and later played for Cambridge. R. Lancaster, another fast bowler of this period, is quite the fastest active Old Rugbeian bowler at the present time. Marlborough were beaten by one wicket in a thrilling one-day match in 1956. From 1958, after the appointment of a first-class groundsman, the wickets improved rapidly and are excellent today. J. L. Cuthbertson, captain in 1959 and 1960, an Oxford Blue for two years, took full advantage of the better batting conditions to break all records. In his four years in the XI he scored 2364 runs, 1123 of them in his last year, when he scored four centuries, two of them in the match against the Meteors and one at Repton, who were beaten in 1959 and 1960. He took 81 wickets for the XI as well, and fielded beautifully in the gully.

In 1961 a weakish side, ably captained by R. Hodder-Williams, did well to hold a very good Marlborough side at Lord's, although the Rugby declaration was as controversial as that in 1946. The 1962 captain, M. R. J. Guest, later an Oxford Blue, scored 944 runs, and in the following year Rugby gained an exciting win at Lord's after being dismissed for 99 in their first innings. R. W. A. Bray scored 94 in the second and N. P. Gray, the son of P. H. Gray the rackets professional, bowled well in a tight finish. The 1964 XI was a good batting side, losing only two matches, but it did not play well at Lord's, only just saving the game. In 1965 Tonbridge were played for the first time by Rugby—both schools had to wait nearly a week for their Lord's matches after the end of the summer term—and were beaten by 4 runs off the last ball. A strong Marlborough side just got home at Lord's, but Rugby played well, with S. D. Bonner, a hard and successful hitter, becoming the third Rugbeian in five years to score 90 at Lord's. Since 1960 G. Geary has been the school professional. He is a fine coach and Rugby has been very lucky to have had his help for six summers.

It is very difficult to select a 'best' side from the last fifty years, but perhaps the following might be pitted against P. F. Warner and his men of the first fifty years of Rugby's fourth century:

B. H. Lyon (S.H. 1918) captain, E. F. Longrigg (S.F. 1925), L. G. H. Hingley (S.F. 1940), M. M. Walford (M. 1934), M. A. Eagar (St. 1952), J. L. Cuthbertson (K. 1960), D. S. Milford (S.F. 1924), W. S. Wardill (W. 1945), G. V. F.

Dawson (S.F. 1928), K. L. T. Jackson (C. 1932), G. A. A. Currie (Sh. 1956) wicket.

Investigation has shown that J. G. Pugh (B. 1922), D. P. G. Elliot (S.F. 1937) and J. R. Bridger (Sh. 1939) have weighty support for inclusion as batsmen, while H. L. Leedham⸍Green (C. 1926) could well have won a slow bowler's place, and many would be most reluctant to leave out R. M. H. Bodding⸍ton (St. 1953).

House cricket in the last hundred years has been crowded out of this record. Between 1867 and 1965 School House lead the Cock House list, but for many years their numbers were very much larger than those in other Houses. The record of Cock House wins from 1867 to 1965 is as follows:

School House	25
School Field	15
Whitelaw	13
Michell	10
Tudor	9
Kilbracken	8
Stanley	7
Cotton	4
Bradley	3

There have been five draws. Town and Sheriff have never been Cock House at cricket.

Since 1945, School Field, despite recent dominance in drawn games, have won only twice. Michell have won five times in the last twenty years and Tudor three. Cotton and Bradley have not been Cock House since the war, in fact Bradley's last win was in 1881!

While Rugby football and cricket held a steady and permanent place in the life of the School, their fortunes varying only with the competence of the performers—perhaps because football was from an early date a compulsory game and cricket became so—other athletic pursuits were subject to periods of prosperity and decline according to the support they were given. This is certainly true of running, which, if only for its antiquity as a Rugby sport, must take third place in the list of games.

The running practised in the earlier years of the nineteenth century was more varied than the cross-country events of today. Boys tended to use the countryside as they found it rather than make up a well-balanced steeplechase course or measure out standard lengths. Hedge-jumping and brook-leaping formed a large part of their exercise; they used ground at some distance from the School as well as neighbouring fields such as those bordering the Barby Road, and it is still possible to pick out the site of Butler's famous leap over the Clifton Brook. Flat races were less popular and were kept, on the whole, to 100 and 200 yards and the quarter-mile.

W. H. D. Rouse describes the type of run in which 'the praepostors were huntsmen or hounds and fags the hares; the huntsmen, arrayed in pink [were] armed with long whips, which made pretty play about the hares' legs if they caught them'. But such rough sport gave way to less barbarous forms of running, chiefly the Bigside Runs, which were paper-chases held over systematically kept courses. The first list of regular runs appeared in 1837, which was the year when the Crick was first run as a race; the fourteen miles of that first Crick course were occasionally covered in eighty minutes.

If numbers can be taken as some indication of interest, support for Bigside Runs soon began to waver, presumably as new games came to be played. The boys were often exhorted—both by the Holder of Bigside Bags, who saw the bags for the paper-trails less used, and by old-boy correspondents to the *Meteor*—to keep up the traditional school runs, but the numbers turning out for them continued to dwindle, even though House runs still formed a regular feature of the week's activities. Once, on the Barby village run, only two out of twenty-four starters came in. It was not until the introduction of the Running Cup in 1881, for which the Houses competed, that the boys began to enter for the Bigside Runs in any numbers. After this, support remained strong until Dr. Percival forbade House running competitions in 1893, when a boy collapsed and died on the 'Short Hillmorton'. Only four went in for the Crick that year.

The Running Cup was eventually restored in 1912, by which time more attention was being paid to training, and the House running order was published. Interest reached a peak soon after this, with fields of 130 for some races. On one occasion the whole school joined in a match against the Inniskillings and the Border Regiment.[1] The Junior Bigside Runs were revived, and the VIII began to have more success.

The Running VIII came into being in 1890, with the Holder of Bigside Bags as captain, and held its first match three years later against the Oxford Hare and Hounds Club. The next year saw the start of its oldest regular fixture, against the Thames

[1] These two regiments and the K.O.S.B. were training in the Rugby district for the Gallipoli attack.

Hare and Hounds, which is still kept up. The VIII's only school opponents for its first forty years were Shrewsbury and Uppingham, and its record against them was not impressive. Around 1935 Bromsgrove and Bradfield were added to the list, and many more schools have been taken on since then, as the fortunes of the team have improved with steadier training. The XVI was started shortly after the First World War, mainly as a form of recognition of the also-rans, since it had no fixtures.

In the tercentenary year of 1867 the school sports were inaugurated in the form we know today. The Athletic Sports have grown up steadily from very simple beginnings to the modern highly organised programme. Up to 1929 they were held in the Lent term, just after the Crick, and the cold weather was often bemoaned and a change of date suggested. Over the years many suggestions have, after frequent repetition, been accepted and have become part of the familiar fabric of the sports; for instance, that the programme of events should be extended; that dress more appropriate to running should be allowed; that the Levée should police the crowds; that there should be a professional timekeeper; that there should be seats for the ladies; and that the school should become affiliated to the A.A.A. It appears that the first few years of the sports were beset by teething troubles of a sort happily rarer now; hurdlers did not always keep to their lanes, and the accuracy of the watch was often questioned: small points in themselves, but taken together giving a good indication of how far the management of the sports has advanced during the first century of their existence.

As to the achievements of the athletes, there has been a steady improvement in most of the school records, with some years of special brilliance, such as 1914, while a few of them have remained unbeaten for over sixty years. As in running, a stimulus was given to athletics by the presentation in 1892 of a House Challenge Cup, in memory of H. C. Wrigley, a member of the Army Class who died while at school. Also the introduction of more scientific methods of training has helped to raise standards, and one consequence is that the school now has an athletics team representing all the usual track and field events, which competes on equal terms with other schools.

Of the 'minor games' the oldest is quite certainly fives, which has been played in the School since before any records of games were kept. 'As to our games here,' wrote E. H. Bradby to his parents in 1839, 'there are none besides cricket, football and fives.' But the game in those days was largely of a spontaneous character, played in the Old Quadrangle, where there is a ledge of a convenient height all round the walls under the cloisters; and games in the porch leading in from High Street, which makes a particularly convenient, almost enclosed area, were a constant nuisance to peaceful passers-by. More formal games could be played in the assorted courts that stood against the north side of the rackets court until eventually replaced by the standard squash courts. These early courts varied in size and design, and it was a middle-sized one with no buttress, regarded as the best, in which School competitions were played, and which, in 1874, was pronounced by a writer to the *Meteor* as 'the right size'; but there were no standard dimensions before the formation of the Rugby Fives Association in 1927. Indeed, when foreign matches came to be played in the early years of this century, it seems repeatedly to have surprised players that

Cheltenham's courts were about ten feet longer than the Rugby ones and that those at Malvern contained buttresses.

There was also a bat-fives court, monopolised by the Upper School as it had been flagged at their expense, which had as its front wall the end of the School buildings next to the Birching Tower, and its back wall the side of a school built on to the vestry of the old Chapel; fags retrieved balls that went out of court on either side. This made for another dangerous thorough-fare. The demand for this court was such that another was built in 1848 on the site of Sally Harrowell's cottages in Lawrence Sheriff Street. When these courts made way for the New Quad-rangle and Chapel, Thomson, 'turner and fives-bat maker', was, in the words of a letter to the *Meteor*, 'saved from impending ruin' by the Rev. L. F. Burrows, who, in 1871, shortly before he left the staff, paid for the paving of a new court against the south wall of the old rackets court; but players could no longer enjoy the fun of throwing their broken bats on the School House roof.

Thomson's bats were made of a single flat piece of willow, some sixteen inches long, with an oval striking area, about the size of a man's hand, rather more than half an inch thick, reducing to only an eighth as it narrowed towards the slim, hand-carved handle: a very good twopence worth. The balls were leather-covered and hand-stitched; as they were only an inch in diameter, play on an unevenly floored court was impos-sible.

These open courts needed constant maintenance, as did the open Eton fives courts presented by two members of the staff in 1863, which stand against the back of the old rackets court, and the two covered Eton courts, the gift of eight more masters, built in 1864. Expense on maintenance and appeals for money to build more courts of the more popular Rugby variety produced—and still produce—lively debate between those who held that the need for new courts would be apparent if the old ones were improved, and those who claimed that such expense on an ill-supported game would be wasteful. For the popularity of fives boomed and slumped long before new grounds and activities made it only one of many possible recreations. In 1868 pressure on courts was such that many schemes were suggested to prevent the fellows from Arnold's (School Field) from occupying the courts by always winning the traditional race from Houses to book courts after third lesson. A massed start was envisaged at the white gate, or even a separate starting point for competitors for each court, so that no one part of the Close would be trampled by the whole of the expected horde. Yet by 1870 Bigside Levée was decreeing that rackets with soft balls could be played in the big and little fives courts, and in 1883 a writer could claim that 'not above twenty fellows in the School play fives'. Although in 1885 a *Meteor* editorial begins: 'Alas for Rugby Fives! To all appearances it . . . is already at its last gasp', by 1893[1] nearly 300 of the School's 450 were said to be players, and the need for new courts seemed to be obvious; yet again, by 1907, it was squash, not fives, that was a nuisance in both Old and New Quadrangles. Revivals after periods of depression were noted also in 1903, 1935, 1941, 1947, 1949 and 1963. Many proposals have been put forward to give more stability; in 1885 colours were suggested, following the example of Bedford; larger prizes were proposed in 1892, although £1

---

[1] Perhaps the date here is significant. It is the year when Percival forbade House running competitions.

for the singles winner and 10*s*. for the runner-up were, in those days, handsome sums. Matches were suggested and the first was played in 1902; and new courts, paid for out of stopped allowances, O.R. grants and other subscriptions were built two at a time in 1877, 1893 and 1898, before the block of six came into being early in this century. A programme of lighting and reroofing is hastening the current revival.

Squash, condemned in 1886 as a 'lazy, pottering game', and hockey, since its inception in some Houses in 1893, have provided alternative forms of exercise for the many and have kept fives in the category of a minor game even for those picked for foreign matches. Fives and rackets pairs often overlapped and the fives match followed the rackets at Cheltenham and Malvern; in 1928 the pairs were the same. Oundle have never been matched since the first encounter was judged a draw 6–6 (when a method of scoring had finally been agreed), even in 1934 when the four included J. F. Hayley and C. M. MacLehose, who both later represented Oxford. Bedford have proved a more possible target to aim at and Marlborough provide a fair match.

Although bat-fives faded away in about 1904 and the Eton fives competition ended in 1913, and there are neither fierce chases across the Close nor rows of following-up caps on the sides of the courts booking them for footballers before Bigsides, internal competitions have survived the disappearance of prize-money and are better supported than ever. The nucleus of players still comes from a few Houses, but domination has moved from Arnold's to Tudor, to Sheriff and to Whitelaw and looks like continuing its round.

While fives has always had the nature of a spontaneous sport, suffering periods of unpopularity and decline, rackets, though a much younger game at Rugby, has, almost since the completion of the first rackets court in 1864, had a more official character. Its history is very largely the story of a remarkable family of professionals, the first of whom, J. B. Gray, was appointed in 1868, the year in which the School first entered for the Public Schools Doubles championship. On that first occasion it had no success, but the following year the pair reached the final, and in 1870 the School won the cup for the first time. Twice more during the time of J. B. Gray—who himself held the world championship title from 1878 to 1887—the pair reached the final.

J. B. Gray retired in 1894 and was succeeded by his son H. B., known universally as 'Harry' Gray, who coached the Rugby players for forty-three consecutive years. During his time there was remarkable success, the pair reaching the finals of the Public Schools Doubles eleven, and winning them six times. From his stable there came D. S. Milford, who held the world championship title from 1937 to 1947; and it was during Harry Gray's second innings during the war, when he did duty for his son and successor, P. H. Gray, from 1939 to 1946, that there emerged G. W. T. Atkins, who has held the title since 1954. Harry Gray had retired, officially, in 1937; but not only did he return during the war, but was prepared again to do duty, at the age of seventy-eight—though this time he did not actually play—in the summer of 1953 when his son was away ill.

The tale of Rugby success has showed no slackening during Peter Gray's period. Peter Kershaw won the Amateur Rackets championship in 1939 and the Royal Tennis championship in 1948. The pair has been six times in the finals, and five times has won the Public Schools Cup; and the Foster Cup for Public Schools singles, started in 1955, has already been won twice by Rugby players.

Old Rugbeians too have had remarkable success at the game. The Noel Bruce Cup for Old Boys' doubles has been won by a Rugby pair twenty times out of the thirty-six competitions since its inception and the Amateur Singles championship has seen Old Rugbeians in the finals twenty-three times, seventeen of them as winners. And there have been a large number of O.R. Blues at the universities.

Generally speaking, rackets has for a century been played at Rugby with great zest and enthusiasm, and it is probably true to say that more matches have been won at Queen's Court by Rugbeians than by boys from any other school.

D. S. Milford, who won the world rackets championship, was also one of the early stars of Rugby hockey. He was one of a team captained in 1923 by J. E. Cairnes (soon to become an Irish international) and was to go on himself to captain England at the game.

Hockey was a late starter at Rugby. Though it had been played sporadically by some Houses since 1893, it was not until 1921 that it was first introduced as a School game. The only match that year was of a combined XI of masters and boys against Rugby town, and was interrupted by a 'a fast-moving flock of sheep, hotly pursued by Mr. Lockhart's dog'—an event which seemed symbolic of the character of the game at Rugby, which, though played seriously, has never lost what an international player on the staff has called 'its aura of holiday and light relief from the business of sport'. Quite recently a

Bacchanalian side, playing against a School XI that included several future internationals, was discovered, some minutes after the game had begun, to contain twelve instead of eleven players.

Once started the game advanced rapidly and quickly developed a high standard of play. House matches began as early as 1923, encouraged by the presentation of a cup by Lord and Lady Stuart, and by 1924 a *Meteor* editorial could speak of the 'complete recognition' of hockey as a School game. The O.R. matches began in the following year and have continued annually. But perhaps the 'complete recognition' of the game was fully achieved when hockey was added to the list of games in which a Countings competition was carried on. It was after a Countings game that W. W. Vaughan was observed, after dark, searching the pitch with a torch for a tooth lost by one of the players. He found it.

From the very beginning the XI was remarkably successful against other schools. From quite early on nine foreigns became the rule, and there was a period of eight years, from 1942 to 1950, when no match was lost. Thereafter, with stiffer opposition from schools such as Marlborough and the Leys, the story was rather different. Perhaps the most notable team of all was that of 1945, under the captaincy of C. G. Bellamy, which scored an average of eight goals a match; their most exciting game was a 7–4 victory over Uppingham.

The hockey players have been fortunate in those who have helped them. H. C. A. Gaunt and Martin Lloyd (both later to be headmasters), W. W. Inge and the Rev. R. Broxton guided them in the earlier days. J. A. M. MacDonogh, who had represented Ireland for some years in what was one of the very greatest of Irish XIs, was in charge of the game for little

short of half of its life so far; other fine players who helped were
I. P. Campbell (England), J. G. Dewes (Cambridge), R. E.
H. Bowdler (Oxford), K. Stagg and P. M. C. Hare. Interest
in the game was increased by occasional international trials on
Caldecott's—surely one of the best grounds owned by any
School—and by the Oxford hockey festival, which became a
regular feature of the Easter holidays and in which the School
always did very well: in 1956 they scored 21 goals to 3 against.
But the Old Rugbeian team was, on occasions, embarrass-
ingly powerful, and in 1951 defeated quite a good School
side 13–0.

In spite of the comparative youth of hockey as a School game,
its tale of distinguished players is already a long one. In addition to those already mentioned, one might cite as international
players two captains of Scotland (P. R. Colville and N.
Livingstone), John Neill (England), M. A. Eagar, who captained Oxford (Ireland) and G. Owen (Wales) from a long
and lengthening list.

But the list of distinctions is not so important as the spirit in
which the game is played. In an age of professionalism it is
refreshing to find a game that is still played, as it is at Rugby,
for the enjoyment of it.

Another late-comer as a regular game at Rugby was lawn
tennis. As early as the spring of 1877, as a result of letters to the
Meteor and a decision of Bigside Levée—passed only after
strenuous debate—a lawn tennis club was formed, and seems to
have attracted widespread support. The following year a
tournament was organised for club members, with money
prizes ranging from 30s. to 15s., and by 1881, if a *Meteor*

correspondent is to be believed, there were 200 members of the tennis club, 'but only three courts, none of these completely true'. But the game came under very severe criticism; it was held that both rackets and cricket would suffer from its competition, and in March 1882 a *Meteor* editorial stated that 'it is an indisputable fact that last year the play of our XI was quite spoiled owing to its members spending the greater part of their time not at the ends improving their play, but in playing Lawn Tennis; the result, of course, was disastrous'.

The cricketers must have proved too strong for the tennis players, for the next reference to the game in the *Meteor* is not until 1907 when a correspondent signing himself 'Miserable Starkey' and declaring that the 'obscure game which rejoices in the name of Lawn Tennis . . . has not yet penetrated into Rugby's primeval gloom', suggested that one of the cricket pitches on Caldecott's should be laid out as courts and the cricketers compensated on Benn's. His plea was unsuccessful, and it was not until after the First World War that six rather rough and very ill-tended courts were laid out on Benn's and the game again became available to the School. Few, however, could escape from cricket to play it, and it is probably true that, throughout the 1920s and 1930s, tennis as a School game was anathema to the cricket-playing members of the staff, who kept a tight hold on the policy of the Games Committee. In 1928 the courts were moved to Springhill, and it was here, on very indifferent courts, that Peter Gray, in 1931, began coaching the few boys who could successfully escape the clutches of the House cricket authorities. The game, none the less, became increasingly popular, and in 1937 three *en-tout-cas* hard courts, the gifts of private donors, were laid down on Caldecott's. The following year three further grey hard courts were provided, and a last was added in 1948.

During these years there was not much progress in the game; the only matches were against the staff, among whom there were a number of keen and excellent players, and the Old Guard won them convincingly. The war years saw inevitable neglect of the hard courts owing to a lack of groundsmen; by 1946 only three courts were available for the whole School. The red courts never recovered and were relaid in 1948, but they needed so much attention that, after twelve years of patient fighting against the dust, they were taken up and replaced by three tarmac, non-upkeep courts. Six grass courts, laid out in 1947 on Hillbrow, however, were a great improvement on those at Springhill, and the following year this number was doubled; tennis was established.

Matches had been arranged during the war against the B.T.H. Company and the R.A.F. College, Cranwell. After the war fixtures began to multiply; the first schools to be played were Repton in 1950 and Stowe in 1951, and to these were added, as the years went by, Oundle, Malvern, King Edward's School, Birmingham, Uppingham, Nottingham High School and Bradfield, as well as the Public Schools Old Boys.

Tennis flourishes today as harmoniously alongside cricket as its optimistic promoters in 1877 could have wished. The standard has varied during the eighteen years since it was fully established, but in two successive years, 1951 and 1952, the Youll Cup was won in the Inter-Public Schools Competition at Wimbledon, with the twins C. G. and D. B. Daniels, G. D. Owen (later a Wimbledon player) and J. W. Neill (later a hockey international) in the first year, and J. G. H.

Hogben and T. N. Wheatcroft replacing the two Daniels in the second. And in the most recent four seasons only three school matches have been lost out of thirty-five played, with T. G. T. Temple and W. J. C. Surtees as the outstanding performers. The game today provides, as its early supporters hoped it might, a happy alternative to, but not a substitute for, cricket— and perhaps an occupation for what, years ago, used to be called 'the loafer'.

Two sports which have had phases of support, but which have suffered long periods of eclipse, are boxing and fencing. Both, in the days before the First World War, were run in con-nection with the gymnastics team and their greatest annual event was the gymnastic competition at Aldershot.

Boxing seems never to have attracted numerous enthusiasts, and a correspondent to the *Meteor* could say, in July 1906, that 'in no Public School is Boxing held in so little esteem as at Rugby'. Yet six years earlier, in 1900, R. H. Edmondson had won the Public Schools heavyweight title, and three years later, in 1909, F. C. Bourne did the same thing. This seems to have been the beginning of a period of success, for Rugby won the gymnastic competition at Aldershot in both 1910 and 1911, and in the latter year I. D. Dewar won the lightweight title, a dis-tinction that had been gained three times before, in successive years 1889 to 1891.

The cessation of the Aldershot camp during the First World War put a stop to School boxing for three years, and it was slow in getting started when war ended. Not until 1925 are House boxing competitions again mentioned in the *Meteor*, and they lost some of their interest for the School as a whole since School

House almost always won them. It is even recorded that in 1936 over half of the competitors came from that one House. Indeed, although the popularity of the sport seemed to increase, and in 1943 there was a record number of entries for the competition, the keenness seemed to be confined always to a few Houses, and for six consecutive years, 1943–8, the cup was won by Sheriff. Thereafter it passed to School Field for two years, to School House again and finally to Whitelaw, who, with the exception of 1955 when Cotton won it, held the cup for the remaining years of the competition. By 1955 the sport was clearly declining, and in 1959 it was abandoned altogether. There had been only one match attempted against another school, when, in March 1942, Rugby won a solitary fight out of seven bouts against Oundle.

Fencing seems to have been less regularly supported even than boxing, and has always had much more the character of a private recreation. It is true that the Public Schools Foils were won at Aldershot in 1904, but after that the *Meteor* makes no mention of the sport until the 1930s, when there appears to have been a considerable revival. On 11 November 1937 there took place 'the first Fencing match to be held in public in Old Big School', against Oxford, and in the same year there was a match against Loughborough College. Thereafter there were yearly foreigns, regularly against Leicester Club and Lawrence Sheriff School, and after the Second War matches multiplied, with other schools such as Stowe—which became a regular fixture—Westminster, Clifton, Cheltenham, Bedford Modern School and Repton, as well as clubs such as those of Leicester and Birmingham. And today there is strongly growing support for the art.

Of sports in and on the water, swimming and diving are of very long standing, and there were competitions even before the erection of the swimming-bath presented by Jex-Blake in 1875. The first record of such a contest comes in the *Meteor* of 1871, but reference to earlier competitions makes it clear that it was no innovation. It consisted of a swimming race over about 400 yards and diving for eggs, the winner being the one who could collect the greatest number of eggs in three dives. This type of diving contest seems to have persisted for at least half a century, though, when a swimming-bath was acquired, the eggs were replaced by coins and later by plates. A diving competition based on style was added in the 1880s.

Jex-Blake's bath, though it was clearly used a great deal, did not at first stimulate much increased interest in the sport. A swimming club was formed, for which the entrance qualification was to swim ten lengths (about 220 yards) in six and a half minutes, but the club does not seem to have flourished. It was complained that membership carried no privilege other than the right to wear a red instead of a blue costume and to use the bath during a mere half-hour each week when non-members were excluded. Even the presentation by Dr. Dukes of a cup for life-saving did not stimulate a great deal of enthusiasm.

It was not until the first decade of the twentieth century that swimming began to prosper, with the institution of a House water-polo competition and of matches against Old Rugbeians and other schools. The first recorded match was against the Old Rugbeians, when the School was successful, but they had to wait seventeen years before they won another match, in 1924, again against the O.R.s. Indeed, during the period of the war and the early twenties, there seems to have been a decline in the sport, in spite of the stimulus provided by foreign matches against Harrow, St. Paul's, King Edward's School, Birming, ham, and the B.T.H. Company. These contests usually con, sisted of a six,man relay, individual events over ten, six and two lengths (the lengths, in the old bath, being about 22 yards), diving and plunge. More schools were added to the fixture list from 1932 when a match was first swum against Oundle, to be followed by Stowe, Repton and Malvern, and in 1934 the first really successful season was experienced with a draw against Stowe and victories in all other matches; and the fact that, swimming against the B.T.H., the relay team beat the existing record by seventeen seconds gives some indication of the improvement that had been achieved.

Of the various styles of swimming, breast,stroke and back, stroke races did not appear in School matches until 1937, though these events had been a part of inter,House competitions for some years previously; 1937 also saw the introduction of the medley relay. From that date until the late fifties there was little change in the events of the School swimming sports, and the only recent changes have been the introduction of butterfly events and of a more elaborate diving competition.

There can be no doubt that the new swimming,bath, opened in 1928, proved a very great spur to the sport at Rugby. For years the old one has been very much too small for the school, many of whom still used the river, and the presentation by the Old Rugbeians of today's 'Tosh' provided the School with one of the finest baths in the country—and one of Rugby's show,pieces.

Apart from basket,ball, which in the last couple of years has achieved considerable popularity as a House competition game, Rugby's youngest sport is sailing.

The sailing club was started in 1950 by Michael McCrum (now Headmaster of Tonbridge) as a private club with a limited membership. Its success was made possible by the kindness of Mr. Edward Cox in making Naseby reservoir available, by a generous financial contribution from Sir Kenneth Preston and a number of Old Rugbeians, by a loan from the School and, not least, by the sympathetic encouragement of the Headmaster.

Four 'Skipper' pram dinghies were bought, two complete, two requiring a good deal of finishing, which was done in the workshop under the supervision of C. P. Mortimer. During the first two years an old hut served as a boatshed and a rather perilous raft as a landing-stage. When McCrum left to be Tutor of Corpus Christi College, Cambridge, the club was taken over by C. H. Silver, who was succeeded in turn by A. R. Lupton (1955) and G. M. Helliwell (1960).

From the beginning the club has been entirely voluntary and —a rare touch of democracy—has elected its own officers. Equipment has, over the fifteen years of its existence, become a little more refined. The original hut has been left to the Naseby Sailing Club, and the Rugby boats are kept at the 'rabbit-warren' end of the embankment, where the gravel bottom and a new, solid (though portable) landing-stage make launching easier. The most important change, however, has been the acquisition of a fleet of 'Fireflys', one presented by the mother of the 1961 commodore (P. G. Lee), and three more bought through the generosity of the Old Rugbeian Society.

Rugby now races six 'Fireflys' against other schools on Saturdays, and on other half-holidays there is added to these a mixed fleet of 'Skippers' and private craft of many classes, from 'Cadets' to 'Ospreys'.

Over the last five years the club has had a membership of fifty to sixty boys, and regular matches have been sailed, with some success, against other schools, and, in the holidays, at Bembridge and Itchenor.

Two events of some importance for the future marked 1965. First, sailing became an 'Alternative Activity',[1] to be pursued, in practice and theory, throughout the year. Second, the Old Rugbeian Sailing Club was founded. Both events augur well.

The games and activities briefly touched on in this chapter by no means exhaust the out-of-school occupations of Rugbeians. There are many more, such as golf, which preserves a steady popularity, but which has always had the character of a personal and individual pastime rather than a School game. And there is the almost infinite variety of the Natural History Society's activities, ranging from brass-rubbing and philately to botany and entomology—but these can hardly be classified as games, and in any case are to have their own history written in the quatercentenary year. The major change that has come over the character of the games during the last century seems to have been twofold. On the one hand there has been a steadily increasing involvement of masters, particularly in the last thirty years; this is due partly to the increasing difficulty in management of grounds and the assumption by the School of responsibility for their upkeep, partly to the introduction of the motor-car and the consequent possibility of activities, if masters are

[1] I.e. one of the permitted occupations for those who have opted out of the Corps.

included, farther afield than was feasible in the old days of the horse and the bicycle. On the other hand there has been a very great increase in the variety of activities, so that the 'great' games—football, cricket, running—though the first two still tower like giants over the rest, no longer hold the position of unquestioned pre-eminence that once they did. And perhaps the attitude towards them is less rigid, more humane, and the boy who cannot be enthusiastic about them is no longer a misfit. They are played with as much vigour as before—and possibly with more enjoyment; but they no longer have the exaggerated importance attached to them that once, perhaps, they did.

Appendixes

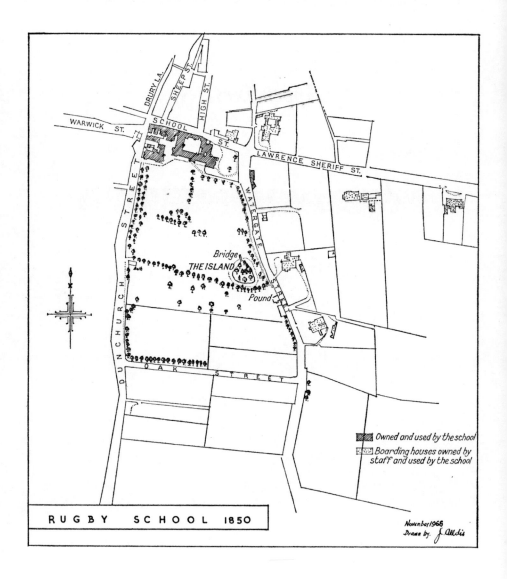

WARWICK ST.

DRURY LA.

SHEEP ST.

HIGH ST.

SCHOOL ST.

LAWRENCE SHERIFF ST.

DUNCHURCH STREET

WATERGATE

Bridge
THE ISLAND
Pound

OAK STREET

Owned and used by the school
Boarding houses owned by
staff and used by the school

RUGBY SCHOOL 1850

November 1968
Drawn by. J. Alldis

I

The Spread of the Rugby Influence

An interesting subject of research, which the present author has not undertaken, would be into the Old Rugbeians who have become headmasters of other schools. It has been a simpler matter to find those men who have served on the Rugby staff and have gone on to headmasterships, and the following list is thought to be a complete one for the period under review:

Date of appointment to headmastership		Service at Rugby	School
1842	Herbert Hill	1836–42	Warwick
1846	John Penrose	1839–46	'A School at Exmouth'[1]
1852	G. E. Lynch Cotton	1837–52	Marlborough
1858	G. G. Bradley	1847–58	Marlborough
1858	E. W. Benson	1852–8	Wellington (1st Master)
1862	Charles Evans	1848–62	King Edward's School, Birmingham
1862	A. G. Butler	1858–62	Haileybury (1st Headmaster)
1862	John Percival	1860–2	Clifton (1st Headmaster) (1887, Rugby)

[1] Name in 1846 unknown. It was a private school later known as 'Pencarwick', after three headmasters (Penrose, Carr and Wickham). It closed in 1908.

Date of appointment to headmastership		Service at Rugby	School
1868	T. W. Jex-Blake	1858–68	Cheltenham (1874, Rugby)
1870	A. W. Potts	1862–9	Fettes (1st Headmaster)
1874	F. E. Kitchener	1862–74	High School, Newcastle, Staffs. (1st Headmaster)
1874	J. S. Phillpots	1862–74	Bedford Grammar School
1877	G. L. Bennett	1875–7	Plymouth College (1st Headmaster) (1883, Sutton Valence)
1877	R. W. Taylor	1869–77	Kelly College
1879	J. M. Wilson	1859–79	Clifton
1883	H. Whitehead	1877–8	Bishop's College, Calcutta
1884	James Robertson	1862–71	Haileybury
1888	C. H. Hodges	1879–88	Townsville Grammar School, Queensland (1901, Church of England Grammar School, Sydney)
1892	F. B. Westcott	1884–92	Sherborne
1898	J. L. A. Paton	1888–98	University College School (1903, Manchester Grammar School)
1898	G. Smith	1892–8	Merchiston (1914, Dulwich)
1899	R. Waterfield	1893–9	Cheltenham
1902	W. H. D. Rouse	1896–1902	Perse School
1903	Frank Fletcher	1894–1903	Marlborough (1911, Charterhouse)
1903	E. Kitchener	1895–1903	Green Bank School, Liverpool (1911, The Golden Parsonage)
1905	A. A. David	1892–8	Clifton (1910, Rugby)
1905	St. J. B. Wynne Wilson	1899–1905	Haileybury (1911, Marlborough)
1906	F. F. S. Williams	1899–1905	Eastbourne College

Date of appoint-ment to headmaster-ship		Service at Rugby	School
1910	H. Costley-White	1903–10	Bradfield (1917, Liverpool College 1919, Westminster)
1911	R. B. Henderson	1902–11	Strand School, King's College (1920, Alleyn's)
1919	H. H. Hardy	1905–19	Cheltenham (1932, Shrewsbury)
1919	J. H. Simpson	1913–19	Rendcomb
1921	E. R. Thomas	1913–21	Royal Grammar School, Newcastle upon Tyne
1922	H. H. Symonds	1912–22	King's School, Chester (1924, Liverpool Institute)
1922	H. N. P. Sloman	1921–2	Tonbridge (previously, 1913–20, Sydney Grammar School)
1925	C. L. Reynolds	1922–5	Nottingham High School
1927	E. W. E. Kempson	1911–19	R.N. College, Dartmouth
1928	E. E. A. Whitworth	1913–28	Bradfield (1939, Tonbridge)
1928	G. A. Riding	1921–8	Warwick (1933, Aldenham)
1932	J. T. Christie	1922–8	Repton (1937, Westminster)
1934	E. F. Bonhote	1911–14 and 1919–34	Haileybury
1936	B. C. Molony	1919–36	Worksop
1937	H. C. A. Gaunt	1929–37	Malvern
1937	H. J. Kittermaster	1928–36	Cargilfield
1938	C. P. C. Smith	1926–38	Glenalmond (1948, Haileybury and I.S.C.)
1938	N. T. Sinclair	1928–38	Royal Masonic School
1939	R. R. Timberlake	1932–9	Royal Grammar School, Lancaster
1940	H. W. F. Franklin	1927–39	Epsom
1943	C. R. Evers	1936–43	Berkhamsted (1953, Sutton Valence)

Date of appointment to headmastership		Service at Rugby	School
1943	R. L. Roberts	1934–43	Blundell's
1944	T. L. Thomas	1923–44	Repton
1944	Martin Lloyd	1930–44	Uppingham
1945	C. M. E. Seaman	1939–45	The Edinburgh Academy (1951, Bedford 1955, Christ's Hospital)
1948	A. Constant	1944–8	Royal College, Mauritius
1949	E. V. Reynolds	1927–49	Stowe
1949	P. G. Mason	1946–9	Aldenham (1962, Manchester Grammar School)
1950	C. H. Potter	1944–50	March Grammar School
1951	R. C. Watt	1926–51	The Edinburgh Academy
1952	J. A. Boyes	1950–2	Kendal Grammar School (1965, City of London School)
1953	M. G. Dolden	1940–53	Hitchin Grammar School
1954	A. W. E. Winlaw	1946–54	Achimota (1959, Government Cadet College, Hasan Abdal, W. Pakistan. 1966, Federal Government College, Warri, Nigeria)
1958	J. G. Dewes	1953–8	Barker College, Sydney
1958	H. A. Staveley	1945–58	Lawrence Sheriff School
1959	D. Ashcroft	1950–9	Cheltenham
1959	L. E. Godfrey-Jones	1944–59	Marling School, Stroud
1962	T. K. Vivian	1954–62	Lucton School
1963	N. A. H. Creese	1955–63	Christ's College, New Zealand
1963	O. R. C. Prior	1930–63	Markham College, Lima
1964	M. McCrum	1948–50	Tonbridge

II

The Housemasters

BRADLEY HOUSE
5 Barby Road

1830 Bonamy Price	1910 B. B. Dickinson
1850 Charles Evans	1923 J. H. Bruce Lockhart
1862 C. B. Hutchinson	1930 H. J. Harris
1884 A. E. Donkin	1945 J. R. A. Smith

1959 G. H. Dazeley

COTTON HOUSE
10 Hillmorton Road

1836 P. W. Powlett	1884 F. D. Morice
1840 G. E. Lynch Cotton	1895 W. H. Payne-Smith
1852 B. Compton	1902 W. N. Wilson
1858 R. B. Smythies	1919 C. P. Evers
1861 (*temporarily*) C. A. Anstey	1935 R. Broxton
1862 C. E. Moberly	(*1941 Requisitioned by*
1874 J. S. Phillpots	*Government*)
1875 H. Lee Warner	1945 R. W. Stott

1956 D. Bulmer

KILBRACKEN HOUSE
33 Bilton Road

1841 J. Penrose

1846 G. G. Bradley

(*1848 Moved to 1 Hillmorton Road*)

1858 T. W. Jex-Blake

1868 C. Elsee

1889 J. Collins

1908 G. F. Bradby

1920 F. W. Odgers

1935 F. C. Slater

(*1941 Moved to 11 Barby Road*)

1943 E. H. L. Jennings

1958 W. W. Inge

1965 J. W. Hele

MICHELL HOUSE
Lawrence Sheriff Street

1841 H. Highton

1852 L. F. Burrows

1872 W. C. Green

1882 W. G. Michell

(*1884 Moved to 3 Hillmorton Road*)

1910 E. A. St. Hill

1920 R. A. Raven

1927 B. C. Molony

1936 G. A. Keay

1951 O. R. C. Prior

1963 J. Ll. R. Baiss

SCHOOL FIELD
16 and 18 Hillmorton Road

1831 J. P. Lee

1838 A. F. Merivale

1841 C. T. Arnold

(*1853 Moved to 2 Barby Road*)

1878 E. A. Scott

1892 W. P. Brooke

1910 H. C. Bradby

1925 E. F. Bonhote

1933 T. L. Thomas

1944 R. C. Watt

1951 J. L. Willans

1964 T. A. Buckney

SHERIFF HOUSE
7 Barby Road

1930 E. H. Johnson	1945 R. H. Walker
1940 J. A. G. Bruce	1956 A. J. Hunt

STANLEY HOUSE
3 Barby Road

1828 C. A. Anstey	(*1942 Requisitioned by*
1854 P. Bowden Smith	*Government*)
1891 C. G. Steel	1944 E. V. Reynolds
1914 F. J. Kittermaster	1949 F. J. A. Chase
1929 A. R. Tatham	1964 P. M. C. Hare

TUDOR HOUSE
4 Horton Crescent

1893 G. Stallard	1928 M. Megson
1913 C. E. M. Hawkesworth	1941 R. Broxton
1924 E. E. A. Whitworth	1949 P. Falk
1964 C. H. Silver	

WHITELAW HOUSE
4 Hillmorton Road
(Original site unknown)

1803 J. H. C. Moor	1841 C. Mayor
(*1811 Moved to 4 Hillmorton Road*)	1846 R. B. Mayor
1832 R. Bird	1863 J. M. Wilson

1879 R. Whitelaw   1936 W. N. Hughes
1913 J. M. Hardwich   1951 W. G. R. Loughery
1929 E. F. Waddy   1965 J. Peirson

TOWN HOUSE

*Until the appointment of H. P. Sparling in 1930, the Headmaster was
Housemaster of the Town, who shared the School House tutors. John
Percival was the first to appoint an official tutor to the Town to do the
work now done by the Housemaster of Town House.*

TUTORS

1891 J. L. A. Paton   1913 E. R. Thomas
1899 W. H. D. Rouse   1916 O. M. Samson
1902 E. Kitchener   1917 W. O. Brigstocke
   (*Town Boys' Hall opened on*   1919 W. A. D. Rudge
    Close)   1921 G. H. Woolley, V.C.
1903 D. E. Shorto   1923 B. C. Molony
1908 O. M. Samson   1924 H. P. Sparling

HOUSEMASTERS

1930 H. P. Sparling   1950 W. W. Inge
(*1946 1 Hillmorton Road opened as*   1958 R. P. Wright
   Town House)

III

Dramatics

For many years the acting of plays has been one of the most popular and regular of the School's activities. As long ago as the headmastership of Dr. John Ingles (1794–1806), W. C. Macready, who later became a distinguished professional actor, was producing plays in School House, but it was not until after the First World War that amateur theatricals became a regular feature of the School calendar. It was owing to the enterprise of a group of School House boys that they became so. Among them were Gyles (now Sir Gyles) Isham, who went on to be President of the O.U.D.S. and to act with the Royal Shakespeare Company at Stratford, J. H. Beausire, Basil Guedalla and C. G. Salinger.

From the time, in March 1919, when *The Bishop's Candle-sticks* and *Vice Versa* were produced in School House, followed in April by the Wilson (Cotton) House production of *The Burglar and the Judge* and *Should this Meet the Eye,* there was a quickening of interest and, one after another, the other Houses began to stage regular productions. P. H. B. Lyon was responsible for the introduction of a regular School play in 1932, when, in July, two performances of *Hamlet* were given in Speech Room.

The Governing Body made a gift of £50 for a framework to make possible the use of the Speech Room stage for acting purposes; it was a clumsy contrivance, requiring two days for erection and one for dismantling, but it did duty until 1937, when a more permanent arrangement was made in New Big School.

From 1932 until the war, development was in the hands of E. V. Reynolds, who also produced the School plays, and J. R. A. Smith, who built up the equipment and the lighting system. Apart from the initial gift from the Governing Body the School stage has had to be responsible for its own finance; but it has been so successfully managed that today the stage amenities are of a very high quality and include, as the result of a recent and most generous anonymous gift, pre-selector lighting equipment of a kind possibly to be found elsewhere only in a professional theatre.

Every term sees dramatics of one kind or another. In the Easter term each House produces its own play; in the summer the School play—usually a serious production—takes place; and in the autumn the masters put on a performance for the amusement of their pupils; this, except during the war years 1939–45, has been an annual event since 1930, when they produced A. A. Milne's *To Have the Honour*.

Although assistance in the boys' plays has from the beginning been given by masters—J. H. Bruce Lockhart and E. W. E. Kempson helped in the 1919 production at School House—the great bulk of the work of production and stage-management is carried out by the boys themselves. There has been progressive improvement in the quality of the performances, and the most recent production by the School, in 1966 (*St. Joan*), was of near-professional standard.

IV

The Chapel Bell (The 'Boomer')

The following information has been provided by Mr. J. Wilshere (O.B.)

The Elsee Bell was dedicated in July 1914 at a ceremony in the Close before being lifted into the Chapel tower. It is a B flat bell, made of thirteen parts copper and four parts tin, weighing nearly three and a quarter tons (exactly, 3 tons 4 cwt. 2 qrs. 20 lb.) and is 5 ft. 9½ in. in diameter. It is one of the heaviest bells in any Midland school, and certainly the heaviest in Rugby, the largest in St. Andrew's Parish Church weighing 25 cwt. (By contrast, Big Ben weighs 13½ tons and the heaviest bell in England, in St. Paul's, 17 tons.)

The Elsee Bell carries, in relief, the School coat of arms and 'Orando Laborando'; also the inscription: 'In remembrance of CHARLES and MARY ANNE ELSEE—their children gave me.' The lettering is a facsimile of medieval lettering (dated 1421) at South Somercotes, Lincolnshire.

During the First World War the 'Boomer' was rung at midday each day during term and all work stopped for five minutes for intercession for Old Rugbeians on active service.

Sources

The following are the principal sources consulted:

A. UNPUBLISHED MATERIAL

1. At the Office of the Clerk to the Governing Body:
   (*a*) Trustee Order Books, 1842–71.
   (*b*) Minutes of the Governing Body, 1871 onwards.
   (*c*) Annual reports to the Governing Body from the Head-master, the Bursar, the Medical Officer, the Sanitary Adviser, the Finance Committee, the School Surveyor, the School Buildings Committee, etc.
   (*d*) The School annual accounts.
   (*e*) A box of papers connected with the Hayman case.
2. At the Public Record Office, London: Written evidence given to the Public Schools Commission (the Clarendon Commission) and letters written by Frederick Temple to the Secretary of the Commission.
3. At St. John's College, Oxford: Papers connected with H. A. James, including autobiographical notes and 'Ludicra'.
4. At the Temple Reading Room:
   (*a*) Collection of letters and other manuscripts.
   (*b*) 'The Rugby Album': a scrap-book in two volumes.
5. Levée minute-books, School House Fasti and annals of other Houses.

6. Material in private hands:

(*a*) The Rev. J. A. G. Haslam and Mrs. Doreen Atkinson: letters dealing with the Haslam family at Rugby.

(*b*) Brigadier J. H. Penrose: a large collection of Arnold and Penrose family letters.[1]

(*c*) Mrs. Denis Buxton: a collection of Jex-Blake material, including his autobiographical notes, now deposited in the Temple Reading Room.

(*d*) Mrs. A. A. David: papers connected with Bishop A. A. David.

(*e*) Mrs. W. W. Vaughan and Mr. H. J. Vaughan: material connected with W. W. Vaughan.

(*f*) Mr. P. H. B. Lyon: correspondence.

B. PUBLISHED MATTER

T. W. Bamford, *Thomas Arnold* (Cresset, 1960).

F. Betts, *Rugby School. A Reconstructed History from the Foundationers' Standpoint* (*Rugby Advertiser*, 1924).

H. C. Bradby, *Rugby* (George Bell, 1900).

Clarendon Commission on Public Schools: *Report* (Stationery Office, 1865).

Maurice Collis, *The Journey Outward* (Faber & Faber, 1952).

Robert Collis, *The Silver Fleece* (Nelson, 1936).

Berdmore Compton, *Edward Meyrick Goulburn* (Murray, 1899).

R. T. Davidson, and W. Benham, *Archibald Campbell Tait* (Macmillan, 1891).

'Day Boy', 'Experiences of a Day Boy at a Public School' (*Macmillan's Magazine*, March 1885).

---

[1] This collection has recently been deposited at the Brotherton Library, Leeds University.

Lord Elton, *Among Others* (Collins, 1938).

C. R. Evers, *Rugby* (Blackie, 1939).

Evidence presented to the Select Committee Sitting on the Public Schools Bill (1865).

Frank Fletcher, *After Many Days* (Hale, 1937).

E. M. Goulburn (ed.), *The Book of Rugby School* (1856).

Christopher Hassall, *Rupert Brooke: a biography* (Faber & Faber, 1964).

Thomas Hughes, 'Rugby', in *Great Public Schools* (Arnold, 1893).

F. A. Iremonger, *William Temple* (O.U.P., 1948).

F. E. Kitchener, 'Rugby Memoir, 1857–1869', in *Life of Frederick Temple,* vol. 1. (Macmillan, 1906).

Edward Marsh, 'Memoir' in *Collected Poems of Rupert Brooke* (Sidgwick & Jackson, 1918).

David Newsome, *A History of Wellington College, 1859–1959* (Murray, 1959).

Vivian Ogilvie, *The English Public School* (Batsford, 1957).

'O.R.' (C. J. Mott), *Rugboeana* (Lomax, Lichfield, 1875).

W. H. D. Rouse, *A History of Rugby School* (Duckworth, 1898).

J. H. Simpson, *Schoolmaster's Harvest . . . 1894–1944* (Faber & Faber, 1954).

A. P. Stanley, *Life and Correspondence of Thomas Arnold* (Fellowes, 1844).

William Temple, *Life of Bishop Percival* (Macmillan, 1921).

W. W. Vaughan, 'Religion at School', in *Cambridge Essays on Education,* ed. A. C. Benson (Cambridge, 1917).

— *The Warp and the Woof in Education* (Address to the British Association, 1925).

W. David Wills, *Homer Lane* (Allen & Unwin, 1964).
J. M. Wilson, *Autobiography* (Sidgwick & Jackson, 1924).
Norman Wymer, *Dr. Arnold of Rugby* (Hale, 1953).

C. PUBLISHED BY RUGBY SCHOOL BOYS
(*dates refer to year of first issue*)

Rugby Miscellany (1845)
Rugbaean (1850)
New Rugbeian (1858)
Meteor (1867)
Crescent (various dates: a School Field publication)
Lion (various dates: Town House publication)
Sibyl (1890)
Laurentian (1898)
Lulu (1900)
Phoenix (1904)
Vulture (1904)
Venture (1905)
Quadrangle (1909)
Puffin (1911)
Comet (1912) (a Cotton House publication)
Sun (1913)
Rugby Opinion (1916) (a School Field publication)
Rugbeian (1918)
Brighter Rugby (1920)
New Rugbeian (1935)

[Not consulted, but completing the list of boys' publications, there were:
Rugby Magazine (1835)
New Rugby Magazine (1864)

T.V.W. (1877)
Leaflet (1884)
Rugbeiensia (1888)
   Only the first lasted more than a year.]

D. MISCELLANEOUS

The annotated registers of Rugby School.
The terminal 'Blue Books' of Rugby School.

Index